GCSE AQA

AF290367

French

There are few things more fun than a stroll along the Seine, but this
CGP Revision Guide is up there.

It explains the entire GCSE AQA French course, with plenty of examples and
practice questions on all the vocab and grammar you'll need for the exams.

It also comes with CGP RevisionHub where you can find quick quizzes, summary tests,
audio, Q&A videos and more — all matched to your book! Yep, we really have made the
crème de la crème of Revision Guides. *Profites-en bien!*

Unlock *CGP RevisionHub*

Just scan a QR code in the book to access the CGP RevisionHub.
Or go to **cgpbooks.co.uk/revise** and enter this code!

3280 9795 9844 4429

By the way, this code only works for one person. If somebody else has
used this book before you, they might have already claimed the code.

Revision Guide
with new *CGP RevisionHub*

Published by CGP

Editors:
Siân Butler
Robbie Claringbold-Driscoll
Elliott Garraway
Nathan Mair
Ilana Pearce
Alex Thompson
Matt Topping

Contributors:
Ben Ffrancon Dowds
Jackie Shaw
Coralie Stewart
Sarah Sweeney

With thanks to Marc Barnard, Eleanor Claringbold-Driscoll, Helen Clements, Pat Dunn, Natalie Handley, Natalie Pomier, Véronique Robine and Jack Tooth for the proofreading.

With thanks to Alice Dent for the copyright research.

Acknowledgements:

Audio produced by Voice Talent Online.

AQA material is reproduced by permission of AQA.

_The worked solutions to questions and commentaries on questions and possible answers
in this book have neither been provided by nor approved by AQA._

ISBN: 978 1 83774 1229
Printed and bound by Bell & Bain Ltd, Glasgow.
Clipart from Corel®

Based on the classic CGP style created by Richard Parsons.

Contents

Contents

Contents

How to Use this Book

This isn't a book. Or rather, this isn't *just* a book. It's full of online resources designed to help you get top marks. To learn how it all works, read these pages or scan the QR code for a walkthrough.

This book follows the AQA specification

1) The content for AQA GCSE French is divided into nine topics. Each topic falls under one of three themes:

| People and lifestyle | Popular culture | Communication and the world around us |

2) In this book, there is usually one section for each topic. However, some topics have been split into two sections to make things more manageable.

3) There are also three grammar sections that cover the grammar you need to know.

4) The resources on the CGP RevisionHub are split up in the same way as the book.

There's also a 'General Stuff' topic in the book and online with content that's useful across the course.

The CGP RevisionHub is full of resources

- You can use the online resources on the CGP RevisionHub alongside this book as you're revising.
- There's audio, quick quizzes and summary tests, as well as printable vocab lists and transcripts.

There are resources for Foundation tier and Higher tier on the CGP RevisionHub. The Hub is automatically set to Higher, but you can switch to Foundation to only see Foundation content.

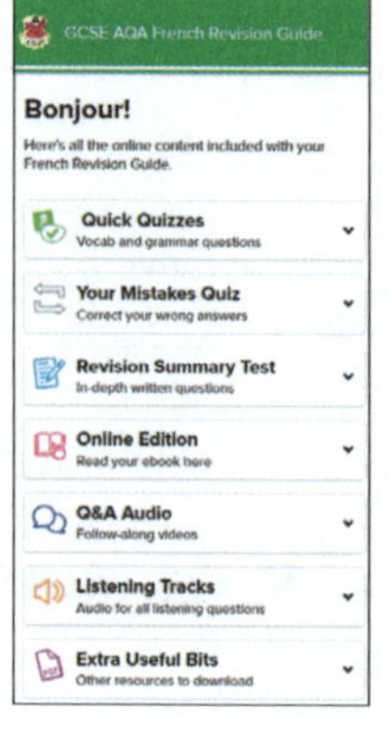

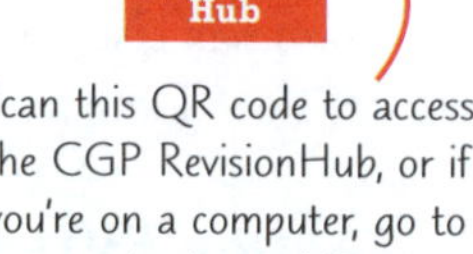

Scan this QR code to access the CGP RevisionHub, or if you're on a computer, go to www.cgpbooks.co.uk/Bonjour.

Get ready for the exams

1) In your exams, you can sit Foundation-tier or Higher-tier papers.

2) In each tier, there are four papers: Listening, Speaking, Reading and Writing. You have to choose the same tier for all four papers.

For more about the exams, see p.151-152.

- In Foundation tier, there's less vocabulary and less grammar to learn and the questions are slightly easier. In this tier, you can earn up to Grade 5.
- In Higher tier, you can achieve Grades 4-9, but you'll need to learn more vocab and more complex grammar.

3) Throughout this book, there's practice for all the key skills you'll need in the exams.

4) Most of this book is helpful for both tiers, but some vocab and questions have been marked with a bracket if they only apply to one tier. →

5) If you aren't sure which tier to take, trying out the questions should help you and your teacher make a decision.

Lola stretched herself to reach the Higher tier.

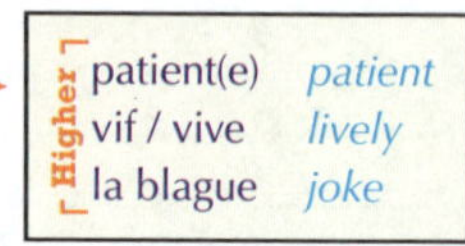

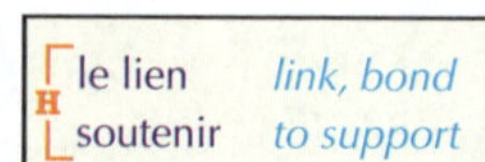

Learn the set vocabulary

- The AQA specification contains a list of words you could be tested on in your Listening and Reading papers, depending on your tier.
- This vocab will also help you in your Speaking and Writing papers. In these two papers, you can use non-specification vocab, too.
- The key vocab is on the main pages of each section. At the end of each section, there's a list of all the vocab relevant to the topic. Every word on the specification is on at least one of these lists.
- There are printable versions of these lists on the CGP RevisionHub.

Practise your listening skills

1) In this book, you'll find questions and example answers:

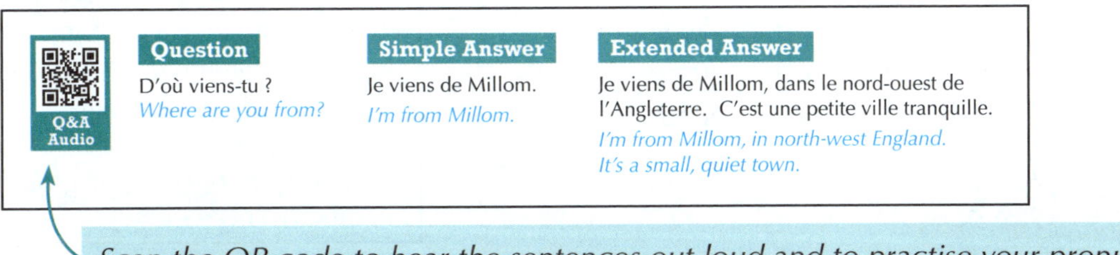

Scan the QR code to hear the sentences out loud and to practise your pronunciation.

2) There are also QR codes that take you to Listening Tracks. Each track comes with questions that test you on what you've heard.

Test your knowledge

Quick Quizzes

- The QR codes at the top of the page take you to a quick quiz.
- These quizzes test you on the vocab (or the grammar in Sections 13-15) on that page.
- They're a great way to keep your knowledge fresh.
- You can easily revisit questions that you answer incorrectly by doing the 'Your Mistakes' quiz.

Revision Summary Tests

- For more of a challenge, try a revision summary test. These are found at the end of each section.
- These tests cover the most important information in a topic and are a good way to see how much you can remember.
- You can do these tests on paper or you can complete them online. Online, you can find sample answers, assess your progress, and look at previous topics to see the areas you need to work on.

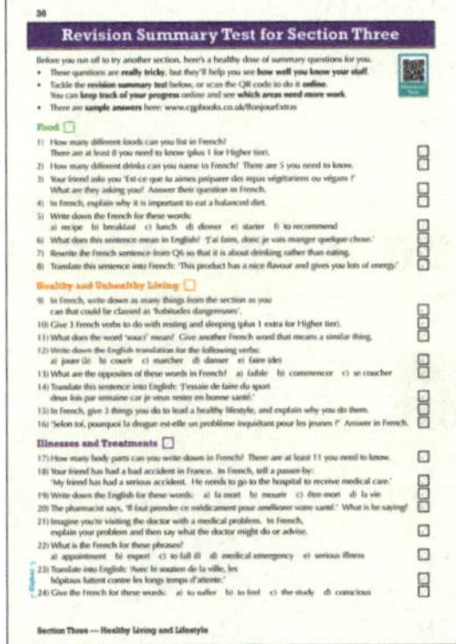

Fun fact — rearrange the letters of 'RevisionHub' and you get...

...'SnoivierUbh', which makes no sense. But do you know what *does* make sense? Using the RevisionHub alongside this book — it'll help you to get the most out of your revision and impress all those examiners.

Numbers and Times

First things first — numbers. You'll need a bit of maths for some of them, but it's all part of the fun...

Un, deux, trois — *One, two, three*

Remember there's also lots of online content here: www.cgpbooks.co.uk/Bonjour

Vocabulary

0	zéro	10	dix
1	un	11	onze
2	deux	12	douze
3	trois	13	treize
4	quatre	14	quatorze
5	cinq	15	quinze
6	six	16	seize
7	sept	17	dix-sept
8	huit	18	dix-huit
9	neuf	19	dix-neuf

Except 'vingt', most of the 'tens' end in 'nte'. Also, '70' is 'sixty-ten', '80' is 'four-twenties', and '90' is 'four-twenty-ten'.

20	vingt
30	trente
40	quarante
50	cinquante
60	soixante
70	soixante-dix
80	quatre-vingts
90	quatre-vingt-dix

21	vingt et un
22	vingt-deux
23	vingt-trois

In-between numbers are formed like English ones, but add 'et un' for numbers ending in '1'.

Grammar — 'un' / 'une'

For feminine nouns, use 'une' and 'et une' instead of 'un' and 'et un':

Il y a <u>vingt et une</u> filles et <u>vingt et un</u> garçons.
There are <u>twenty-one</u> girls and <u>twenty-one</u> boys.

11 to 16 all end in 'ze'. But 17, 18 and 19 are 'ten-seven' etc.

71	soixante et onze	91	quatre-vingt-onze
72	soixante-douze	98	quatre-vingt-dix-huit

For the 70s and 90s, add 11-19 to 'soixante' and 'quatre-vingt' (like 'quatre-vingts' (*80*) but without the 's'). '81' and '91' miss out the 'et', e.g. quatre-vingt-un (*81*).

100	cent	10 000	dix mille
1000	mille	1 000 000	un million

623	six cent vingt-trois
1947	mille neuf cent quarante-sept

For hundreds and thousands, put cent, deux cent, mille (etc.) before the number.

In French, long numbers are broken up by full stops or spaces instead of commas.

Add '-ième' to the number to say second, third, etc.

Use 'premier' for masculine nouns and 'première' for feminine ones.

Numbers ending in 'e' lose the e.

A 'u' is added to 'cinq'.

The 'f' in 'neuf' changes to a 'v'.

1st	premier / première	4th	quatrième	7th	septième	10th	dixième
2nd	deuxième	5th	cinquième	8th	huitième	99th	quatre-vingt-dix-neuvième
3rd	troisième	6th	sixième	9th	neuvième		

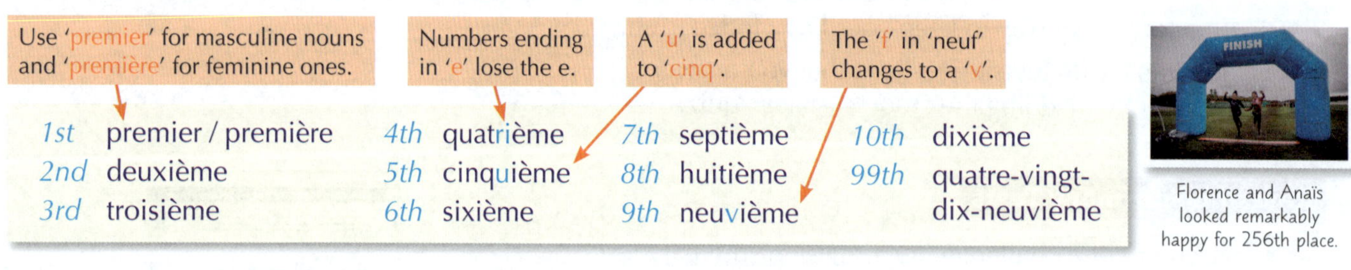

Florence and Anaïs looked remarkably happy for 256th place.

Here are a few more handy number words...

Vocabulary

le nombre	*number*
environ	*about*
la moitié	*half*
compter	*to count*
le chiffre	*figure, number*
une dizaine	*about ten*
une centaine	*about a hundred*

Higher

J'ai compté environ six chiens.
I counted about six dogs.

Le nombre d'habitants a augmenté.
The number of residents has increased.

Il a une dizaine de tableaux.
He has about ten paintings.

La moitié des étudiants étudient l'anglais.
Half of the students are studying English.

Quelle heure est-il ? — *What time is it?*

1) There are different ways to tell the time in French. Make sure you <u>learn</u> all of them. To say 'it's...o'clock', use '<u>il est...heure(s)</u>'.

> Il est une heure. *It's 1 o'clock.*   Il est vingt heures. *It's 8 pm.*

The French use the 24-hour clock a lot — so make sure you can use it.

2) To say '...minutes past', you say the hour, then the number of minutes. You don't need any <u>extra</u> words.

> Il est trois heures douze. *It's 03:12.*
> Il est vingt heures trente-trois. *It's 20:33.*

To say 'in the evening' without referring to a specific hour of the day, just say 'le soir'. E.g. 'Le soir, j'ai dormi.' (*In the evening, I slept.*) The same rule applies for 'in the morning' and 'in the afternoon'.

3) Use '<u>moins...</u>' (*less*) to say '<u>...to</u>'.

> Il est onze heures moins dix. *It's ten to eleven.*

Grammar — 'à' with times

You use '<u>à</u>' with times to say '<u>at</u>'.
<u>à</u> dix heures   *<u>at</u> ten o'clock*

4) Use this vocab to say '<u>quarter past</u>', '<u>half past</u>' and '<u>quarter to</u>'.

Vocabulary

le quart	*quarter*
demi	*half*
moins le quart	*quarter to*
du matin	*in the morning*
de l'après-midi	*in the afternoon*
du soir	*in the evening*

> Il est deux heures et quart. *It's quarter past two.*
> Il est deux heures et demie. *It's half-past two.*
> Il est trois heures moins le quart. *It's quarter to three.*
> Il est six heures du soir. *It's six in the evening.*

'Demi' needs to agree with the gender of the noun before. 'Heures' is feminine, so you add an 'e' to make it 'demi<u>e</u>'.

Practice Questions

Q1 *Listen to these four sentences and write down in French exactly what you hear.*
Use your knowledge of French to make sure that what you have written is accurate.   [8 marks]

Q2 *Read this activity board for a summer camp, then answer the questions in English.*

> **Foot :** *quinze heures quarante-cinq*
> **Musique :** *treize heures trente*
> **Théâtre :** *dix-neuf heures quinze*
> **Natation :** *seize heures cinquante*
> **Cours de cinéma :** *vingt heures*

a) At what time does swimming start?   [1 mark]
b) Which activity happens last?   [1 mark]
c) Which activity starts before football?   [1 mark]
d) Which activity happens in between swimming and film class?   [1 mark]

You should never eat a clock — it's very time-consuming...

Being able to use numbers and times in French will prove really handy — it's the kind of thing that comes up again and again in a lot of topics. They can seem daunting at first, so practise them until they get easier.

Days and Dates

Learn this time and date vocab and you'll never miss a party in France...

Les jours (m) de la semaine — *The days of the week*

In French, the days of the week are always <u>lower case</u>. They're also all <u>masculine</u>.

Vocabulary

lundi	*Monday*
mardi	*Tuesday*
mercredi	*Wednesday*
jeudi	*Thursday*
vendredi	*Friday*
samedi	*Saturday*
dimanche	*Sunday*
à (lundi) !	*see you on (Monday)!*

Grammar — 'le lundi' (Mondays)

To say something happens regularly on a certain day, use the <u>masculine definite article</u> ('le') with the day — <u>not a plural</u>.

<u>Le lundi</u>, je fais du sport.
On Mondays, I do sport.

To say something happened on one specific day, you don't need the <u>article</u>.

<u>Jeudi</u>, j'ai acheté un vélo.
On Thursday, I bought a bike.

aujourd'hui	*today*
le jour / la journée	*day*
quotidien(ne)	*daily*
demain	*tomorrow*
hier	*yesterday*
le lendemain	*next day*
la semaine	*week*
le week-end	*weekend*

Je pars mardi.

I'm leaving on Tuesday. — the day after tomorrow — après-demain

Vendredi, j'ai fait mes devoirs, donc aujourd'hui je peux me relaxer.

On Friday, I did my homework, so today I can relax.

Je vais à la synagogue avec ma mère le week-end.

I go to synagogue with my mother at the weekend. — during the week — pendant la semaine

Elle voit son père le dimanche.

She sees her father on Sundays. — every day — tous les jours

Les mois (m) de l'année — *The months of the year*

Months and seasons are <u>masculine</u> and <u>don't</u> begin with <u>capital letters</u>.

Vocabulary

le mois	*month*	juillet	*July*
janvier	*January*	août	*August*
février	*February*	septembre	*September*
mars	*March*	octobre	*October*
avril	*April*	novembre	*November*
mai	*May*	décembre	*December*
juin	*June*		

la saison	*season*
l'hiver (m)	*winter*
le printemps	*spring*
l'été (m)	*summer*
l'automne (m)	*autumn*

To say 'in + a season', you say 'en hiver', 'en été', and 'en automne'. But watch out — 'in spring' is '<u>au printemps</u>'.

Question

As-tu une saison préférée ?
Do you have a favourite season?

Simple Answer

Oui, j'aime l'hiver parce que j'adore la neige et Noël.
Yes, I like winter because I love snow and Christmas.

Extended Answer

Oui, je trouve l'hiver très agréable parce que j'aime beaucoup les traditions de la période de Noël. En plus, mon anniversaire est en janvier, donc c'est une saison que j'apprécie beaucoup.

Yes, I find winter really nice because I like the traditions of the Christmas period a lot. In addition, my birthday is in January, so it's a season that I really appreciate.

Quelle est la date ? — *What's the date?*

In French, you say 'the nine April' or 'the seventeen November'. The exception to this rule is the first day of a month, where you use 'le premier' (*the first*), like you would in English.

Aujourd'hui c'est le quinze mai.

Today is the 15th May.

Mon frère est né le vingt-cinq février deux mille dix.

My brother was born on the 25th February 2010.

the 1st August — le premier août

in the 90s — dans les années quatre-vingt-dix

in 2006 — en deux mille six

Faire des projets — *Making plans*

These words are really useful for making arrangements... and for your exams.

Vocabulary

le matin	*morning*
le midi	*noon*
l'après-midi (m)	*afternoon*
le soir / la soirée	*evening*
la nuit	*night*

Grammar — forming adverbs

To form adverbs in French, you normally add '-ment' to the feminine form of the adjective (see p.125):

rare ➡ **rarement** (*rarely*)

générale ➡ **généralement** (*generally*)

Qu'est-ce que tu fais ce matin ?

What are you doing this morning?

Le soir, je vais souvent au cinéma.

In the evening, I often go to the cinema.

La semaine prochaine, je vais danser.

Next week, I'm going to dance.

Je suis rarement en retard.

I am rarely late.

this weekend — ce week-end

This afternoon — Cet après-midi

Practice Questions

Q1 *Write to a French friend about your typical week. You should write about 90 words in French. Make sure you cover:*

- *what you normally do each day*
- *what time each activity starts*
- *what you will do next week.* [15 marks]

Top Tip for Higher Students
✓ Use adverbs like 'régulièrement' (*regularly*) to talk about what you do often.

Higher

Q2 *Listen to these announcements made in a French school, then answer the questions in English.*

a) On what date will the show take place? [1 mark]

b) In which month do the exams finish? [1 mark]

c) On which days do language classes take place? [1 mark]

d) When was the school established? [1 mark]

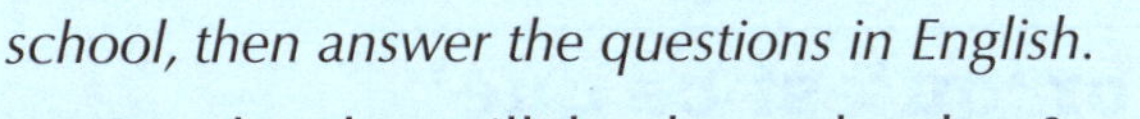

The school's audio equipment was about as state of the art as its toilets.

My favourite date? That soft, brown one I ate on holiday...

Adding in a day or a date can be a great way to make your answers more detailed. But be sure to match your tenses to your time phrases — if you say something happened last week, you'll need the past tense.

Questions

Questioning your decision to take French? Well, this page will come in very handy...

Poser des questions — *Asking questions*

Vocabulary

la question	*question*	combien ?	*how much / many?*
quand ?	*when?*	qui ?	*who?*
pourquoi ?	*why?*	quoi ?	*what?*
où ?	*where?*	que / qu' ?	*what?*
comment ?	*how?*	quel / quelle ?	*which?*

These are known as interrogatives.

'It's behind you!'

Qui vient avec moi ? *Who's coming with me?*

Où est la plage ? *Where is the beach?*

Ask questions by changing your tone of voice

The <u>easiest</u> way to ask a <u>question</u> in French is to say a normal sentence, but <u>make your voice go up</u> at the end.

Le pain coûte combien ? *How much is the bread?*

C'est loin ? *Is it far?*

Tu travailles où ? *Where do you work?*

Il arrive ? *He's arriving?*

In writing, the only difference between this question and the statement 'C'est loin.' (*It's far.*) is the question mark.

Ask questions by putting the verb after the question word

When the sentence starts with a <u>question word</u>, you can also <u>swap</u> the <u>verb</u> and the <u>subject</u> (the person or thing doing the action) around. Don't forget to add a <u>hyphen</u> between the <u>verb</u> and the <u>subject pronoun</u>.

Pourquoi es-tu en retard ?	*Why are you late?*
Où travailles-tu ?	*Where do you work?*
Qui est-il ?	*Who is he?*
Qu'as-tu mangé ?	*What did you eat?*

If the verb ends in a <u>vowel</u> and is followed by '<u>il</u>', '<u>elle</u>' or '<u>on</u>', you add a '<u>t</u>' to make it <u>easier to say</u>.

Quand a-t-il fini ses devoirs ?
When did he finish his homework?

Ask questions using 'est-ce que' or 'qu'est-ce que'

1) You can turn a <u>statement</u> into a yes or no <u>question</u> by using '<u>est-ce que</u>'.

Est-ce que tu as des frères et sœurs ?	*Do you have any brothers or sisters?*
Est-ce que tu aimes jouer au tennis ?	*Do you like playing tennis?*

2) You usually use '<u>qu'est-ce que</u>' if your question starts with '<u>what</u>'.

Qu'est-ce que tu fais le samedi ? *What do you do on Saturdays?*

Qu'est-ce que c'est ? —*What is it?*

Here are some useful <u>questions</u> that you might want to ask:

Quelle heure est-il ?	*What time is it?*
Pendant combien de temps ?	*For how long?*
D'où vient votre famille ?	*Where is your family from?*
Qu'est-ce que vous avez dit ?	*What did you say?*
À quelle heure tu voudrais aller à la fête ?	*At what time would you like to go to the party?*

how many days — combien de jours

do — fait
ask — demandé

Grammar — prepositions

You can use a preposition <u>before</u> a question word, e.g.
<u>Avec qui</u> habites-tu ?
<u>Who</u> do you live <u>with</u>?

'<u>C'est</u>' can also be used to form lots of different questions:

C'est de quelle couleur ?	*What colour is it?*
C'est combien ?	*How much is it?*
C'est quelle date aujourd'hui ?	*What is the date today?*
C'est quel jour de la semaine ?	*What day of the week is it?*

When — quand
Who — qui
Where — où

Question
D'où viens-tu ?
Where are you from?

Simple Answer
Je viens de Millom.
I'm from Millom.

Extended Answer
Je viens de Millom, dans le nord-ouest de l'Angleterre. C'est une petite ville tranquille.
I'm from Millom, in north-west England. It's a small, quiet town.

Practice Questions

Q1 *Imagine you are at a restaurant with your friend. Ask the following questions out loud in French.*

- *Ask what time the restaurant closes.*
- *Ask your friend if they want chips.*
- *Ask how much an ice cream costs.*
- *Ask where the toilets are.* [4 marks]

'That's another chunk of the children's inheritance spent on ice cream.'

Higher

Q2 *You are interviewing some teachers for a school project. Write a list of questions in French that you will use for the interviews. You should find out:*

- *how long they have been a teacher for*
- *where they work*
- *what subject they teach*
- *why they like being a teacher*
- *what their favourite part of the school day is.* [10 marks]

If the question is 'Can I stop revising yet?', the answer is 'Non'…

In the speaking exam, you'll have to ask the examiner a question. This page covers lots of different ways to pose questions, so practise coming up with questions for all the topics until you've got them down.

Find the CGP RevisionHub at cgpbooks.co.uk/Bonjour

Section One — General Stuff

Being Polite

'I want' never gets — unless you want more exciting French vocab, that is. Learn the words and expressions on these pages and wow everyone with your French charm. Please.

Bonjour...au revoir — *Hello...goodbye*

Learn these phrases — they're crucial.

Vocabulary

bonjour	*hello*	ça va	*it's fine, I'm fine*
bienvenue	*welcome*	félicitations	*congratulations*
voici	*here is*	monsieur	*sir, Mr, gentleman*
bonsoir	*good evening*	madame	*Mrs, Ms, madam, lady*
au revoir	*goodbye*	mademoiselle	*Miss, Ms*
à bientôt	*see you soon*	salut	*hi, bye*
à demain	*see you tomorrow*	enchanté(e)	*pleased to meet you*
ça va ?	*how are you?*		

Stephen practised his French by greeting himself every morning.

Comment ça va ? — *How are you?*

Comment ça va ?	*How are you? (informal)*
Je me sens super bien.	*I feel super.*
Pas mal.	*Not bad.*
Félicitations pour votre succès !	*Congratulations on your success!*
Bienvenue à l'hôtel.	*Welcome to the hotel.*
Voici votre chambre.	*Here is your room.*
À bientôt !	*See you later!*

How are you? (formal) — Comment allez-vous?

awful — très mal

well — bien

Grammar — using 'tu' and 'vous'

There are two ways of saying 'you' in French.

- 'Tu' is singular and informal. You should use it with a friend or family member.
- 'Vous' is for more than one person, or for one person in a formal situation, e.g. a stranger or someone older than you.

The conversation below shows some common phrases in use:

Madame Rollet:	Bonjour Nour, comment ça va ?	*Hello Nour, how are you?*
Nour:	Ça va bien. Comment allez-vous ?	*I'm fine. How are you?*
Madame Rollet:	Pas mal, merci.	*Not bad, thanks.*
Nour:	Est-ce que je peux vous présenter Sahil ?	*May I introduce Sahil?*
Madame Rollet:	Enchantée. Ça va ?	*Pleased to meet you. How are you?*
Sahil:	Ça ne va pas très bien.	*I'm not very well.*
Madame Rollet:	Pourquoi ?	*Why?*
Sahil:	Je me sens un peu triste aujourd'hui.	*I feel a bit sad today.*

Nour uses the polite 'vous' form — Madame Rollet is older than her.

If you're talking to someone you call 'tu', say 'est-ce que je peux te présenter' — it's informal.

Je voudrais... — *I would like...*

1) '<u>Je voudrais</u>' (*I would like*) is <u>more polite</u> than '<u>je veux</u>' (*I want*).

> Je voudrais un verre d'eau.   *I would like a glass of water.*
>
> Je voudrais du pain.   *I would like some bread.*

> *He would like* — Il voudrait
> *She would like* — Elle voudrait

'Je voudrais' is in the conditional tense — see p.139 for more.

2) '<u>Est-ce que je peux...</u>' means '<u>Can I...</u>' or '<u>May I...</u>'.

> Est-ce que je peux m'asseoir ?   *Can I sit down?*

See p.8-9 for more about forming questions.

S'il vous plaît — *Please*

Don't forget these useful <u>polite words</u> — they could make all the difference...

Vocabulary

s'il te plaît	*please (informal)*	attention	*watch out*
s'il vous plaît	*please (formal)*	(quel) dommage	*what a shame*
merci (beaucoup)	*thank you (very much)*	désolé(e)	*sorry*
d'accord	*okay, alright*		

Don't forget to say 's'il te plaît' instead of 's'il vous plaît' if you're talking to someone you call 'tu.'

Grammar — 'désolé' or 'désolée'?

Like 'enchanté', 'désolé' has to <u>agree</u> with the <u>subject</u>. You add an extra '<u>e</u>' if you're female:

Je suis désol<u>é</u>. *I'm sorry.* (male)   **Je suis désol<u>ée</u>.** *I'm sorry.* (female)

Practice Questions

Q1   *Read the following email that Amelia has written to her party planner, then answer the questions below.*

> *Bonsoir ! Je voudrais organiser une grande fête pour l'anniversaire de mon mari. Je voudrais du jazz, un gâteau et des lumières dans le jardin pour l'événement. Est-ce qu'on peut aussi avoir un feu d'artifice à la fin de la soirée, s'il vous plaît ? Merci !*

a)   What occasion is the party celebrating?   *[1 mark]*

b)   What food would Amelia like to order for the party?   *[1 mark]*

c)   Where does Amelia want the lights to be put?   *[1 mark]*

d)   What will happen at the end of the party?   *[1 mark]*

Q2   *Write a script about two people informally meeting and introducing themselves for the first time. Write about 50 words in French. Then edit your script to make it more formal. Make sure your two characters:*

- *greet one another*
- *introduce themselves*
- *ask one another how they're doing.*   *[10 marks]*

WRITING

Top Tip for Higher Students
✓ Try to include some Higher-only adjectives to show off your vocabulary.

How many words does French have for 'you'? Tu many...

You don't want to begin every conversation on the wrong foot. Being able to adjust the politeness and formality of your language depending on who you're talking to is a useful skill to have under your belt.

Opinions

Having an opinion is a great way to pick up lots of marks in the exam, so don't hold back on giving your views. Just make sure your rants are peppered with exciting phrases and vocab...

Qu'est-ce que tu penses de... ? — *What do you think of...?*

There are lots of ways to ask someone their opinion in French.

Vocabulary

l'opinion (f)	*opinion*
l'avis (m)	*opinion, mind*
penser (à / de)	*to think (about / of)*
exprimer	*to express*
selon	*according to*
H poser	*to ask (a question)*
ajouter	*to add*

Qu'est-ce que tu penses de cette chanson ? — *What do you think of this song?*

Quel est ton avis sur cette émission ? — *What's your opinion of this TV show?*

Est-que je peux te poser une question sur le sport ? — *Can I ask you a question about sport?*

Selon toi, quelle est la meilleure saison ? — *In your opinion, what is the best season?*

Speak your mind to sound impressive

Vocabulary

oui	*yes*	adorer	*to love, really like*
non	*no*	aimer	*to like*
absolument	*absolutely*	préférer	*to prefer*
peut-être	*perhaps*	préféré(e)	*favourite*
l'intérêt (m)	*interest*	détester	*to hate, detest*
ça m'est égal	*I'm not bothered*	**H** apprécier	*to appreciate*

Be careful — 'j'aime Pierre' can mean 'I like Pierre' OR 'I love Pierre'. If you only like him, it's safer to say 'je trouve Pierre sympathique' (*I think Pierre is nice*) or 'j'aime bien Pierre' (*I like Pierre*). Otherwise you might be giving out the wrong message...

J'aime bien lire. — *I like reading.*

Je m'intéresse à la musique. — *I'm interested in music.*

Je déteste vraiment danser. — *I absolutely hate dancing.*

Tu es d'accord avec moi ? — *Do you agree with me?*

Non, à mon avis le shopping en ligne est moins pratique que les magasins. — *No, in my opinion online shopping is less practical than shops.*

I'm not interested in — Je ne m'intéresse pas à

with that — avec ça

in my view — selon moi

Parce que — *Because*

The best way to justify your opinion is to give a reason.

Vocabulary

parce que	*because*
car	*because*
à cause de	*because of*

J'aime ce film parce que les acteurs sont formidables. — *I like this film because the actors are terrific.*

Je trouve ce film nul car l'histoire est ennuyeuse. — *I think this film is rubbish because the story is boring.*

Use describing words to explain your opinions

Here are some <u>describing words</u> that you can use to <u>explain</u> your opinion. If you don't have an opinion on something, just make one up. There aren't any marks available for <u>shrugging</u>...

Vocabulary

bon(ne)	*good*	affreux / affreuse	*awful*
super	*great*	embêtant(e)	*annoying*
génial(e)	*great*	ennuyeux / ennuyeuse	*boring*
parfait(e)	*perfect*	mauvais(e)	*bad*
excellent(e)	*excellent*	nul(le)	*rubbish*
passionnant(e)	*exciting*	terrible	*terrible, dreadful*
extraordinaire	*extraordinary*	étonnant(e)	*surprising, amazing*
amusant(e)	*funny, enjoyable*	formidable	*terrific, astounding*
intéressant(e)	*interesting*		

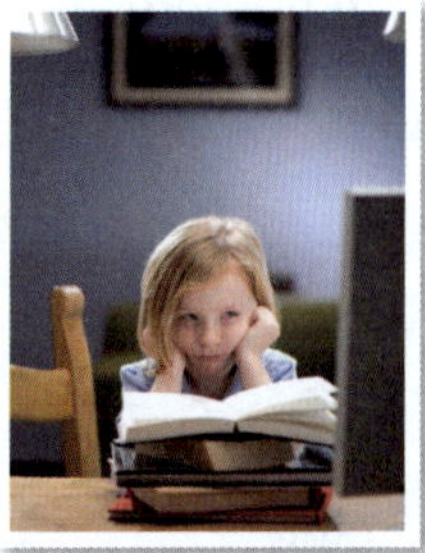
'Zero stars. Would not recommend.'

Je pense que c'est très intéressant.	*I think that it's very interesting.*
J'aime bien cette série. Je trouve l'histoire passionnante et elle me touche beaucoup.	*I like this series. I find the story exciting and it moves me a lot.*

Grammar — 'ce'/'cette'/'cet'

'<u>Ce</u>' (*this / that*) becomes '<u>cette</u>' in front of feminine nouns.

For masculine nouns starting with a vowel, you use '<u>cet</u>'. See p.123 for more info.

Q&A Audio

Question

Qu'est-ce que tu penses de la musique classique ?

What do you think of classical music?

Simple Answer

J'adore ça — c'est super.

I love it — it's great.

Extended Answer

Je ne m'intéresse pas à la musique classique parce qu'à mon avis, c'est ennuyeux.

I'm not interested in classical music because, in my opinion, it's boring.

Practice Questions

Q1 Listen to this recording from your French partner school. Blandine and Marc are talking about what they do at the weekend. Decide whether the statements below are true or false.

LISTENING

    a) i) Blandine has fun with her sports team.   *[1 mark]*

        ii) Marc dislikes all sports.   *[1 mark]*

    b) i) The book Marc is reading is boring.   *[1 mark]*

        ii) Blandine often reads novels.   *[1 mark]*

    c) i) Blandine likes different kinds of films.   *[1 mark]*

        ii) Marc enjoys watching action films.   *[1 mark]*

Listening Track 3

Q2 Answer the following questions out loud in French. You should talk for about 20 seconds for each question.

SPEAKING

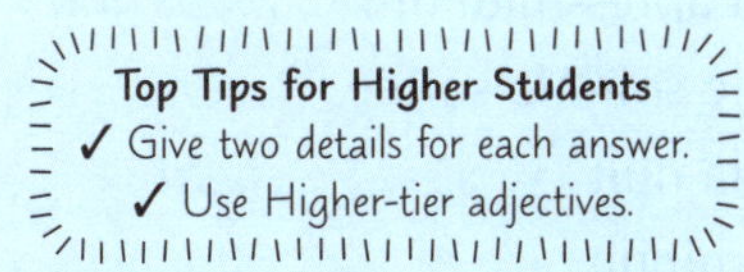

- *Quel est ton film préféré et pourquoi ?*
- *Que penses-tu de ton école ?*
- *Qui est ton chanteur ou groupe préféré ?*   *[6 marks]*

No, I don't want to hear your opinion on my jokes...

Giving your opinion is a fantastic way to pick up extra marks. You can use adjectives to support your opinions with reasoning — if you say you like or dislike something, try to explain why that's the case.

General Stuff — Vocabulary

These pages are full of useful vocab that you'll find yourself using all the time, so make sure you've nailed the basics.

Numbers

le nombre	*number*
le numéro	*number*
un	*one*
deux	*two*
trois	*three*
quatre	*four*
cinq	*five*
six	*six*
sept	*seven*
huit	*eight*
neuf	*nine*
dix	*ten*
onze	*eleven*
douze	*twelve*
treize	*thirteen*
quatorze	*fourteen*
quinze	*fifteen*
seize	*sixteen*
dix-sept	*seventeen*
dix-huit	*eighteen*
dix-neuf	*nineteen*
vingt	*twenty*

'Number' can be translated as 'nombre' or 'numéro', depending on the context. E.g. you say 'elle habite au <u>numéro</u> sept' (*she lives at number 7*), but 'le <u>nombre</u> de personnes a augmenté' (*the number of people has increased*).

Remember to add 'et un' to numbers ending in '1'.

vingt et un	*twenty-one*
vingt-deux	*twenty-two*
trente	*thirty*
quarante	*forty*
cinquante	*fifty*
soixante	*sixty*
soixante-dix	*seventy*
quatre-vingts	*eighty*
quatre-vingt-dix	*ninety*
cent	*one hundred*
mille	*one thousand*
le millier	*thousand*
le million	*million*

premier / première	*first*
deuxième	*second*
troisième	*third*
quatrième	*fourth*
cinquième	*fifth*
sixième	*sixth*
septième	*seventh*
huitième	*eighth*
neuvième	*ninth*
dixième	*tenth*
centième	*hundredth*
environ	*about*
la moitié	*half*
compter	*to count*

Higher

une dizaine	*about ten*
une centaine	*about a hundred*
la majorité	*majority*
la plupart (de)	*most, majority (of)*
le chiffre	*figure, number*
le compte	*account, count*
le milieu	*middle*

Times

l'heure (f)	*hour, time*
la minute	*minute*
demi	*half*
le quart	*quarter*
le matin	*morning*
midi	*noon*
l'après-midi (m)	*afternoon*
le soir / la soirée	*evening*
la nuit	*night*
minuit	*midnight*
le moment	*moment*
en ce moment	*at the moment*
tard	*late*
en retard	*late*
toujours	*always*

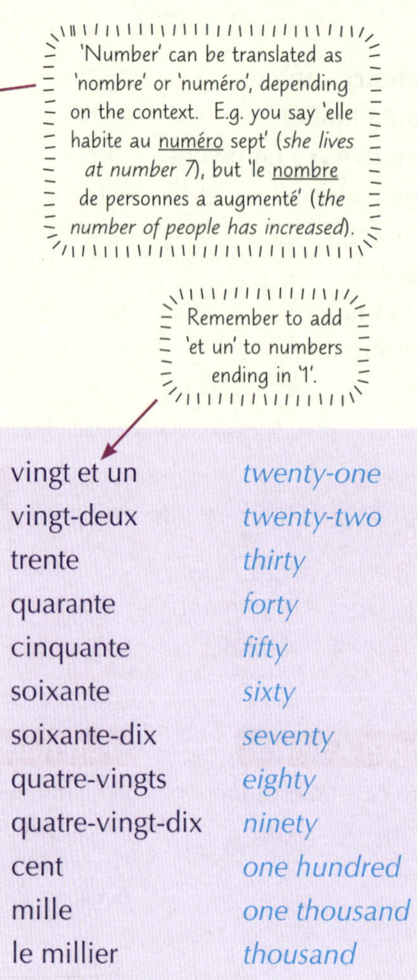

To say what time it is, you say 'il est ... heure(s)', e.g. 'il est trois heures'.

'Le soir' usually refers to the time at which something happens, while 'la soirée' means the duration of the evening, e.g. 'toute la soirée' (*all evening*).

'Tard' refers to it being late in the day, while 'en retard' refers to being behind schedule.

maintenant	*now*
après	*after*
avant	*before*
pendant	*during*
enfin	*finally*
parfois	*sometimes*
souvent	*often*
normalement	*normally*
généralement	*generally*
presque	*almost*
immédiatement	*immediately*
finalement	*finally*
longtemps	*a long time, a long while*
H l'instant (m)	*instant, moment*

Dates

la date	*date*	la semaine	*week*	le siècle	*century*
lundi	*Monday*	le week-end	*weekend*	la saison	*season*
mardi	*Tuesday*	janvier	*January*	le printemps	*spring*
mercredi	*Wednesday*	février	*February*	l'été (m)	*summer*
jeudi	*Thursday*	mars	*March*	l'automne (m)	*autumn*
vendredi	*Friday*	avril	*April*	l'hiver (m)	*winter*
samedi	*Saturday*	mai	*May*	la fois	*time*
dimanche	*Sunday*	juin	*June*	le présent	*present*
à (lundi) !	*see you on (Monday)!*	juillet	*July*	le passé	*past*
		août	*August*	l'avenir (m)	*future*
aujourd'hui	*today*	septembre	*September*	le futur	*future*
le jour / la journée	*day*	octobre	*October*	bientôt	*soon*
		novembre	*November*	dernier / dernière	*last*
demain	*tomorrow*	décembre	*December*	prochain(e)	*next*
hier	*yesterday*	le mois	*month*	récent(e)	*recent*
le lendemain	*next day*	l'an (m) / l'année (f)	*year*	récemment	*recently*
quotidien(ne)	*daily*			**H** l'époque (f)	*era, period, time*

Questions

la question	*question*	qui ?	*who?*
quand ?	*when?*	quoi ?	*what?*
pourquoi ?	*why?*	que, qu' ?	*what?*
où ?	*where?*	quel / quelle ?	*which?*
comment ?	*how?*	est-ce que, est-ce qu'	*expression put before a verb that makes a sentence into a question*
combien ?	*how much / many?*		

Being Polite

bonjour	*hello, good morning*	(quel) dommage	*what a shame*
bienvenue	*welcome*	félicitations	*congratulations*
voici	*here is*	monsieur	*sir, Mr, gentleman*
bonsoir	*good evening*	madame	*Mrs, Ms, madam, lady*
au revoir	*goodbye*	mademoiselle	*Miss, Ms*
à bientôt	*see you soon*	s'il te plaît	*please (informal)*
à demain	*see you tomorrow*	s'il vous plaît	*please (formal)*
ça va ?	*how's it going?, how are you?*	merci (beaucoup)	*thank you (very much)*
		d'accord	*okay, alright*
ça va	*it's fine, I'm fine, it's OK*	**H** salut	*hi, bye*
désolé(e)	*sorry*	enchanté(e)	*pleased to meet you*
attention	*watch out, attention*		

General Stuff — Vocabulary

Opinions

l'opinion (f)	*opinion*
l'avis (m)	*opinion, mind*
le côté	*side*
l'idée (f)	*idea*
oui	*yes*
non	*no*
bien	*well*
mal	*badly*
probablement	*probably*
absolument	*absolutely*
malheureusement	*unfortunately*
peut-être	*maybe, perhaps*
ça m'est égal	*I'm not bothered*

la raison	*reason*
l'intérêt (m)	*interest*
le tort	*wrong*
le doute	*doubt*
l'espoir (m)	*hope*
la peur	*fear*
selon	*according to*
c'est-à-dire	*in other words, that is to say*
la pensée	*thought*
le plaisir	*pleasure*
l'argument (m)	*argument*
le contraire	*opposite, contrary*

Higher (c'est-à-dire to le contraire)

'Wrong' is an adjective in English, but it's a noun in French. It's used with 'avoir', e.g. 'il a tort' (*he is wrong*).

Opinions — Verbs

adorer	*to love, really like, adore*
aimer	*to like*
préférer	*to prefer*
détester	*to hate, detest*
exprimer	*to express*
raconter	*to tell, narrate*
intéresser	*to interest*
s'intéresser à	*to be interested (in)*
penser (à / de)	*to think (about / of)*

poser	*to ask, put (a question)*
apprécier	*to appreciate, like*
souligner	*to underline, stress*
remarquer	*to remark, notice*
noter	*to mark, write down, notice*
ajouter	*to add*
concerner	*to affect, concern, relate to*

Higher (poser to concerner)

Opinions — Adjectives

bon(ne)	*good*
super	*great*
génial(e)	*great, brilliant*
préféré(e)	*favourite*
parfait(e)	*perfect*
excellent(e)	*excellent*
passionnant(e)	*exciting, thrilling*
extraordinaire	*extraordinary*
amusant(e)	*funny, enjoyable, fun, amusing*
intéressant(e)	*interesting*
heureux / heureuse	*happy*
content(e)	*glad, pleased*
certain(e)	*certain, sure*

clair(e)	*clear*
triste	*sad*
affreux / affreuse	*dreadful, awful, horrible*
embêtant(e)	*annoying*
ennuyeux / ennuyeuse	*boring*
mauvais(e)	*bad*
nul(le)	*rubbish*
terrible	*terrible, dreadful*
étonnant(e)	*surprising, amazing, incredible*
formidable	*terrific, astounding*

Higher (étonnant(e) to formidable)

Useful Nouns

l'accent (m)	*accent*	la liste	*list*		la demande	*request, demand*
l'article (m)	*article, item*	le moyen	*means, way*		le désir	*desire*
la chose	*thing*	l'ordre (m)	*order*		le détail	*detail*
le début	*beginning*	la possibilité	*possibility*		le document	*document*
la décision	*decision*	la situation	*situation*		l'émotion (f)	*emotion, feeling*
la difficulté	*difficulty*	le sens	*sense, meaning*		la manière	*manner, way*
l'exemple (m)	*example*	la sorte	*sort, kind*		la mémoire	*memory*
la façon	*way, manner*	le système	*system*		l'origine (f)	*origin, source*
la fin	*end*	la vérité	*truth*		la perte	*loss*
les gens (m)	*people*	le cas	*case, scenario*		la production	*production*
l'importance (f)	*importance*	le contexte	*context*		le reste	*rest*
l'intention (f)	*intention*	la définition	*definition*			

Higher: le cas, le contexte, la définition

Higher: la demande → le reste

Useful Verbs

apporter	*to bring (something)*	s'asseoir	*to sit down*
changer	*to change*	avouer	*to admit to, confess to*
créer	*to create*	décevoir	*to disappoint*
croire	*to believe*	définir	*to define*
décrire	*to describe*	démontrer	*to demonstrate*
devenir	*to become*	dépendre de	*to depend on*
dire	*to say, tell*	hésiter	*to hesitate*
(avoir) dit	*(have) said, (have) told*	inclure	*to include*
espérer	*to hope*	(avoir) inclus	*to (have) included*
mettre	*to put*	interrompre	*to interrupt, halt*
(avoir) mis	*(to have) put*	laisser	*to leave, let*
se mettre à	*to start, begin*	occuper	*to fill*
oublier	*to forget*	s'occuper (de)	*to keep busy, take care (of)*
prononcer	*to pronounce*	oser	*to dare*
proposer de	*to propose (to), offer, suggest*	placer	*to put, place*
se servir de	*to use, make use of*	se placer	*to position yourself*
signifier	*to mean*	produire	*to produce, make*
sourire	*to smile*	remercier	*to thank*
trouver	*to find*	rendre	*to return something, give something back, make*
admettre	*to admit*	reposer	*to put down*
amener	*to bring (someone)*	souhaiter	*to wish*
appartenir	*to belong*	tenir	*to hold*
asseoir	*to sit (someone)*	toucher	*to touch*

Higher: admettre, amener, appartenir, asseoir

Higher: s'asseoir → toucher

Useful Phrases

il y a	*there is / there are*	il est (difficile) de	*it is (difficult) to*
il y aura	*there will be*	il manque	*it is missing*
il y avait	*there was / there were*	il vaut la peine de	*it is worth*
il faut	*it is, it's necessary, must*	il vaut mieux	*it is better (to)*

Higher: il est (difficile) de, il manque, il vaut la peine de, il vaut mieux

Revision Summary Test for Section One

Put your knowledge of the basics to the test with these summary questions for Section One.

* These questions are **hard**, but they'll really help you see **how well you know your stuff**.
* Tackle the **revision summary test** below, or scan the QR code to do it **online**.
  You can **track your progress** online and see **which areas need more work**.
* There are **sample answers** for the test here: www.cgpbooks.co.uk/BonjourExtras

Numbers and Times

1) In words, write the numbers 1-20 in French.

2) Write down the French for these numbers:
   a) fifty-two   b) seventy-four   c) ninety-three   d) five hundred and eighty   e) six thousand

3) How would you say the following words in French?   a) first   b) fourth   c) ninth   d) tenth

4) Say the current time in French. Then write the French for each of these times:
   a) 11:30 am   b) 18:00   c) 20:47   d) 10 pm   e) 00:00

5) Translate this sentence into French: 'It is almost four in the afternoon,
   so I must leave immediately or I am going to be late.'

6) What do the words below mean in English?
   a) une centaine   b) le chiffre   c) le milieu   d) la plupart   e) le compte   f) l'instant

Days and Dates

7) List the days of the week in French. Then list them again, backwards.

8) Give all of the months of the year in French, then list the four seasons.

9) What do these words mean in English?
   a) bientôt   b) quotidien   c) le lendemain   d) hier   e) semaine   f) prochain

10) 'Quand est l'anniversaire de ton meilleur ami ?' Write your answer in words and in French.

11) What is the French for these words?
    a) century   b) recent   c) last   d) tomorrow   e) time   f) past

Questions

12) List as many question words as you can in French. There are at least 9 you need to know.

13) What do these questions mean in English?
    a) Pourquoi tu manges ?   c) Qu'est-ce que tu manges ?   e) Avec qui manges-tu ?
    b) Où est-ce que tu manges ?   d) Quand est-ce que tu manges ?   f) Quel légume manges-tu ?

Being Polite

14) What's the French for the following phrases? a) see you soon   b) see you tomorrow   c) I'm sorry

15) Write down a short conversation between two people in French. Have them
    say hello to each other, ask each other how they are and then say goodbye.

16) What's the English for these phrases?   a) dire la vérité   b) il se met à sourire   c) s'il vous plaît

17) Translate these words and phrases into French: a) hi   b) pleased to meet you   c) with pleasure

Opinions

18) In French, give 5 adjectives you could use to express a positive opinion
    and 5 adjectives you could use to express a negative opinion.

19) Translate these phrases about opinions on sport into French:
    a) I adore playing sport.   c) I'm interested in sport.   e) I find football thrilling.
    b) I don't like sport.   d) Sport is a good way to relax.   f) Sport changed my life.

20) Answer this question in French: 'Quel est ton avis sur les films d'action ?'

Quick Quiz

About Yourself

Learning to tell the examiner about yourself is really important. If you don't have much to say, just make stuff up. As long as you don't say you were born in 3020, they'll never know...

Je m'appelle... — *My name is...*

Don't forget you can access your online content here: www.cgpbooks.co.uk/Bonjour

Vocabulary

le nom	*surname, name*	espagnol(e)	*Spanish*
s'appeler	*to be named*	européen(ne)	*European*
l'âge (m)	*age*	bi(sexuel) /	*bi(sexual)*
la date	*date*	bi(sexuelle)	
(être) né(e)	*(to have been) born*	gay	*gay*
		hétéro	*straight*
la langue	*language*	l'enfance (f)	*childhood*
français(e)	*French*	africain(e)	*African*
anglais(e)	*English*	arabe	*Arabic, Arab*
britannique	*British*	francophone	*French-speaking*
allemand(e)	*German*		

(Higher: l'enfance, africain(e), arabe, francophone)

Grammar — saying your age

In French, you don't say how old you <u>are</u> — you say how many years you <u>have</u>. This means you need to use the verb '<u>avoir</u>' (to have).

Quel âge <u>as</u>-tu ? ⟹ J'<u>ai</u> seize ans.

How old <u>are</u> you? ⟹ *I <u>am</u> sixteen.*

For more on numbers and dates, see p.4-7.

Je m'appelle Sara et j'habite à Natland.

I'm called Sara and I live in Natland.
> near to Kendal — près de Kendal

J'ai quinze ans, et je suis né(e) le neuf juin 2010.

I'm fifteen years old, and I was born on the ninth of June 2010.
> 'Né(e)' needs an extra 'e' on the end if you're female (see p.121).

Mon anniversaire, c'est le deux février.

My birthday is on the second of February.

Je suis britannique mais ma famille est d'origine espagnole.

I'm British but my family is of Spanish origin.
> English — anglais(e)
> Welsh — gallois(e)
> Scottish — écossais(e)
> Irish — irlandais(e)

Pendant mon enfance, j'habitais au Maroc. C'est là que j'ai appris l'arabe.

During my childhood, I lived in Morocco. It's there that I learnt Arabic.

Practice Question

Q1 *Read the following text out loud, then answer the questions below in French.*

> Je m'appelle Sophie et j'ai quinze ans. Mon anniversaire, c'est le dix-sept mars. J'habite avec ma famille à Manchester, en Angleterre. Cependant, je suis allemande. Mes parents sont nés à Munich.

SPEAKING

[5 marks]

Family photos in the Claus household were always a festive affair.

a) *Comment t'appelles-tu ?*

b) *Quel âge as-tu ?*

c) *C'est quand ton anniversaire ?*

d) *Où habites-tu ?* *[10 marks]*

Top Tip for Higher Students
✔ Develop your answers by using different tenses, e.g. talking about where you would like to live in the future.

It's always about 'me', 'me', 'me' — typical...

The vocab on this page will help you answer questions about yourself. And if you run out of things to say about yourself, you could add extra detail about where your parents are from or what your town is called.

My Family and Friends

Despite what's on the previous page, it's not *always* about you... You'll need to be able to describe your family and friends as well. Here's some handy vocab to soothe your sorrows.

La famille proche — *Close relatives*

Vocabulary

la famille	*family*	le frère	*brother*
familial(e)	*family (adj.)*	la sœur	*sister*
le membre	*member*	l'oncle (m)	*uncle*
le parent	*parent*	la tante	*aunt*
le père	*father*	le cousin /	*cousin*
la mère	*mother*	la cousine	
le beau-père	*step-father, father-in-law*	l'animal (m)	*animal, pet*
la belle-mère	*step-mother, mother-in-law*	le chien	*dog*
la fille	*daughter*	la maman	*mum, mummy*
le fils	*son*	garder	*to take care of, look after*

When you're talking about something or someone that belongs to you, e.g. 'my sister', you need to use a possessive adjective (see p.123).

Parle-moi de ta famille — *Tell me about your family*

Question

Est-ce que tu as une grande famille ?

Have you got a big family?

Simple Answer

J'ai une petite famille — nous sommes quatre.

I've got a small family — there are four of us.

Grammar — comparisons

To compare one person or thing to another, use 'plus / moins...que' (*more / less...than*) with an adjective in the middle. See p.124.

Elle est plus jeune que moi.
She is younger than me.

Extended Answer

J'ai une petite famille et nous sommes très proches. J'ai un frère qui est plus jeune que moi et une cousine. Nous avons aussi un chien qui s'appelle Felix.

I've got a small family and we are very close. I have a younger brother and one cousin (female). We also have a dog called Felix.

The photographer forgot to tell the Grey family to say 'cheese'.

Dans ma famille, il y a neuf personnes.	*In my family, there are nine people.*	
J'ai une grande famille car mes parents sont séparés et j'ai un beau-père et une belle-mère.	*I have a big family because my parents are separated and I have a step-father and a step-mother.*	*don't live together —* ne vivent pas ensemble *are divorced —* sont divorcés
J'ai deux frères qui sont plus grands que moi.	*I have two brothers who are taller than me.*	*older —* plus âgés *younger —* plus jeunes
Le partenaire de ma mère vient du Canada, donc j'ai de la famille à l'étranger.	*My mum's partner comes from Canada, so I have some family abroad.*	*isn't British —* n'est pas britannique
Ma mère a trois sœurs, mais mon père est fils unique.	*My mum has three sisters, but my dad is an only child.*	*my grandmother is an only child —* ma grand-mère est fille unique

Tu t'entends bien avec... ? — *Do you get on well with...?*

Vocabulary

l'ami(e)	*friend*	aider	*to help*
s'entendre (avec)	*to get on, get along (with)*	comprendre	*to understand*
rencontrer	*to meet, run into*	encourager	*to encourage*
proche	*nearby, close*	écouter	*to listen*
connaître	*to know, be familiar with*	excuser	*to excuse, forgive*
passer	*to spend time, pass*	s'excuser	*to apologise*
parler	*to speak, talk*	**H** le lien	*link, bond*
discuter	*to discuss, talk about*	soutenir	*to support*

Je connais beaucoup de gens dans ma ville. — *I know lots of people in my town.*

Tu t'entends avec ta famille ? — *Do you get on with your family?*

Je m'entends bien avec mes parents. — *I get on well with my parents.*

Mon amie n'est pas gentille, parce qu'elle ne s'excuse jamais après une dispute. — *My friend is unkind because she never apologises after a dispute.*

Mes amis me soutiennent toujours — nous avons des liens très forts. — *My friends always support me — we have a very strong bond.*

I've made friends — Je me suis fait des amis

I have a good relationship — J'ai un bon rapport

spend a lot of time together — passons beaucoup de temps ensemble

Practice Questions

Q1 Write a description of your family and friends.
You should write about 50-90 words in French. Describe:

- the size of your family
- the members of your family
- whether you get along with your family and friends
- what activities you like to do with your friends. **[10 marks]**

Top Tips for Higher Students
✓ Use plural reflexive pronouns, e.g. 'nous <u>nous</u> entendons bien'.
✓ Add more detail to your sentences using relative pronouns like 'qui' and 'que'.

Higher

Q2 Read this email that your penfriend Manon wrote about her family and answer the questions below in English.

Dans ma famille, il y a trois personnes — ma mère, mon père et moi. Je n'ai ni frères ni sœurs, mais heureusement, j'ai un oiseau qui s'appelle Marcel. J'ai aussi beaucoup de cousins et je passe souvent du temps avec eux. Le week-end dernier, par exemple, nous sommes allés au cinéma car nous avons l'habitude d'aller voir un film ensemble tous les mois. C'est une tradition familiale.

a) Who is in Manon's immediate family? *[1 mark]*
b) What animal does Manon have as a pet? *[1 mark]*
c) What did Manon do last weekend? *[1 mark]*
d) Why did Manon choose to do this? *[1 mark]*

You won't find poached *père* on many dessert menus...

Describing the members of your family will help score you extra marks, so keep a few handy adjectives in your pocket that you can use to add interest to your answers. That's where the next page comes in...

Describing People

Now you know how to name people in French, you can begin to describe them. This is a great opportunity to learn how to insult an annoying sibling in flawless French, so don't let it slip by.

Décrire les autres — *Describing others*

Vocabulary

le visage	*face*	noir(e)	*black*
les yeux (m)	*eyes*	blanc(he)	*white*
les cheveux (m)	*hair*	brun(e)	*brown*
long(ue)	*long*	rouge	*red*
court(e)	*short*	bleu(e)	*blue*
grand(e)	*tall, big, large*	vert(e)	*green*
petit(e)	*short, small*	ressembler à	*to look like*
la taille	*size, height*	se ressembler	*to look alike*
joli(e)	*pretty, attractive*	l'air (m)	*air, appearance*
beau / bel / belle	*beautiful*	gris(e)	*grey*
la couleur	*colour*	grandir	*to grow*

[Higher] — applies to l'air, gris(e), grandir

Grammar — agreements

Adjectives <u>agree</u> with the <u>person or thing</u> they're describing — if it's <u>feminine</u>, you need to add an 'e' onto the <u>end of the adjective</u>. If it's <u>plural</u>, add an '<u>s</u>'. If it's <u>feminine and plural</u>, add '<u>es</u>'.

Ma copine est très petite.
My girlfriend is very short.

Elle a les cheveux longs.
She has long hair.

Watch out for <u>irregular</u> adjectives though, e.g. '<u>blanc</u>' becomes '<u>blanche</u>' when it agrees with a feminine noun.

Ma sœur est assez grande et jolie. Elle a les yeux bleus et les cheveux longs.

My sister is quite tall and pretty. She has blue eyes and long hair.

Mon meilleur copain a les yeux verts et les cheveux noirs.

My best friend has green eyes and black hair.

Je ressemble à mon père car je suis petit et j'ai les yeux verts comme lui.

I look like my dad because I am short and I have green eyes like him.

Mon père avait les cheveux bruns quand il était jeune, mais maintenant il a les cheveux gris.

My dad had brown hair when he was young, but now he has grey hair.

fat —	grosse
slim —	mince
a beard —	une barbe
wears glasses —	porte des lunettes
average height —	de taille moyenne
blonde —	blonds
ginger —	roux

Décris-toi — *Describe yourself*

Question

À quoi ressembles-tu ?
What do you look like?

Simple Answer

Je suis grand(e) et j'ai les yeux bleus.
I am tall and I have blue eyes.

Extended Answer

Je suis grand(e) mais je suis plus petit(e) que mon frère. Comme ma mère, j'ai les yeux verts. Mes cheveux sont courts et bruns. Pourtant, je voudrais changer la couleur de mes cheveux, car je trouve que les cheveux noirs sont plus jolis.

I am tall but I am shorter than my brother. Like my mother, I have green eyes. My hair is short and brown. However, I would like to change the colour of my hair because I think that black hair is prettier.

Grammar — false friends

Some French words sound like English words, but have a <u>different</u> meaning.

sensible	*sensitive (not sensible)*
grand(e)	*big / tall (not grand)*
joli(e)	*pretty (not jolly)*
sympathique	*nice (not sympathetic)*

La personnalité — *Personality*

Vocabulary

timide	*timid, shy*	méchant(e)	*nasty, naughty*	strict(e)	*strict*
bavard(e)	*chatty*	inquiet / inquiète	*worried*	spécial(e)	*special*
fier / fière	*proud*	sérieux / sérieuse	*conscientious*	intelligent(e)	*intelligent*
drôle	*funny*	travailleur / travailleuse	*hard-working*	patient(e)	*patient*
gentil(le)	*kind*	paresseux / paresseuse	*lazy*	vif / vive	*lively*
sympathique	*nice, kind*	ennuyeux / ennuyeuse	*boring*	la blague	*joke*
agréable	*pleasant*				
calme	*calm, quiet*				
fort(e)	*strong, loud*				
embêtant(e)	*annoying*				

Higher: patient(e), vif / vive, la blague

Grammar — imperfect tense

To describe someone in the <u>past</u>, use the <u>imperfect tense</u> (see p.137).
Elle <u>était</u> vive et bavarde.   She <u>was</u> lively and talkative.

Mes parents sont vraiment patients et agréables. — *My parents are really patient and nice.*

Mon père pense qu'il est drôle, mais je trouve ses blagues ennuyeuses. — *My dad thinks that he is funny, but I find his jokes boring.*

Mon frère est paresseux et il ne pense jamais aux autres. Cependant, je suis très fier / fière de ma famille. — *My brother is lazy and he never thinks about others. However, I'm very proud of my family.*

Mon amie Li est vraiment sympa. Elle est toujours là pour moi quand j'ai un problème. — *My friend Li is really nice. She is always there for me when I have a problem.*

Practice Questions

Q1 *In this extract from a podcast, Fabien is being interviewed about his family.*

*There are two true statements in each list below.
Choose the correct statements from each list.*

a) **A.** It's never quiet at Fabien's house.   **C.** His sisters have blue eyes.
    B. Fabien is the youngest child at home.   **D.** Fabien is shorter than his brother.   *[2 marks]*

b) **A.** Fabien's mother has short hair.   **C.** His father has white hair.
    B. His father is tall.   **D.** Fabien looks like his father.   *[2 marks]*

c) **A.** Fabien's mother has a lot of siblings.   **C.** His father has three sisters.
    B. Fabien has a lot of cousins.   **D.** Fabien lives near his grandparents.   *[2 marks]*

Q2 *Write a description of your best friend for your blog.
You should write about 90 words in French. Describe:*

- *the appearance and personality of your friend*
- *why they are your best friend*
- *an activity you recently did together.*   *[15 marks]*

Top Tips for Higher Students
✓ Use a range of tenses, e.g. talk about when you first met your friend.
✓ Include a wide range of adjectives, e.g. superlatives to talk about your friend's best qualities.

My brother's so *agréable* — when he's asleep...

If you think you've said all there is to say about the people in your life, you can always describe how their appearance or personality has changed over time, or any activities you hope to do with them in future.

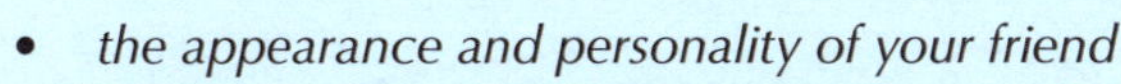

Relationships and Partnerships

The examiners are also pretty interested in your relationships with other people. Luckily, these pages will give you the chance to practise those pesky reflexive verbs you know and love. Get reading...

Être en couple — *Being in a couple*

Vocabulary

le copain	*friend, boyfriend*	supporter	*to tolerate*
la copine	*friend, girlfriend*	se séparer	*to break up*
le / la partenaire	*partner*	regretter	*to be sorry*
le couple	*couple*	le problème	*problem*
seul(e)	*alone*	se disputer	*to argue*
ensemble	*together*	le rapport	*relationship*
désirer	*to want, desire*	la relation	*relationship*
la communication	*communication*	le conflit	*conflict*
communiquer	*to communicate*	mentir	*to lie*
la conversation	*conversation*	tromper	*to cheat, deceive*
l'amour (m)	*love*	critiquer	*to criticise*
la confiance	*trust*		

*(le rapport, la relation, le conflit, mentir, tromper, critiquer are marked **Higher**)*

Grammar — reflexive verbs

Reflexive verbs (see p.140) have an extra part — a reflexive pronoun.

Tu te disputes...
You argue…

In the perfect tense (see p.135), the pronoun goes before the present tense part of 'être' (*to be*).

Je me suis marié(e).
I got married.

J'étais seul(e) pendant deux ans, et puis j'ai rencontré ma copine, Usma.

I was alone for two years, and then I met my girlfriend, Usma.

Mon ami va m'aider à trouver un partenaire.

My friend is going to help me find a partner.

Je sors avec mon copain depuis un an. Il écoute quand je parle de mes problèmes.

I've been going out with my boyfriend for a year. He listens when I talk about my problems.

Le mariage — *Marriage*

Vocabulary

célibataire	*single, unmarried*	égal(e)	*equal*
la femme	*wife*	la société	*society*
le mari	*husband*	la tradition	*tradition*
le mariage	*marriage, wedding*	traditionnel(le)	*traditional*
se marier (avec)	*to marry, get married (to)*	promettre	*to promise*
le mariage du même sexe	*same-sex marriage*	la promesse	*promise*
le PACS	*civil partnership*	unir	*to unite, join*

*(la promesse, unir are marked **H**)*

Claudia was struggling to resist Alain in his new jumper.

À mon avis il est possible d'être un couple fort sans se marier.

In my opinion it is possible to be a strong couple without getting married.

Les mariages sont trop chers. Moi, je préférerais acheter une maison.

Weddings are too expensive. Personally, I would prefer to buy a house.

Aujourd'hui, le PACS est plus courant.

Today, civil partnerships are more common.

I think that — Je pense qu'

In my opinion — Selon moi

These days — De nos jours

Tu voudrais te marier ? — *Do you want to get married?*

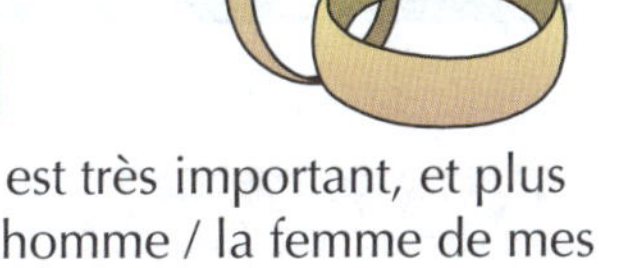

Q&A Audio

Question

Tu voudrais te marier un jour ?

Do you want to get married one day?

Simple Answer

Oui, plus tard, je voudrais me marier et avoir des enfants.

Yes, in the future I'd like to get married and have children.

Extended Answers

Oui, pour moi le mariage est très important, et plus tard, j'espère rencontrer l'homme / la femme de mes rêves et rester avec lui / elle pour toujours. Je ne comprends pas les gens qui ne désirent pas se marier.

Yes, marriage is very important for me, and in the future I hope to meet the man / woman of my dreams and stay with him / her forever. I don't understand people who don't want to get married.

Moi, je ne veux absolument pas me marier. Par contre, pour moi, ce qui est plus important c'est l'amour et la confiance. On peut être avec quelqu'un et avoir des enfants sans se marier.

I absolutely don't want to get married. On the other hand, for me, what's more important is love and trust. You can be with someone and have children without getting married.

Grammar — talking about the future

There are lots of different ways to talk about your <u>future plans</u>. You can use:

The <u>immediate future</u> (see p.138):

Je vais rencontrer quelqu'un. *I am going to meet someone.*

Or the <u>conditional</u> (see p.139):

Je voudrais avoir une famille. *I would like to have a family.*

Or use '<u>j'espère</u>' (*I hope*) <u>+ infinitive</u>:

J'espère me marier un jour. *I hope to get married one day.*

> If you're taking Higher tier, you can also use the proper future (see p.138).

Practice Questions

Q1 Look at the two photos below. Talk in French about what is in the photos. You should talk for about a minute and say something about both photos.

[5 marks]

Q2 Read these headlines about marriage from a French news website, then answer the questions below in English.

Les mariages étaient moins chers dans le passé — aujourd'hui, ça coûte trop cher	Selon les recherches, les couples qui se marient sont plus heureux que les autres	Le nombre de mariages entre personnes du même sexe a récemment augmenté

a) Give one advantage to getting married mentioned in a headline. [1 mark]

b) Give one disadvantage to getting married mentioned in a headline. [1 mark]

c) Name one way that marriage has changed according to the headlines. [1 mark]

Higher

Emotions run high at weddings — even the cakes are in tiers...

...and if the sight of reflexive verbs is causing your stress levels to rise — fear not. They're simple once you know how to form them, and they'll be really useful when describing your relationships with other people.

Identity & Relationships with Others — Vocabulary

Your relationship with vocab may be a bit rocky, but it's important that you know how to talk about yourself and others.

About Yourself

le nom	name, surname, full name
appeler	to call
s'appeler	to be named
l'âge (m)	age
la date	date
(être) né(e)	(to have been) born
la naissance	birth
la jeunesse	youth
l'identité (f)	identity
handicapé(e)	disabled
la langue	language
français(e)	French

anglais(e)	English
britannique	British
américain(e)	American
canadien(ne)	Canadian
allemand(e)	German
espagnol(e)	Spanish
suisse	Swiss
européen(ne)	European
bi(sexuel) / bi(sexuelle)	bi(sexual)
gay	gay
hétéro	straight, heterosexual

non-binaire	non-binary
queer	queer
transgenre	transgender

Higher:

l'enfance (f)	childhood
le sexe	sex
le handicap	disability
africain(e)	African
chinois(e)	Chinese
marocain(e)	Moroccan
belge	Belgian
arabe	Arabic, Arab
francophone	French-speaking
québécois(e)	from Quebec

My Family and Friends

la famille	family
familial(e)	family (adj.)
la génération	generation
le membre	member
le parent	parent
le père	father
la mère	mother
le beau-père	step-father, father-in-law
la belle-mère	step-mother, mother-in-law
la fille	daughter
le fils	son
le frère	brother
la sœur	sister
l'oncle (m)	uncle
la tante	aunt
le cousin / la cousine	cousin

l'animal (m)	animal, pet
les animaux (m)	animals, pets
le chien	dog
l'ami(e)	friend
s'entendre (avec)	to get on, get along (with)
rencontrer	to meet, run into
proche	nearby, close
connaître	to know, be familiar with
passer	to spend time, pass
parler	to speak, talk
chatter / tchatter	to chat (online)
discuter	to discuss, talk about
aider	to help
l'aide (f)	help
comprendre	to understand

encourager	to encourage
entendre	to hear
écouter	to listen
excuser	to excuse, forgive
s'excuser	to apologise

Higher:

la maman	mum, mummy
la connaissance	acquaintance
unique	unique
garder	to take care of, look after, keep
le lien	link, bond
soutenir	to support
permettre	to allow, permit
(avoir) permis	(to have) allowed, (to have) permitted
manquer	to miss
l'oiseau (m)	bird

When using 'manquer' to talk about missing someone, invert the subject and object. E.g. 'tu me manques' (I miss you).

Describing People — Appearance

la personne	person
l'adulte (m/f)	adult
l'enfant (m/f)	child
le garçon	boy
la fille	girl
l'ado (m/f), l'adolescent(e)	teenager, adolescent
l'homme (m)	man
la femme	woman
la dame	lady
jeune	young
vieux / vieil / vieille	old

le visage	face
les yeux (m)	eyes
les cheveux (m)	hair
long(ue)	long
court(e)	short
grand(e)	tall, big, large
petit(e)	short, small, little
la taille	size, height
joli(e)	pretty, attractive
beau / bel / belle	beautiful
la couleur	colour

noir(e)	black
blanc(he)	white
brun(e)	brown
rouge	red
bleu(e)	blue
vert(e)	green
ressembler à	to look like
se ressembler	to look alike

Higher:

l'air (m)	air, appearance
gris(e)	grey
grandir	to get bigger, get taller, grow

Describing People — Personality

la personnalité	*personality*
le sentiment	*feeling*
timide	*timid, shy, bashful*
bavard(e)	*chatty, talkative*
fier / fière	*proud*
drôle	*funny*
gentil(le)	*kind*
sympa, sympathique	*nice, kind, friendly*
agréable	*pleasant, nice, agreeable*
calme	*calm, quiet*
fort(e)	*strong, loud*
embêtant(e)	*annoying*
méchant(e)	*nasty, naughty, mean*
inquiet / inquiète	*worried, anxious*
sérieux / sérieuse	*conscientious, responsible*
travailleur / travailleuse	*hard-working*
paresseux / paresseuse	*lazy*
ennuyeux / ennuyeuse	*boring*

strict(e)	*strict*
spécial(e)	*special*
intelligent(e)	*intelligent*
la colère	*anger*
l'indépendance (f)	*independence*

Higher

patient(e)	*patient*
vif / vive	*lively*
la blague	*joke*
le type	*type, guy*
le respect	*respect*
respecter	*to respect*
sembler	*to seem*
se sentir	*to feel*
la responsabilité	*responsibility*
responsable	*responsible*
libéral(e)	*liberal*
sensible	*sensitive*
indépendant(e)	*independent*

Relationships and Partnerships

le copain	*friend, boyfriend*
la copine	*friend, girlfriend*
le / la partenaire	*partner*
le couple	*couple*
seul(e)	*alone*
ensemble	*together*
désirer	*to want, desire*
la communication	*communication*
communiquer	*to communicate, pass on*
la conversation	*conversation*
l'amour (m)	*love*
la confiance	*trust*
supporter	*to tolerate, bear, put up with*
séparer	*to separate*
se séparer	*to break up*
regretter	*to be sorry, regret*
le problème	*problem*
différent(e)	*different*
disputer	*to scold, tell off*
se disputer	*to argue*

Some words for family members have more than one meaning, e.g. 'femme' (wife <u>and</u> woman) and 'fille' (*daughter* <u>and</u> *girl*).

célibataire	*single, unmarried*
la femme	*wife*
le mari	*husband*
le mariage	*marriage, wedding*
marier	*to marry (someone to someone)*
se marier (avec)	*to marry, get married (to)*
le mariage du même sexe	*same-sex marriage*
le PACS	*civil partnership*
égal(e)	*equal*
la société	*society*
la tradition	*tradition*
traditionnel(le)	*traditional*
promettre	*to promise*

Higher

le rapport	*relationship*
la relation	*relationship*
le conflit	*conflict*
mentir	*to lie*
tromper	*to cheat, deceive*
critiquer	*to criticise*
la promesse	*promise*
unir	*to unite, join*

The happy couple managed to pose for one good photo before Rover spotted a squirrel.

'rapport' and 'relation' are often used in the plural, e.g. 'j'ai de bonnes relations avec mon père' (*I have a good relationship with my father*).

Revision Summary Test for Section Two

It's time for some summary questions to test just how well you've got on with this section.

- Yep, these questions are **hard** — they'll really help you see **how well you know your stuff**.
- Tackle the **revision summary test** below, or scan the QR code to do it **online**.
  Use the CGP RevisionHub to **track your progress** and see **which areas need more work**.
- You can find **sample answers** here: www.cgpbooks.co.uk/BonjourExtras

About Yourself ☐

1) How many nationalities can you name in French?
   There are at least 8 you need to know (plus 3 for Higher tier).

2) How would you give your name and age to a French person you've just met?

3) Now tell them where you live and what nationality you are, giving as much detail as you can.

4) How would you say these words in French?   a) language   b) youth   c) identity   d) disabled

5) List as many French words related to gender and sexuality as you can.
   There are at least 6 you need to know (plus 1 for Higher tier).

H 6) 'J'habite en France mais je suis d'origine québécoise.' What's Élodie saying? Answer in English.

My Family and Friends ☑

7) How many words for family members can you name in French?
   There are at least 12 you need to know (plus 1 for Higher tier).

8) 'As-tu une grande famille ? À quoi ressemble ta vie de famille ?' Answer in French.

9) How would you say the words below in French?
   a) to meet   b) to understand   c) to apologise   d) to hear   e) generation   f) help (noun)

H 10) Explain how you met your closest friend and describe what makes them unique. Answer in French.

Describing People ☑

11) Describe two of your friends. Give details about their personality as well as their appearance.

12) How would you say the following words in French?   a) short   b) young   c) small   d) old

13) 'Tu ressembles à tes parents ?' Translate this question into English and then answer it in French.

14) How many words can you think of to describe someone's personality in French?
    There are at least 18 you need to know (plus 6 for Higher tier).

Higher
15) 'La vie adulte me semble dure. On a trop de responsabilités.'
    Do you agree with Étienne? Why? / Why not? Answer in French.

16) 'Ma sœur est intelligente, responsable et vraiment indépendante. Pourtant,
    à mon avis elle est trop sensible.' Translate Mari's sentences into English.

Relationships and Partnerships ☑

17) How would you say the verbs below in French?
    a) to break up   b) to promise   c) to argue   d) to get married   e) to be sorry   f) to tolerate

18) How would you say the words below in French?
    a) alone   b) trust   c) same-sex marriage   d) single   e) boyfriend   f) love

19) In French, give two arguments for marriage and two arguments against it.

Higher
20) Imagine you don't get on with some of your classmates. Which of the
    sentences below would best describe your relationship with them?
    a) Tu le trouves assez bavard et drôle.   c) Vous vous disputez souvent.
    b) Vous avez un lien fort et un rapport facile.   d) Tu n'as aucun problème avec lui.

21) 'J'espère trouver une partenaire bientôt, mais je vais attendre jusqu'à l'âge de trente ans avant de me
    marier. Je veux être sûr qu'elle est la femme de mes rêves.' Translate Jean's sentences into English.

Food

Grab a croissant, then munch your way through the tasty vocab on this page.

Head to the CGP RevisionHub for all your online content: www.cgpbooks.co.uk/Bonjour

La nourriture — *Food*

Vocabulary

manger	*to eat*	la boisson	*drink, beverage*	frais / fraîche	*fresh*
la faim	*hunger*	la soif	*thirst*	équilibré(e)	*balanced*
le pain	*bread*	l'eau (f)	*water*	végétarien(ne)	*vegetarian*
le poisson	*fish*	le café	*coffee, café*	préparer	*to prepare*
la viande	*meat*	le thé	*tea*	la cuisine	*cooking, kitchen*
le légume	*vegetable*	le lait	*milk*	le poulet	*chicken*
le fruit	*fruit*	le repas	*meal*	contenir	*to contain, include*
le fromage	*cheese*	le petit-déjeuner	*breakfast*		
les frites (f)	*chips*	le déjeuner	*lunch*	le plat	*dish*
boire	*to drink*	le dîner	*dinner*	le régime	*diet*

(Higher: le poulet, contenir, le plat, le régime)

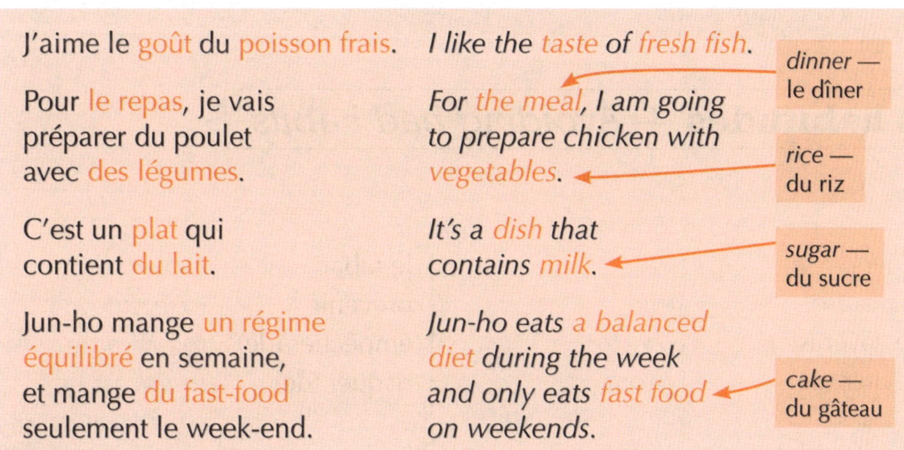

J'aime le goût du poisson frais.
I like the taste of fresh fish.

Pour le repas, je vais préparer du poulet avec des légumes.
For the meal, I am going to prepare chicken with vegetables.

C'est un plat qui contient du lait.
It's a dish that contains milk.

Jun-ho mange un régime équilibré en semaine, et mange du fast-food seulement le week-end.
Jun-ho eats a balanced diet during the week and only eats fast food on weekends.

dinner — le dîner

rice — du riz

sugar — du sucre

cake — du gâteau

Grammar — hungry & thirsty

In French, you don't say that you **are** hungry or thirsty. Instead, you say that you **have** hunger or thirst.

J'ai faim.   *I'm hungry.*
Elles ont soif.   *They are thirsty.*

Q&A Audio

Question

Quelle est ta boisson préférée ?

What's your favourite drink?

Simple Answer

Ma boisson préférée, c'est le café, mais j'aime aussi le thé.

My favourite drink is coffee, but I like tea too.

Extended Answer

J'adore les boissons chaudes, surtout quand il fait froid dehors. J'aime bien le thé, mais je préfère le café au lait.

I love hot drinks, especially when it's cold outside. I quite like tea, but I prefer milky coffee.

Practice Question

Q1   *Listen to Selina, Ahmed and Élodie talking about food. Choose the correct answer to complete each statement.*

a) Selina likes to eat...	A. cheese	B. fish	C. bread	[1 mark]
b) Ahmed likes...	A. fruit	B. chips	C. cheese	[1 mark]
c) Élodie's sister eats...	A. fresh food	B. unhealthy food	C. fast food	[1 mark]
d) Ahmed doesn't eat...	A. meat	B. ice cream	C. vegetables	[1 mark]

Listening Track 5

If I have a tuna milkshake, am I drinking a poisson boisson? 

Almost everyone has opinions on food. In French, tell a friend or family member about what you had for dinner last night, and give your opinion on what you ate and drank. Make sure you use full sentences.

Healthy and Unhealthy Living

A healthy lifestyle is something that many people aspire to — if only pizza and TV didn't get in the way. For this topic, try to think about the choices you make on a daily basis and why — deep stuff.

Le mode de vie — *Lifestyle*

Vocabulary

la santé	*health*	se coucher	*to go to bed*	se relaxer	*to relax*
sain(e)	*healthy*	dormir	*to sleep*	fatigué(e)	*tired*
bon(ne)	*good*	se lever	*to get up*		
mauvais(e)	*bad*	tôt	*early*		
rester	*to stay, remain*	le lit	*bed*		

Je **me lève** à 6h30 le matin et je **me couche** à 10h30 le soir.

I get up at 6:30 am and I go to bed at 10:30 pm.

wake up — me réveille

Bien **dormir** est important pour rester en bonne santé.

Sleeping well is important for staying healthy.

eating — manger

Bernard credited his good health to his morning routine.

Éviter les mauvaises habitudes — *Avoiding bad habits*

Vocabulary

l'habitude (f)	*habit*	tuer	*to kill*	le tabac	*tobacco*
la drogue	*drug(s)*	la cause	*cause*	prévenir	*to let know, warn*
l'alcool (m)	*alcohol*	essayer (de)	*to try (to)*	empêcher (de)	*to prevent (from)*
fumer	*to smoke*	éviter (de)	*to avoid (doing something)*	risquer (de)	*to risk (doing something)*
la cigarette	*cigarette*				
vapoter	*to vape*	arrêter (de)	*to stop (doing something)*	le risque	*risk*
la menace	*threat*			refuser (de)	*to refuse (to)*
le danger	*danger*	difficile	*difficult*	causer	*to cause*
dangereux / dangereuse	*dangerous*	le souci	*worry, concern*	dépendre (de)	*to depend (on)*
		l'inquiétude (f)	*worry, anxiety*	persuader (de)	*to persuade (to)*

(Higher: le tabac, prévenir, empêcher (de), risquer (de), le risque, refuser (de), causer, dépendre (de), persuader (de))

Mon frère a arrêté de fumer parce que c'est mauvais pour la santé.

My brother stopped smoking because it's bad for your health.

vaping — vapoter

Je crois que l'alcool et la drogue sont une menace pour la société.

I believe that alcohol and drugs are a threat to society.

obesity — l'obésité

Il faut prévenir les jeunes des risques du tabac.

We must warn young people of the risks of tobacco.

of sugary drinks — des boissons sucrées

Question

Qu'est-ce que tu penses de la drogue ?

What do you think of drugs?

Simple Answer

Je pense que la drogue est très dangereuse.

I think that drugs are very dangerous.

Extended Answer

Je crois que la drogue est beaucoup plus dangereuse que l'alcool, surtout pour les jeunes. C'est pourquoi il faut les persuader de l'éviter.

I think that drugs are much more dangerous than alcohol, especially for young people. That's why we must persuade them to avoid them.

Faire de l'exercice — *Doing exercise*

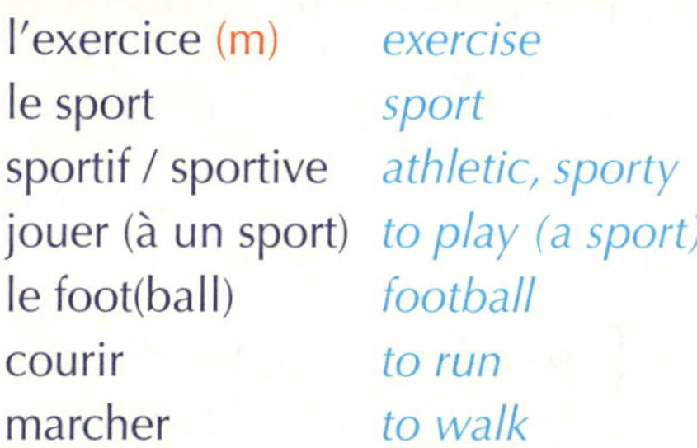

Vocabulary

l'exercice (m)	*exercise*	danser	*to dance*	fort(e)	*strong*
le sport	*sport*	faire (de)	*to do, play*	faible	*weak*
sportif / sportive	*athletic, sporty*	la natation	*swimming*	l'équipe (f)	*team*
jouer (à un sport)	*to play (a sport)*	l'activité (f)	*activity*	bouger	*to move*
le foot(ball)	*football*	actif / active	*active, energetic*	nager	*to swim*
courir	*to run*	l'effort (m)	*effort*	l'esprit (m)	*mind, spirit*
marcher	*to walk*	la forme	*form, shape*	mener	*to lead*

(bouger, nager, l'esprit, mener — Higher)

Elle est assez sportive — elle aime courir et faire de la natation.

She is quite sporty — she likes to run and swim.

Pour rester en bonne forme, il faut faire un effort pour mener une vie active.

To stay in good shape, you must make an effort to lead an active life.

Le gouvernement essaie de nous encourager à bouger plus.

The government is trying to encourage us to move more.

J'adore jouer au football parce que j'aime bien l'esprit d'équipe.

I love playing football because I really like the team spirit.

go skateboarding — du skate

healthy — en bonne santé

rugby — au rugby

Practice Questions

Q1 *Answer these questions out loud in French.* **(SPEAKING)**

- *Qu'est-ce que tu penses de l'alcool ?*
- *Pourquoi les jeunes boivent-ils ?*
- *Selon toi, quels sont les dangers des cigarettes ?* [6 marks]

Top Tips for Higher Students
- ✓ Explain your answers fully.
- ✓ Use a wide range of vocab, including some Higher-tier words.

Q2 *Read this passage and answer the questions below.* **(READING)**

(Higher)

> *Le nouveau centre sportif dans ma ville est maintenant ouvert. Vous pouvez y faire beaucoup de sports différents. Par exemple, il y a une grande piscine où on peut apprendre à nager. Moi, j'aime bien la natation parce que je me sens heureux quand je nage. À mon avis, le sport et l'exercice sont de bons moyens de se relaxer et de rester en bonne forme.*

a) What has recently opened in the writer's town? [1 mark]

b) Which sport does the writer enjoy? [1 mark]

c) Why do they enjoy this sport? [1 mark]

d) Give one benefit of physical activity mentioned in the text. [1 mark]

A couch potato is a vegetable — it has to be healthy...

When using 'faire' to talk about the kind of sport or exercise you do, you have to include 'de' after 'faire'. And while you're here, don't forget that 'de' combines with 'le' to make 'du' and with 'les' to make 'des'.

Illnesses and Treatments

Knowing how to talk about illnesses could save your life — it's also really useful for pulling a sickie. Add in the fact that it crops up in French exams and you can be sure it's worth learning well...

Je me sens malade — *I feel ill*

Vocabulary

la maladie	*illness*	mourir	*to die*	se casser	*to break (a body part)*
malade	*ill*	(être) mort(e)	*(to have) died*		
tomber	*to fall*	mort(e)	*dead*	**Higher** lutter	*to fight, struggle*
le mal	*ache*	se sentir	*to feel*	l'attaque (f)	*attack*
l'accident (m)	*accident*	l'incident (m)	*incident*	souffrir	*to suffer*
grave	*serious, grave*	blesser	*to hurt, injure*	conscient(e)	*conscious, aware*
		se blesser	*to hurt oneself, injure oneself*	vivant(e)	*alive, living*
la mort	*death*				

(Higher: se sentir, l'incident, blesser, se blesser)

Elle est tombée malade d'une maladie du sang rare.

She fell ill with a rare blood disease.

Deux personnes sont mortes à cause d'un accident grave.

Two people died as a result of a serious accident.

is fighting — lutte contre

is suffering from — souffre d'

were injured — ont été blessées

J'ai mal au corps — *My body hurts*

Vocabulary

la tête	*head*	le corps	*body*	la jambe	*leg*
les yeux (m)	*eyes*	le cœur	*heart*	le pied	*foot*
l'oreille (f)	*ear*	le dos	*back*	l'œil (m)	*eye*
la bouche	*mouth*	le bras	*arm*	la peau	*skin*
la langue	*tongue*	la main	*hand*	le sang	*blood*

(Higher: l'œil, la peau, le sang)

When talking about body parts in French, you often use the definite article ('le' / 'la' / 'les') instead of a possessive adjective. E.g. 'Il s'est cassé <u>la</u> jambe' (He broke <u>his</u> leg).

J'ai mal à la tête.

I have a headache.

Elle s'est cassé les jambes.

She broke her legs.

Bilal a mal au dos parce qu'il est tombé de son vélo.

Bilal's back hurts because he fell off his bike.

a tummy ache — mal au ventre

a cold — un rhume

her wrist — le poignet

her finger — le doigt

Skydiving is one way to make an entrance at your wedding, but maybe not the *best* way.

Grammar — avoir mal + au / à l' / à la / aux

The preposition '<u>à</u>' combines with <u>definite articles</u> (see p.110):

- à + le = <u>au</u> ⟹ J'ai mal <u>au</u> dos. (*I have backache.*)
- à + l' = <u>à l'</u> ⟹ J'ai mal <u>à l'</u>oreille. (*My ear hurts.*)
- à + la = <u>à la</u> ⟹ J'ai mal <u>à la</u> main. (*My hand hurts.*)
- à + les = <u>aux</u> ⟹ J'ai mal <u>aux</u> pieds. (*My feet ache.*)

À l'hôpital — *At the hospital*

Vocabulary

l'urgence (f)	*emergency*		les hôpitaux (m)	*hospitals*
médical(e)	*medical*		l'attente (f)	*wait*
l'hôpital (m)	*hospital*		le traitement	*treatment*
le soin	*care*		bénéficier de	*to get, receive, benefit from*
le / la médecin	*doctor*		gérer	*to manage, handle, deal with*
l'expert(e)	*expert*		le conseil	*advice, counsel, council*
le rendez-vous	*appointment*		sauver	*to save, rescue*
le médicament	*medicine, drug*		efficace	*efficient, effective*
			le soutien	*support*
prendre	*to take*		l'étude (f)	*study*
améliorer	*to improve*			

(Higher: les hôpitaux, l'attente, le traitement, bénéficier de, gérer, le conseil, sauver, efficace, le soutien, l'étude)

J'ai bénéficié **des soins médicaux** à l'hôpital.

*I received **medical care** at the hospital.*

L'expert m'a donné de bons conseils pendant mon rendez-vous à l'hôpital.

The expert gave me some good advice during my appointment at the hospital.

The nurse — L'infirmier / L'infirmière

L'étude **a montré** que ce nouveau médicament est efficace.

*The study **showed** that this new drug is effective.*

Le médicament peut être utilisé par les médecins pour gérer les maladies **de longue durée**.

*The medicine can be used by doctors to manage **long-term** illnesses.*

mental — mentales

Practice Questions

Q1 *Mathieu is talking about visiting the hospital. Read the text, then answer the question below.*

> Je vais souvent à l'hôpital pour voir ma tante, qui est malade. J'étais triste, mais le médecin lui a donné un nouveau médicament et donc elle va bientôt quitter l'hôpital. À l'avenir, je voudrais être scientifique et trouver de nouveaux médicaments pour aider les personnes malades.

READING

Choose the two correct statements from the list below.

A. Mathieu often goes to the hospital.

B. Mathieu's aunt's health is declining.

C. Mathieu wants to work in medical research when he is older.

D. Mathieu wants to work with old people in the future.

[2 marks]

Q2 *You are writing an article for a French website. You should write about 90 words in French. Describe:*

- *the role of a doctor*
- *whether you would like to be a doctor when you grow up, and why.*

WRITING

Top Tip for Higher Students
✓ Use the conditional.

[15 marks]

The hop-ital — where kangaroos go to recover...

Remember, 'à' + 'le' = 'au' and 'à' + 'les' = 'aux'. It might all seem a bit of a headache, but it's important you've got this down — you may need it in the exam if you're asked to talk about which part of you hurts.

Healthy Living and Lifestyle — Vocabulary

You don't just need a healthy lifestyle — for the exam, you'll also need a healthy knowledge of the words on these pages.

Food

la nourriture	*food*
manger	*to eat*
le produit	*product*
la faim	*hunger*
le pain	*bread*
le poisson	*fish*
la viande	*meat*
le légume	*vegetable*
le fruit	*fruit*
le fromage	*cheese*
les frites (f)	*chips*
la glace	*ice cream, ice*
le fast-food	*fast food*
boire	*to drink*
la boisson	*drink, beverage*
la soif	*thirst*
l'eau (f)	*water*
le café	*coffee, café*
le thé	*tea*
le lait	*milk*
le vin	*wine*
le goût	*taste, flavour*
le repas	*meal*

le petit-déjeuner	*breakfast*
le déjeuner	*lunch*
le dîner	*dinner*
l'entrée (f)	*starter*
l'énergie (f)	*energy*
frais / fraîche	*fresh*
équilibré(e)	*balanced*
végan(e)	*vegan*
végétarien(ne)	*vegetarian*
préparer	*to prepare*
couper	*to cut*
recommander	*to recommend*
la recette	*recipe*
la cuisine	*cooking, kitchen*

Higher

le poulet	*chicken*
sentir	*to smell*
contenir	*to contain, include*
le contenu	*contents*
nourrir	*to feed*
le plat	*dish*
le verre	*glass*
le couteau	*knife*
le régime	*diet*

Healthy and Unhealthy Living — Habits and Lifestyle

la santé	*health*
sain(e)	*healthy*
bon(ne)	*good*
mauvais(e)	*bad*
rester	*to stay, remain*
coucher	*to put (someone) to bed*
se coucher	*to go to bed, lie down, sleep*
dormir	*to sleep*
lever	*to lift, raise*
se lever	*to get up, stand up*
tôt	*early*
le lit	*bed*
se relaxer	*to relax*
fatigué(e)	*tired*
l'habitude (f)	*habit*
la fois	*time (occasion)*
la drogue	*drug(s)*
l'alcool (m)	*alcohol*
fumer	*to smoke*
la cigarette	*cigarette*
vapoter	*to vape*

la menace	*threat*
le danger	*danger*
dangereux / dangereuse	*dangerous*
tuer	*to kill*
la cause	*cause*
essayer (de)	*to try, attempt (to)*
éviter (de)	*to avoid (doing something)*
arrêter (de)	*to stop (doing something)*
difficile	*difficult*
le souci	*worry, concern*
l'inquiétude (f)	*worry, anxiety*
inquiétant(e)	*worrying, disturbing*

Higher

le tabac	*tobacco*
se reposer	*to rest*
prévenir	*to let know, warn*
empêcher (de)	*to prevent (someone from)*
risquer (de)	*to risk (doing something)*
le risque	*risk*
refuser (de)	*to refuse (to)*
causer	*to cause*
dépendre (de)	*to depend (on)*
persuader (de)	*to persuade (to)*

Healthy and Unhealthy Living — Sport and Exercise

l'exercice (m)	*exercise*
le sport	*sport*
sportif / sportive	*athletic, sporty, competitive, sporting*
jouer (à un sport)	*to play (a sport)*
le foot(ball)	*football*
courir	*to run*
marcher	*to walk*
la promenade	*walk*
danser	*to dance*
faire (de)	*to do, play*
la natation	*swimming*
l'activité (f)	*activity*

actif / active	*active, energetic*
l'effort (m)	*effort*
la forme	*form, shape*
peser	*to weigh*
la vie	*life*
fort(e)	*strong*
faible	*weak*
l'équipe (f)	*team*

Higher

garder	*to keep, take care of, look after*
bouger	*to move*
nager	*to swim*
l'esprit (m)	*mind, spirit*
mener	*to lead*

Illnesses and Treatments

la maladie	*illness*
malade	*ill*
tomber	*to fall*
le mal	*ache*
l'accident (m)	*accident*
grave	*serious, grave*
la mort	*death*
mourir	*to die*
(être) mort(e)	*(to have) died*
mort(e)	*dead*
la tête	*head*
les yeux (m)	*eyes*
l'oreille (f)	*ear*
la bouche	*mouth*
la langue	*tongue*
le corps	*body*
le cœur	*heart*
le dos	*back*
le bras	*arm*
la main	*hand*
la jambe	*leg*
le pied	*foot*
l'urgence (f)	*emergency*
médical(e)	*medical*
l'hôpital (m)	*hospital*
le soin	*care*
le / la médecin	*doctor*
l'expert(e)	*expert*
le rendez-vous	*appointment*
le médicament	*medicine, drug*

prendre	*to take*
la science	*science*
améliorer	*to improve*

Higher

l'incident (m)	*incident*
se blesser	*to hurt oneself, injure oneself*
se casser	*to break (a body part)*
se sentir	*to feel*
lutter	*to fight, struggle*
l'attaque (f)	*attack*
la bataille	*battle*
souffrir	*to suffer*
conscient(e)	*conscious, aware*
vivant(e)	*alive, living*
l'œil (m)	*eye*
la peau	*skin*
le sang	*blood*
les hôpitaux (m)	*hospitals*
l'attente (f)	*wait*
le traitement	*treatment*
bénéficier de	*to get, receive, benefit from*
gérer	*to manage, handle, deal with*
le conseil	*advice, counsel, council*
conseiller (à... de)	*to advise, recommend (someone to do something)*
sauver	*to save, rescue*
efficace	*efficient, effective*
le soutien	*support*
l'étude (f)	*study*

Revision Summary Test for Section Three

Before you run off to try another section, here's a healthy dose of summary questions for you.

- These questions are **really tricky**, but they'll help you see **how well you know your stuff**.
- Tackle the **revision summary test** below, or scan the QR code to do it **online**.
  You can **keep track of your progress** online and see **which areas need more work**.
- There are **sample answers** here: www.cgpbooks.co.uk/BonjourExtras

Food ☐

1) How many different foods can you list in French?
   There are at least 8 you need to know (plus 1 for Higher tier). ☑

2) How many different drinks can you name in French? There are 5 you need to know. ☑

3) Your friend asks you 'Est-ce que tu aimes préparer des repas végétariens ou végans ?'
   What are they asking you? Answer their question in French. ☑

4) In French, explain why it is important to eat a balanced diet. ☑

5) Write down the French for these words:
   a) recipe   b) breakfast   c) lunch   d) dinner   e) starter   f) to recommend ☑

6) What does this sentence mean in English? 'J'ai faim, donc je vais manger quelque chose.' ☑

7) Rewrite the French sentence from Q6 so that it is about drinking rather than eating. ☑

8) Translate this sentence into French: 'This product has a nice flavour and gives you lots of energy.' ☑

Healthy and Unhealthy Living ☐

9) In French, write down as many things from the section as you
   can that could be classed as 'habitudes dangereuses'. ☑

10) Give 3 French verbs to do with resting and sleeping (plus 1 extra for Higher tier). ☑

11) What does the word 'souci' mean? Give another French word that means a similar thing. ☑

12) Write down the English translation for the following verbs:
    a) jouer (à)   b) courir   c) marcher   d) danser   e) faire (de) ☑

13) What are the opposites of these words in French?   a) faible   b) commencer   c) se coucher ☑

14) Translate this sentence into English: 'J'essaie de faire du sport
    deux fois par semaine car je veux rester en bonne santé.' ☑

15) In French, give 3 things you do to lead a healthy lifestyle, and explain why you do them. ☑

16) 'Selon toi, pourquoi la drogue est-elle un problème inquiétant pour les jeunes ?' Answer in French. ☑

Illnesses and Treatments ☑

17) How many body parts can you write down in French? There are at least 11 you need to know. ☑

18) Your friend has had a bad accident in France. In French, tell a passer-by:
    'My friend has had a serious accident. He needs to go to the hospital to receive medical care.' ☑

19) Write down the English for these words: a) la mort   b) mourir   c) être mort   d) la vie ☑

20) The pharmacist says, 'Il faut prendre ce médicament pour améliorer votre santé.' What is he saying? ☑

21) Imagine you're visiting the doctor with a medical problem. In French,
    explain your problem and then say what the doctor might do or advise. ☑

22) What is the French for these phrases?
    a) appointment   b) expert   c) to fall ill   d) medical emergency   e) serious illness ☑

⌐ Higher ⌐
23) Translate into English: 'Avec le soutien de la ville, les
    hôpitaux luttent contre les longs temps d'attente.' ☑

24) Give the French for these words: a) to suffer   b) to feel   c) the study   d) conscious ☑

School Subjects

Ah, school subjects... I'm sure you're bursting to say that you adore all things French-related.
Explaining your opinion will get you more marks, so use this page to prepare properly.

Les matières (f) — *Subjects*

Vocabulary

l'anglais (m)	*English*		l'espagnol (m)	*Spanish*
les mathématiques (f),	*maths*		l'allemand (m)	*German*
les maths (f)			le théâtre	*drama*
les sciences (f)	*science*		la musique	*music*
la physique	*physics*		l'art (m)	*art*
l'informatique (f)	*computer science*			
l'histoire (f)	*history*			
la géographie	*geography*			
la religion	*religion*			
les langues modernes (f)	*modern languages*			
le français	*French*			

Remember there's also lots of online content here: www.cgpbooks.co.uk/Bonjour

Grammar (Higher only) — 'depuis'

To say you've been doing something since a certain age, use the present tense with 'depuis' (*since*). See p.133 for more on this.

J'étudie le français depuis l'âge de six ans.
I've been studying French since the age of six.

Moi, j'adore l'histoire parce que j'aime étudier le passé.

I love history because I like studying the past.

À mon avis, la physique est une matière bien trop difficile.

In my opinion, physics is a far too difficult subject.

Je trouve la géographie très intéressante.

I find geography very interesting.

chemistry — la chimie
biology — la biologie

stimulating — stimulante

Ma matière préférée, c'est... — *My favourite subject is...*

Question

Quelle est ta matière préférée ?

What's your favourite subject?

Simple Answer

J'aime bien les maths. Les réponses sont toujours claires.

I like maths. The answers are always clear.

Extended Answer

J'aime les maths car c'est facile, mais je préfère l'anglais parce que j'aime lire des romans passionnants.

I like maths because it's easy, but I prefer English because I like to read exciting novels.

Practice Question

Q1 You are writing an email to a friend to give your opinion on school subjects. You should write about 90 words in French. Describe:

- the subjects you like and why
- the subjects that you have found difficult this year
- what you want to study in the future.

[15 marks]

Top Tips for Higher Students
✓ Use superlatives, e.g. 'le plus grand', 'le moins vite'.
✓ Link phrases together with conjunctions.

I think all of these opinions are pretty subjective...

Everyone has subjects they love and subjects they just can't stand — whatever they are for you, make sure you can say them in French and fully explain why that's the case. Have a go now — you'll thank me later.

School Life

You probably already know everything there is to know about life at your school. Well, now's your opportunity to learn how to speak about it in French. It's thrilling stuff, so time to get cracking.

Aller à l'école — *Going to school*

Vocabulary

l'école (f)	*school*	la seconde	*Year 11*	arriver (à)	*to arrive (at)*
le collège	*secondary school*	le cours	*course, lessons*	quitter	*to leave (somewhere)*
le lycée	*college, sixth form*	la leçon	*lesson*		
l'éducation (f)	*education*	la classe	*class*	rentrer	*to go in*
étudier	*to study*	la récré(ation)	*breaktime*	assister (à)	*to attend*
travailler	*to work*	commencer (à)	*to start (to)*	l'étude (f)	*study*
l'élève (m/f)	*pupil*	durer	*to last*	la rentrée	*return to school*

(Higher: assister (à), l'étude (f), la rentrée)

Ma première leçon commence à 8h30.	*My first lesson starts at 8:30 am.*	
J'assiste à cinq cours chaque jour.	*I attend five classes every day.*	
Nous retournons à l'école à la fin du mois.	*We go back to school at the end of the month.*	leave school — quittons l'école
Cette année, je rentre en seconde.	*This year, I'm going into year 11.*	

> ### Grammar — feminine nouns starting with a vowel
> <u>Feminine</u> nouns beginning with <u>vowels</u> always take <u>masculine possessive adjectives</u> — it's easier to say.
> - **Mon** école ⟶ *My school*
> - **Son** éducation ⟶ *His/her education*

Professor Smith's youth potion had worked exactly as planned.

En classe — *In class*

Vocabulary

l'enseignement (m)	*teaching*	écrire	*to write*	l'explication (f)	*explanation*
le / la prof(esseur)	*teacher*	l'intérêt (m)	*interest*	l'instruction (f)	*instruction*
apprendre (à)	*to learn (to), teach (someone)*	l'exercice (m)	*written exercise*	enseigner (à)	*to teach*
		comprendre	*to understand*	l'objectif (m)	*objective*
expliquer	*to explain*	pratique	*practical*	pratiquer	*to practise*
demander	*to ask*	discuter	*to discuss*	réaliser	*to achieve*
la réponse	*reply, answer*	la discussion	*discussion*	mériter (de)	*to deserve (to)*

(Higher: l'explication (f), l'instruction (f), enseigner (à), l'objectif (m), pratiquer, réaliser, mériter (de))

En cours d'anglais, nous avons discuté des thèmes du roman.	*In the English lesson, we discussed the themes of the novel.*	the message of the poem — du message du poème
Il m'a demandé d'expliquer mes réponses, mais je n'avais pas les connaissances nécessaires.	*He asked me to explain my answers, but I didn't have the necessary knowledge.*	He made me — Il m'a obligé à

À mon école, il y a... — *At my school, there is...*

Vocabulary

l'espace (f)	*space*	l'écran (m)	*screen*	l'activité (f)	*activity*
la salle	*room*	la règle	*ruler*	l'équipe (f)	*team*
la bibliothèque	*library*	le cahier	*exercise book*	organiser	*to organise*
la cour	*playground*	prêter	*to lend*	divers(e)	*varied, diverse*
les toilettes (f)	*toilets*	emprunter (à)	*to borrow (from)*	**H** bénéficier de	*to benefit from, receive*
le tableau	*board*	le club	*club*		

La récré dure quinze minutes — nous aimons *jouer au football en équipe*.

Break lasts fifteen minutes — we like to play football in teams.

Je peux emprunter *ta règle* ?

Can I borrow your ruler?

Mon école bénéficie d'*une grande bibliothèque*.

My school benefits from a large library.

your pencil — ton crayon

a new canteen — une nouvelle cantine

Q&A Audio

Question

Il est comment, ton collège ?

What is your school like?

Simple Answer

C'est une grande école avec beaucoup de salles de classe et une bibliothèque très utile.

It's a big school with lots of classrooms and a very useful library.

Extended Answer

C'est un petit collège, mais nous avons tout ce qu'il faut. Par exemple, nous avons une bibliothèque géniale, une grande cour où nous passons la récré, et une piscine.

It's a little school, but we have everything we need. For example, we have a great library, a big playground where we spend breaktime, and a swimming pool.

Practice Questions

Q1 *Read the passages and answer the question below.*

Alain : *Dans mon collège, tout le monde doit étudier l'anglais. Je déteste ça : le prof est vraiment ennuyeux, donc je n'arrive pas à m'intéresser aux cours.*

Karine : *Je vais au lycée et je suis en seconde. J'adore les cours de sciences parce que je m'intéresse au monde naturel et j'aime faire des expériences*.*

READING

**expériences — experiments*

Choose the right person for each sentence.
Write 'K' for Karine or 'A' for Alain.

a) This student enjoys learning about the environment around them. [1 mark]

b) The teacher plays an important role in whether this student enjoys the subject. [1 mark]

c) This student is in Year 11. [1 mark]

Q2 *Listen to Nicolas speak about his time at school.*
Complete the following sentences in English.

 LISTENING

 Listening Track 6

Higher

a) Nicolas thinks that physics will be very ....·

b) Nicolas arrives late to school because ....·

c) Nicolas feels .... after his classes on Tuesday.

d) After lunch, Nicolas ....· [4 marks]

What did the measuring stick say to the pen? "I am your ruler..."

Examiners may well ask questions about your school and what you think of it, so if you've got all this vocab learnt and some opinions stored up and ready to go, you'll be well on your way to acing the exam. Nice.

School Pressures and Difficulties

School can be pretty stressful — you're trying to juggle studying and getting the grades you need whilst maintaining a social life and doing your hobbies. Perfect training for the circus...

Les examens (m) — *Exams*

Vocabulary

examiner	*to examine*	l'effort (m)	*effort*
le / la candidat(e)	*candidate*	le but	*goal, aim, objective*
le bac(calauréat)	*high school final exam*	le défi	*challenge*
préparer	*to prepare*	la chance	*luck*
se préparer	*to get ready*	intelligent(e)	*intelligent*

Question

Qu'est-ce que tu penses des examens ?

What do you think of exams?

Simple Answer

Je trouve les examens difficiles, et donc j'essaie de bien me préparer.

I find exams hard, so I try to prepare well.

Extended Answer

Les examens sont très difficiles, mais à mon avis, le pire, c'est de devoir attendre les résultats ! J'espère que je n'ai pas fait trop d'erreurs.

Exams are very difficult, but in my opinion, what's worse is having to wait for results! I hope that I haven't made too many mistakes.

J'ai obtenu de bons résultats — *I got good results*

Vocabulary

réussir (à)	*to succeed (in), pass*	gagner	*to earn*	répéter	*to repeat*
le succès	*success*	l'erreur (f)	*mistake*	le contrôle	*test, inspection*
le résultat	*result*	nul(le)	*rubbish*	l'échec (m)	*failure*
la note	*mark, grade*	faible	*weak*	se tromper	*to make a mistake*
célébrer	*to celebrate*	fort(e)	*strong*	obtenir	*to get, obtain*

(Higher: le contrôle, l'échec (m), se tromper, obtenir)

J'ai réussi l'examen de maths, donc je vais célébrer mon succès !

I passed the maths exam, so I'm going to celebrate my success!

sat / took — passé

Le prof a corrigé mon contrôle et m'a donné une bonne note.

The teacher marked my test and gave me a good grade.

'ne…que' means 'only'. See p.141 for more.

Quel candidat n'a fait qu'une erreur ?

Which candidate only made one mistake?

Fatou s'est trompée pendant l'examen, mais elle a réussi à obtenir son bac.

Fatou made a mistake in the exam, but she succeeded in getting her baccalaureate.

didn't get ready for — ne s'est pas préparée pour

Grammar — 'quel'

'Quel', meaning 'which' or 'what', agrees in number and gender with the noun following it.

- **Quels** candidats ont réussi ?   *Which candidates passed?*
- **Quelle** chance !   *What luck!*

'What an amazing piece of paper!'

Les règles (f) scolaires — *School rules*

Vocabulary

attendre	*to expect*	le règlement	*rules, regulation*
interdire (à)	*to forbid, ban*	permettre (à...de)	*to allow*
l'uniforme (m)	*uniform*		*(someone to do something)*
porter	*to wear, carry*	harceler	*to bully, harass*
le vêtement	*item of clothing*	obliger	*to require, force*
les devoirs (m)	*homework*	la responsabilité	*responsibility*
H le comportement	*behaviour*	responsable	*responsible*

Higher: le règlement, permettre, harceler, obliger, la responsabilité, responsable

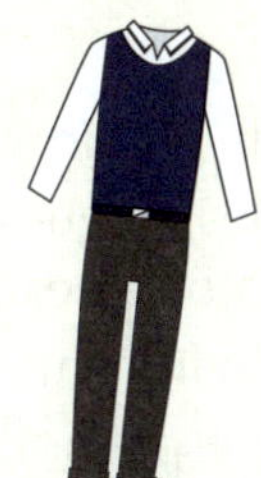

Le collège nous oblige à porter un uniforme qui a l'air très professionnel.

The school makes us wear a very professional-looking uniform.

very ugly — très laid
very smart — très chic / élégant

L'objectif de l'école est de réduire le nombre d'absences et d'améliorer le comportement des élèves.

The school's objective is to reduce the number of absences and improve the behaviour of pupils.

equality among pupils — l'égalité entre les élèves

Les défis (m) à l'école — *Challenges at school*

Vocabulary

terrible	*terrible, dreadful*	la confiance	*confidence*	respecter	*to respect*
affreux / affreuse	*dreadful, awful, horrible*	aider	*to help*	le respect	*respect*
méchant(e)	*nasty, naughty*	l'aide (f)	*help*	le soutien	*support*

Higher: respecter, le respect, le soutien

Sékou est très intelligent, mais il est aussi paresseux.

Sékou is very intelligent, but he is also lazy.

doesn't have much confidence — n'a pas beaucoup de confiance en lui

L'école offre son soutien aux élèves inquiets.

The school offers support to worried students.

Practice Questions

Q1 *Respond to the following questions out loud.*
You should talk for about 30-60 seconds for each question.

  a) Comment te prépares-tu pour les examens ?

  b) Que penses-tu de ton uniforme scolaire ?

  c) Selon toi, quel est le plus grand problème dans ton école ?

  d) Qu'est-ce que tu penses des règles à ton collège ? *[8 marks]*

Penny chose the morning of Tommy's maths exam to steal his lucky socks.

Q2 *Listen to these four sentences and write down in French exactly what you hear.*
Use your knowledge of French to make sure that what you have written is accurate. *[8 marks]*

Assez 'stressed', you say 'out' — stressed, out, stressed, out...

You might have to talk about your exams in the exams. Get yourself ready by learning all these words and making sure you know how to pronounce them. Cue hours of talking to yourself in French. Delightful.

Education — Vocabulary

Education is all about learning things. And it just so happens there are three whole pages of words for you to learn here...

School Subjects

la matière	*subject*
l'anglais (m)	*English*
les mathématiques (f),	*maths*
les maths (f)	
les sciences (f)	*science*
la physique	*physics*
l'informatique (f)	*computer science, computing*
la technologie	*technology*
l'histoire (f)	*history*
la géographie	*geography*

la religion	*religion*
les langues modernes (f)	*modern languages*
le français	*French*
l'espagnol (m)	*Spanish*
l'allemand (m)	*German*
le théâtre	*drama*
la musique	*music*
H le sujet	*subject, topic*
l'art (m)	*art*

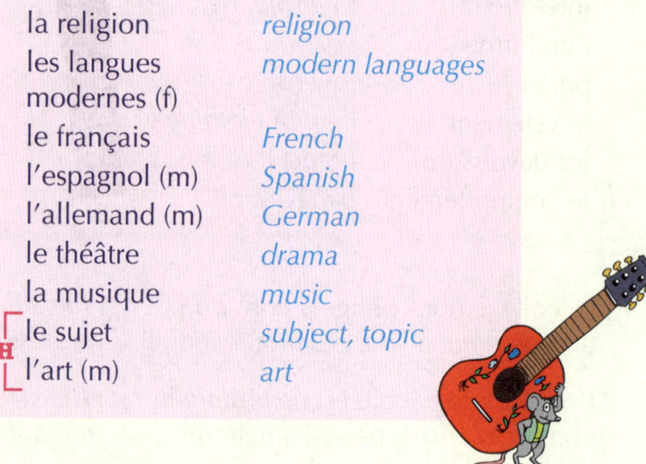

School Life — Going to School

l'école (f)	*school*
le collège	*secondary school*
le lycée	*college, sixth form*
l'éducation (f)	*education*
scolaire	*school (adj.)*
étudier	*to study*
l'élève (m/f)	*pupil, student*
l'étudiant(e)	*student*
l'ami(e)	*friend*
jeune	*young*
l'ado (m/f), l'adolescent(e)	*teenager, adolescent*
travailler	*to work*
la quatrième	*Year 9*
la seconde	*Year 11*
la première	*Year 12*
le cours	*course, lessons*
la leçon	*lesson*
la classe	*class*
la récré(ation)	*breaktime*
septembre	*September*
la journée	*day*
la semaine	*week*
l'année (f)	*year*
les vacances (f)	*holidays*
le voyage	*journey*
commencer (à)	*to start, begin (to)*
arriver (à)	*to arrive (at), manage (to), succeed (in)*

quitter	*to leave (somewhere), take off (clothes)*
se quitter	*to leave each other*
durer	*to last*
la fois	*time (occasion)*
continuer	*to continue, carry on*
laver	*to wash (something)*
se laver	*to get washed*
rentrer	*to go in, come in, come back (in), go back (in)*

Higher

assister (à)	*to attend*
l'étude (f)	*study*
le retard	*delay*
la troisième	*Year 10*
la rentrée	*reopening, return to school*
la diversité	*diversity*
divers(e)	*varied, diverse*

The school's new policy of compulsory smiling had done wonders for student attitudes.

School Life — In Class

l'enseignement (m)	*education, teaching*
le / la prof(esseur)	*teacher*
savoir	*to know (how to), can*
connaître	*to know (a person)*
apprendre (à)	*to learn (to), teach (someone)*
expliquer	*to explain*
demander	*to ask*
se demander	*to wonder*
la réponse	*reply, response, answer*
écrire	*to write*
la tâche	*task, chore*
les devoirs (m)	*homework*
l'intérêt (m)	*interest*
le thème	*theme, topic*
la communication	*communication*
l'information (f)	*information*
lire	*to read*
la lecture	*reading*
le livre	*book*
le roman	*novel*
le texte	*text*
l'histoire (f)	*story*
l'exercice (m)	*written exercise*
le niveau	*level*
la compétence	*competence, skill*
capable	*able, capable*
imaginer	*to imagine, invent*
encourager (à)	*to encourage (to)*
comprendre	*to understand*

lever	*to lift, raise*
utile	*useful*
inutile	*useless*
passionnant(e)	*exciting, thrilling*
difficile	*difficult*
dur(e)	*hard (adj.)*
dur	*hard (adv.)*
facile	*easy*
simple	*simple*
pratique	*practical*
idéal(e)	*ideal*
discuter	*to discuss*
la discussion	*discussion*
conscient(e)	*conscious, aware*
se lever	*to get up, stand up*

Higher

la connaissance	*knowledge*
l'explication (f)	*explanation*
l'instruction (f)	*instruction*
distribuer	*to hand out, give out*
le chapitre	*chapter*
le poème	*poem*
la scène	*scene*
pratiquer	*to practise*
enseigner (à)	*to teach*
l'objectif (m)	*objective*
réaliser	*to achieve, realise*
mériter (de)	*to deserve (to), have earned*
inspirer	*to inspire*
la passion	*passion*
s'asseoir	*to sit down*

School Life — Facilities and Equipment

l'espace (f)	*space*
la salle	*room*
la bibliothèque	*library*
la cour	*courtyard, playground*
les toilettes (f)	*toilets*
la piscine	*swimming pool*
l'autobus (m) / le bus	*bus*
l'équipement (m)	*equipment*
le sac	*bag*
le dictionnaire	*dictionary*
le tableau	*board, picture, painting*
l'écran (m)	*screen*
le mail / l'e-mail (m)	*email*
la lettre	*letter*
le stylo	*pen*
la règle	*ruler*

le cahier	*exercise book*
prêter	*to lend*
emprunter (à)	*to borrow (from)*
ranger	*to tidy, put away*
le club	*club*
le football	*football*
l'activité (f)	*activity*
l'équipe (f)	*team*
organiser	*to organise*
s'organiser	*to get organised*

Higher

la feuille	*sheet*
la scène	*stage*
bénéficier de	*to benefit from, receive*
la poche	*pocket*

School Pressures and Difficulties — Exams

l'examen (m)	*exam*
examiner	*to examine*
le / la candidat(e)	*candidate*
le bac(calauréat)	*high school final exam*
réussir (à)	*to succeed (in), pass*
le succès	*success*
préparer	*to prepare*
se préparer	*to get ready*
corriger	*to correct, mark*
le résultat	*result, follow-up*
la note	*mark, grade*
améliorer	*to improve*
célébrer	*to celebrate*
gagner	*to win, earn, gain*
l'effort (m)	*effort*
l'erreur (f)	*mistake, error*
la faute	*mistake, error, fault*

nul(le)	*rubbish*
faible	*weak*
fort(e)	*strong*
le courage	*courage*
le but	*goal, aim, objective, purpose*
le défi	*challenge*
accepter	*to accept, admit*
la chance	*luck*
répéter	*to repeat*
intelligent(e)	*intelligent*
sérieux	*conscientious, responsible*
essayer (de)	*to try, attempt (to)*
l'essai (m)	*attempt, try, test*

Higher

le contrôle	*test, check, inspection*
l'échec (m)	*failure*
se tromper	*to make a mistake*
obtenir	*to get, obtain*

School Pressures and Difficulties — Rules and Behaviour

devoir	*to have to, must*
attendre	*to expect, wait (for)*
la règle	*rule*
interdire (à)	*to forbid, ban*
interdit(e)	*prohibited, banned*
l'uniforme (m)	*uniform*
porter	*to wear, carry*
le vêtement	*item of clothing*
le pantalon	*trousers*
se changer	*to get changed*
la mode	*fashion*
frapper	*to hit, knock*
terrible	*terrible, dreadful*
affreux / affreuse	*dreadful, awful, horrible*
strict(e)	*strict*
ennuyeux / ennuyeuse	*boring*
travailleur / travailleuse	*hard-working*
paresseux / paresseuse	*lazy*
méchant(e)	*nasty, naughty*
concentrer	*to concentrate*
la confiance	*confidence, trust*
l'égalité (f)	*equality*

égal(e)	*equal*
l'indépendance (f)	*independence*
aider	*to help*
l'aide (f)	*help*
le souci	*worry, concern*
inquiéter	*to bother, disturb*
s'inquiéter (de)	*to be worried (about)*
l'inquiétude (f)	*worry, anxiety*
inquiet / inquiète	*worried*

Higher

le comportement	*behaviour*
le règlement	*rules, regulation*
permettre (à...de)	*to allow (someone to do something)*
(avoir) permis	*(have) allowed*
harceler	*to bully, harass*
obliger	*to require, force, oblige*
abandonner	*to abandon, give up*
l'absence (f)	*absence*
le silence	*silence*
la responsabilité	*responsibility*
responsable	*responsible*
respecter	*to respect*
le respect	*respect*
indépendant(e)	*independent*
le soutien	*support*

Revision Summary Test for Section Four

Now you've educated yourself on education, it's time to crack on with these summary questions.

- These questions are **hard**, but they'll really help you see **how well you know your stuff**.
- Tackle the **revision summary test** below, or scan the QR code to do it **online**.
  You can **track your progress** online and see **which areas need more work**.
- There are **sample answers** for the test here: www.cgpbooks.co.uk/BonjourExtras

School Subjects ☐

1) How many school subjects can you name in French?
   There are at least 15 you need to know (plus 1 for Higher tier).

2) Translate this sentence into English: 'Mes matières préférées, ce sont les langues
   modernes — ce sont des matières difficiles, mais c'est important de pouvoir communiquer.'

School Life ☐

3) Your French friend is complaining: 'Je ne sais pas faire cet exercice.' What is he saying?

4) Translate these school years into French: a) Year 9   b) Year 11   c) Year 12

5) 'What time does your school day start and finish? How long is the school day?' Answer in French.

6) In French, give three adjectives you could use to describe a teacher.
   Then give three different adjectives you could use to describe a lesson.

7) Write down the English for these words:
   a) se demander   b) quitter   c) connaître   d) comprendre   e) se laver   f) lever   g) expliquer

8) 'Quel équipement y a-t-il dans ta salle de classe ?' Translate the question and respond in French.

9) 'Qu'est-ce que tu fais pendant la récréation ?' Answer in French.

10) Translate this sentence into English: 'Quand on s'est assis, le prof a distribué les feuilles
    — cette année, on étudie les poèmes de guerre, car c'est une passion du prof.'

11) Give the English for these words:
    a) réaliser   b) l'objectif   c) mériter   d) inspirer   e) pratiquer   f) la connaissance

School Pressures and Difficulties ☐

12) In French, describe a rule in your school. Then give your opinion on your school's rules.

13) Your friend tells you: 'L'école m'oblige à porter un uniforme scolaire — par exemple, je dois
    avoir un pantalon noir. Et toi, qu'est-ce que tu portes à l'école ?' Translate her words.

14) Give a different French word that means a similar thing to these words:
    a) l'erreur   b) dur   c) parler   d) les cours   e) l'étudiant   f) quitter

15) Give the French translation of these words:
    a) weak   b) awful   c) lazy   d) hard-working   e) nasty   f) boring   g) strong   h) banned

16) Translate this sentence into English:
    'Louis se prépare pour ses examens parce qu'il veut obtenir de bonnes notes.'

17) Someone tells you: 'The candidates improved their grades and passed the exam —
    now they will celebrate their success!' Translate his words into French.

18) Write down the adjective forms of these nouns: a) l'égalité   b) l'inquiétude

19) What do these words mean in English?
    a) le défi   b) le courage   c) la chance   d) frapper   e) la confiance   f) le but

20) 'In your opinion, what are the biggest two problems at your school?' Answer in French.

21) Translate this sentence into English: 'Les nouvelles règles n'ont amélioré ni
    le comportement des élèves ni le nombre d'absences.'

Education Post-16

You've probably thought lots about the future already — all that's left is to talk about it in French. Here's a little something to help you on your way...

Don't forget you can access your online content here: www.cgpbooks.co.uk/Bonjour

Après le collège, je veux... — *After school, I want to...*

Vocabulary

le lycée	*college, sixth form*	rêver (à / de)	*to dream (of / about)*
le stage	*work experience*	le rêve	*dream*
l'apprentissage (m)	*apprenticeship*	prêt(e)	*ready*
l'occasion (f)	*chance, opportunity*	la formation	*training*
le projet	*plan*	conseiller (à... de)	*to advise, recommend (someone to do something)*
choisir	*to choose*		
le choix	*choice*	le conseil	*advice, counsel*
décider (de)	*to decide (to)*	réfléchir (à)	*to reflect (on), think (about)*
se décider (à)	*to make the decision (to)*	la recherche	*research, search*
		l'industrie (f)	*industry*

(Higher: la formation, conseiller, le conseil, réfléchir, la recherche, l'industrie)

Je veux aller au lycée l'année prochaine pour passer le bac.

I want to go to sixth form next year to do A-levels.

to vocational college — au lycée technique / lycée professionnel

On m'a conseillé de faire un stage industriel pour m'aider à décider quoi faire.

I've been advised to do some work experience in industry to help me decide what to do.

have chosen to do — ont choisi de faire

Ils rêvent de faire un apprentissage parce qu'ils veulent suivre une formation pratique.

They dream of doing an apprenticeship because they want to undertake practical training.

are ready to — sont prêts à

Faire des choix — *Making choices*

Question

Pourquoi as-tu choisi de passer / ne pas passer le bac ?

Why have you chosen to do / not do A-levels?

Simple Answers

J'ai besoin du bac pour faire mon métier idéal.

I need A-levels to do my ideal job.

J'ai décidé de faire un apprentissage car je préfère la formation pratique.

I decided to do an apprenticeship because I prefer practical training.

Extended Answers

Je viens de commencer le lycée. Il faut aller à l'université pour faire mon métier idéal, et pour faire ça, j'ai besoin du bac.

I've just started at sixth form. You have to go to university to do my ideal job, and to do that, I need A-levels.

J'aimerais trouver un emploi et gagner de l'argent. J'y ai réfléchi et j'ai décidé que la meilleure façon de réaliser ça, c'est de faire un apprentissage.

I would like to find a job and earn money. I've thought about it and I've decided the best way to achieve that is by doing an apprenticeship.

Grammar (Higher only) — venir + de + infinitive

'Venir + de + infinitive' means 'to have just done something'. Don't forget that 'venir' (*to come*) is an irregular verb.

Je viens de terminer le collège.

I have just finished secondary school.

Inès vient de décider ses projets pour l'avenir.

Inès has just decided her future plans.

Aller à l'université — *Going to university*

Vocabulary

l'avenir (m)	*future*	l'entretien (m)	*interview, maintenance*
le futur	*future*	l'étape (f)	*stage, step*
l'université (f)	*university*	l'année sabbatique (f)	*gap year*
la carrière	*career*	le champ	*field, realm*
finir	*to end, finish*	s'inscrire à	*to join, enrol in*
terminer	*to end, finish*	admettre	*to admit*
le concours	*entrance exam, competition*	la concurrence	*competition (rivalry)*
		la durée	*length, duration*
le rendez-vous	*appointment*	la condition	*condition*

(l'étape, l'année sabbatique, le champ, s'inscrire à, admettre, la concurrence, la durée, la condition are marked **Higher**)

Avant d'aller à l'université, je voudrais prendre une année sabbatique pour découvrir le monde.

Before going to university, I would like to take a gap year to discover the world.

finding a job — de trouver un boulot

Claire n'a pas l'intention de s'inscrire à l'université car ce n'est pas nécessaire pour sa future carrière.

Claire doesn't intend to enrol at university because it's not necessary for her future career.

to get a degree — d'obtenir une licence

Il faut passer un concours pour aller à certaines universités — il y a beaucoup de concurrence.

You have to take an entrance exam to go to some universities — there's lots of competition.

go for an interview — passer un entretien

Grammar — avoir l'intention de

'Avoir l'intention de' means 'to intend to' do something.
It is followed by an infinitive (see p.133).

Elle a l'intention d'aller à l'université.
She intends to go to university.

Amil couldn't get many on board his apprenticeship.

Practice Questions

Q1 *Translate these sentences into French.*
  a) In September, I will go to college.
  b) I have the chance to go to the university of my dreams.
  c) My best friend wants to do an apprenticeship.
  d) She organised an appointment to discuss her career. *[8 marks]*

WRITING

Q2 *Answer the questions below out loud in French. Try to answer as fully as you can.*
  • *What do you want to do after your GCSEs? Why?*
  • *What are the main differences between doing an apprenticeship and doing A-levels?*
  • *Describe a work experience placement you have done or would like to do.*
  • *In your opinion, is going to university worth it?* *[4 marks]*

SPEAKING

Top Tips for Higher Students
✓ Use the conditional and future tenses.
✓ Use subject-specific vocabulary.

Work experience always gives me *stage* fright...

You'll need to use the future tense to describe your plans, so why not spend some time now brushing up on it? If you're doing Higher, you need to be able to use both forms of the future — see page 138 for more.

Career Choices and Ambitions

Unless you want to pilot yachts for a living, planning your future is often far from plain sailing.
Don't worry about revealing your plans to the world in French. If you're uncertain — make it up.

Le monde du travail — *The world of work*

Vocabulary

travailler	*to work*	le / la collègue	*colleague*
le travail	*work, job, task*	la grève	*strike*
employer	*to employ, use*	l'argent (m)	*money*
l'employé(e)	*employee, worker*	le bureau	*desk, office*
l'emploi (m)	*job*	le chômage	*unemployment*
le métier	*job, occupation*	fabriquer	*to manufacture, produce, make*
le boulot	*work, job*	le rôle	*role*
les affaires (f)	*business, matters*	le service	*service*
l'entreprise (f)	*company*	le commerce	*trade, commerce*
l'organisation (f)	*organisation*	l'économie (f)	*economy*

(Higher: le rôle, le service, le commerce, l'économie)

Je travaille dans une grande entreprise qui fabrique de la nourriture pour animaux, mais nous sommes actuellement en grève.

I work for a big company that manufactures pet food, but we are currently on strike.

Quand l'économie était faible, elle n'avait pas d'emploi mais maintenant elle travaille dans un bureau.

When the economy was weak, she didn't have a job but now she works in an office.

was unemployed — était au chômage

for a charity — dans une association caritative

Ton métier idéal — *Your ideal job*

Vocabulary

le directeur / la directrice	*headteacher, manager*	le chanteur / la chanteuse	*singer*
le facteur / la factrice	*postman / postwoman*	le serveur / la serveuse	*waiter, server*
le policier / la policière	*police officer*	la construction	*construction, building*
le / la journaliste	*journalist*	l'usine (f)	*factory*
l'auteur(e)	*author*	la direction	*direction, management*
l'artiste (m/f)	*artist*	la police	*police*
le / la médecin	*doctor*	l'avocat(e)	*lawyer*
l'acteur / l'actrice	*actor*	le / la ministre	*minister*

(Higher: la direction, la police, l'avocat(e), le / la ministre)

For more jobs, see the vocab list on p.51.

Mon métier idéal, c'est d'être chanteur car j'aime faire de la musique.

My ideal job is to be a singer because I like making music.

Travailler dans une boulangerie, c'est le rôle pour moi — j'adore parler aux clients.

Working in a bakery is the role for me — I love talking to customers.

at the vet's — chez le vétérinaire

À l'avenir, je veux être… — *In the future, I want to be…*

Mon frère veut être policier
mais moi, je serai avocat(e).

*My brother wants to be a police
officer but I will be a lawyer.*

Ma mère travaillait dans une banque,
mais maintenant elle est factrice.

*My mum used to work in a bank,
but now she is a postwoman.*

Il va être ministre du gouvernement.

*He is going to be a
government minister.*

Question

Quel est ton métier
idéal ? Pourquoi ?

*What is your ideal
job? Why?*

Simple Answer

Je veux être acteur / actrice
car ils / elles gagnent
beaucoup d'argent.

*I want to be an actor
because they earn
a lot of money.*

Extended Answer

Je crois que diriger ma propre entreprise
de construction serait idéal pour moi —
être son propre patron, ce serait génial !

*I believe that running my own construction
company would be ideal for me —
being your own boss would be great!*

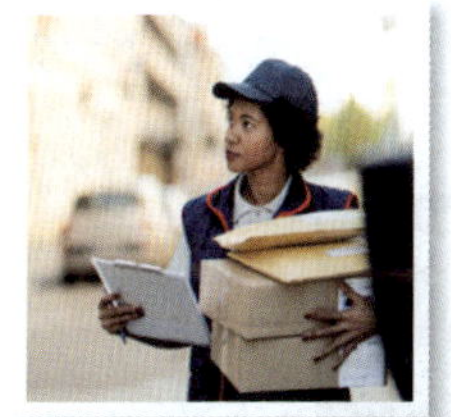

Celine thought the job advert said *actrice*…

Grammar — articles with jobs / professions

In French, you don't use an indefinite article
('un' / 'une') when you describe someone's job.

Ma mère est avocate.   ***My mother is a lawyer.***
Je veux être médecin.   ***I want to be a doctor.***

Practice Questions

Q1 Read this email that Ismaïl, your Algerian penfriend, has
sent you. Then answer the questions below in English.

> Quand j'étais jeune, mon rêve était de travailler dans une boulangerie parce que j'adorais
> faire du pain. Aujourd'hui, je continue à m'intéresser à la cuisine, et je voudrais être
> chef après l'école. En ce moment, j'ai un boulot d'été dans la cuisine d'un restaurant.
> Je ne gagne pas beaucoup d'argent, mais j'espère que l'expérience va être utile.

a) What did Ismaïl want to do when he was younger?   *[1 mark]*

b) What does he want to do when he leaves school?   *[1 mark]*

c) Where does he currently work?   *[1 mark]*

d) Give one positive and one negative of his current job.   *[2 marks]*

Q2 In this extract from a podcast, Fabienne is being interviewed about her career.

There are two true statements in each list below.
Choose the correct statements from each list.

Higher

a) **A.** Fabienne works in finance.   **b)** **A.** Fabienne worked when she was a student.
  B. Fabienne's job lets her travel.   **B.** Fabienne used to be a police officer.
  C. Fabienne finds her job easy.   **C.** Fabienne took a gap year.   *[4 marks]*

I'm called Sue — my parents are both lawyers…

There are lots of job options out there — and so there are lots of things you can say in French. Now, go find
a friend and, in French, tell them what job or jobs you want to do in the future and why they appeal to you.

Future Study and Work — Vocabulary

There's nothing worse than not knowing what to do next — so here's some vocab to keep you busy.

Education Post-16 — Next Steps

le lycée	college, sixth form
le bac(calauréat)	high school final exam (like A-levels)
la note	mark, grade
le résultat	result, follow-up
la première	year 12
le stage	work experience
l'apprentissage (m)	apprenticeship
progresser	to progress
le progrès	progress
le chemin	way, path
l'occasion (f)	chance, opportunity
le projet	plan
choisir	to choose
le choix	choice
décider (de)	to decide (to)
se décider (à)	to make the decision (to)
rêver (à / de)	to dream (of / about)
le rêve	dream
prêt(e)	ready

Higher

la formation	training
conseiller (à... de)	to advise, recommend (someone to do something)
le conseil	advice, counsel, council
réfléchir (à)	to reflect (on), think (about)
réaliser	to achieve
l'objectif (m)	objective
la recherche	research, search
l'industrie (f)	industry
l'enquête (f)	survey, investigation

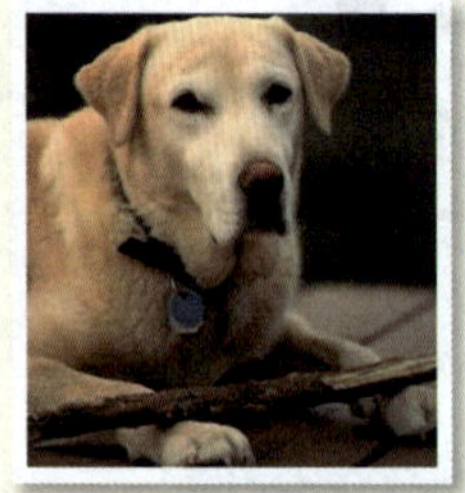

Reggie was in training for the position of regional branch manager.

Education Post-16 — University

l'avenir (m)	future
le futur	future
l'université (f)	university
étudier	to study
l'étudiant(e)	student
l'éducation (f)	education
l'expérience (f)	experience
l'indépendance (f)	independence
la carrière	career
commencer (à)	to start, begin (to)
finir	to end, finish
terminer	to end, finish
le concours	entrance exam, competition
réussir (à)	to pass, succeed (in)
le rendez-vous	appointment
l'entretien (m)	interview, maintenance

Higher

l'étape (f)	stage, step
l'établissement (m)	establishment, organisation
sabbatique (adj.)	sabbatical
l'année sabbatique (f)	gap year
indépendant(e)	independent
le champ	field, realm
inscrire	to write down
s'inscrire à	to join, enrol in
admettre	to admit
la concurrence	competition (rivalry)
la durée	length, duration
la condition	condition

Career Choices and Ambitions — At Work

l'adulte (m/f)	*adult*
travailler	*to work*
le travail	*work, job, task*
employer	*to employ, use*
l'employé(e)	*employee, worker*
l'emploi (m)	*job*
le métier	*job, occupation*
le boulot	*work, job*
les affaires (f)	*business, matters*
l'entreprise (f)	*company*
l'organisation (f)	*organisation*
la firme	*firm*
le / la collègue	*colleague*
le salaire	*salary, wage*
le / la client(e)	*customer, client*
la réunion	*meeting*
l'uniforme (m)	*uniform*
la grève	*strike*
l'argent (m)	*money*
riche	*rich*

le bureau	*desk, office*
vendre	*to sell*
le chômage	*unemployment*
fabriquer	*to manufacture, produce, make*
traduire	*to translate*
servir	*to serve*

Higher

le rôle	*role*
l'échelle (f)	*ladder, scale*
le service	*service*
le commerce	*trade, commerce*
l'économie (f)	*economy*
inventer	*to invent, make up*
la loi	*law*
l'appel (m)	*call*
la coopération	*cooperation*
nettoyer	*to clean*
le développement	*development*
technique (adj.)	*technical*

Career Choices and Ambitions — Jobs

le chef	*boss, cook*
le / la patron(ne)	*boss*
le directeur / la directrice	*headteacher, manager*
le / la prof(esseur)	*teacher*
le / la secrétaire	*secretary*
le facteur / la factrice	*postman / postwoman*
le policier / la policière	*police officer*
le / la journaliste	*journalist*
l'écrivain(e)	*writer*
l'auteur(e)	*author*
l'artiste (m/f)	*artist*
le / la médecin	*doctor*
l'aidant(e)	*carer*
le / la propriétaire	*owner*
l'acteur / l'actrice	*actor*
le chanteur / la chanteuse	*singer*
l'influenceur / l'influenceuse	*influencer*
le serveur / la serveuse	*waiter, waitress, server*

le / la scientifique	*scientist*
l'expert(e)	*expert*
le / la bénévole	*volunteer*
le / la président(e)	*president*
le gouvernement	*government*
la politique	*politics*
la poste	*post office*
la banque	*bank*
la boulangerie	*bakery*
l'usine (f)	*factory*
construire	*to build, construct*
la construction	*construction, building*

Higher

la cheffe	*boss, cook*
le leader	*leader*
l'avocat(e)	*lawyer*
le / la soldat(e)	*soldier*
le chercheur / la chercheuse	*researcher*
le / la ministre	*minister*
professionnel(le)	*professional*
la direction	*management, direction*
la réception	*reception*
la police	*police*
le parlement	*parliament*

Revision Summary Test for Section Five

Now that you've tackled this section — it's time to check your knowledge. On your marks, set...

- Yep, these questions are **hard** — they'll really help you see **how well you know your stuff**.
- Tackle the **revision summary test** below, or scan the QR code to do it **online**.
  Use the CGP RevisionHub to **track your progress** and see **which areas need more work**.
- You can find **sample answers** here: www.cgpbooks.co.uk/BonjourExtras

Education Post-16 ☐

1) You read this sentence on a university website: 'If you want to go to university,
   you must improve your grades and pass an entrance exam'. Translate it into French.

2) 'Do you think work placements are useful?' Explain your answer in French.

3) Write down a French synonym for these words: a) finir   b) le futur

4) 'Would you like to take a gap year? Why? / Why not?' Answer in French.

5) 'Quels sont tes projets après le collège ?' Translate the question and answer in French.

6) Translate this sentence into French: 'The student passed
   the interview, but she decided to continue her education.'

7) Nicolas has been advised to try out a particular job before he decides on his future career.
   Which piece of career advice below best applies to him?
   a) Vous devez continuer à étudier.   c) Vous devez faire un stage.
   b) Vous devez aller à l'université.   d) Vous devez avoir de bons résultats.

8) Translate these words into English:
   a) le progrès   b) le chemin   c) le rêve   d) la carrière   e) le rendez-vous   f) l'occasion

9) In French, ask your friend if they are ready to leave school and enrol at university. **[H]**

10) Give the English for these words: a) l'étape   b) réfléchir à   c) l'enquête   d) le champ

Career Choices and Ambitions ☐

11) A French friend asks this: 'How do you want to progress in your career?'
    Translate the question and then answer it in French.

12) How many jobs can you name in French?
    There are at least 18 you need to know (plus 5 for Higher tier).

13) You read this headline in a Belgian newspaper: 'Selon les experts, le chômage va
    augmenter en Belgique cette année.' What is it saying?

14) How many different places of work can you name in French?
    There are at least 4 you need to know (plus 1 for Higher tier).

15) What does 'le travail' mean? Can you give three synonyms in French?

16) 'In your opinion, why is it important to have a job?' Answer in French.

17) In French, name a job you would like to do and say why you would be good at it.

18) Translate these verbs into French.
    a) to translate   b) to manufacture   c) to build   d) to sell   e) to employ   f) to work

19) A friend asks you, 'Comment est-ce que tu vas gagner de l'argent comme adulte ?'
    Translate the question and respond in French.

20) What do these words mean?
    a) l'uniforme   b) le chômage   c) l'entreprise   d) la grève   e) le salaire   f) le gouvernement

21) Translate this sentence into English: 'La direction de l'entreprise veut
    augmenter la coopération entre les services techniques et les autres rôles.' **[Higher]**

22) Translate these words into French: a) gap year   b) competition   c) research   d) to admit

Music

Quick Quiz

Is that the sweet sound of a new section all about free-time activities I hear? There's lots of vocab about music to get your head around, so take your time learning it.

La musique — *Music*

Head to the CGP RevisionHub for all your online content: www.cgpbooks.co.uk/Bonjour

Vocabulary

jouer (de)	*to play (an instrument)*	la radio	*radio*
l'instrument (m)	*instrument*	le concert	*concert*
apprendre (à)	*to learn (to)*	le membre	*member*
chanter	*to sing*	le groupe	*group*
la chanson	*song*	populaire	*popular*
les paroles (f)	*lyrics*	télécharger	*to download*
écouter	*to listen (to)*	le rythme	*rhythm, rate*
		le genre	*type, kind, sort*

Grammar — 'jouer de'

'Jouer' is followed by 'de l'', 'du', 'de la' or 'des' when you're talking about playing a musical instrument.

Je joue du violon et de la flûte.
I play the violin and the flute.

Q&A Audio

Question

Est-ce que tu joues d'un instrument de musique ?
Do you play a musical instrument?

Simple Answer

Oui, je joue de la guitare et je chante.
Yes, I play the guitar and I sing.

Extended Answer

Oui, je joue du piano depuis cinq ans et j'apprends à jouer de la trompette. Je suis aussi membre d'un groupe de jazz.

Yes, I have been playing the piano for five years and I'm learning to play the trumpet. I am also a member of a jazz group.

Pierre plays in the horn section of his local orchestra.

Écouter de la musique — *Listening to music*

La musique est ma passion et je vais souvent à des concerts avec mes copains.

Je préfère chanter, mais parfois c'est difficile de me souvenir des paroles.

Ma sœur écoute la radio tout le temps et elle télécharge beaucoup de musique populaire.

Music is my passion and I often go to concerts with my friends.

I prefer singing, but sometimes it's difficult to remember the lyrics.

My sister always listens to the radio and she downloads lots of popular music.

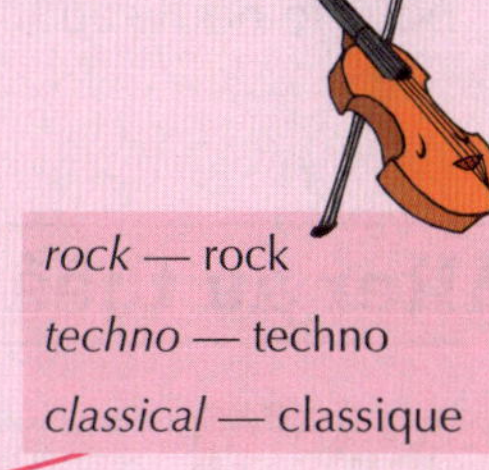

rock — rock
techno — techno
classical — classique

Practice Question

Q1 Listen to three people talk about their attitudes to music and answer the questions below.

a) What does Camille regularly do? *[1 mark]*

b) i)   How long has Dorian been singing for? *[1 mark]*

   ii) What has Dorian started doing this year? *[1 mark]*

c) i)   How did Inès find learning an instrument at first? *[1 mark]*

   ii) How does she feel about learning an instrument now? *[1 mark]*

Listening Track 9

I write songs for French artists — some call me a *parole* officer...

'Jouer' is followed by 'de l'' / 'du' / 'de la' / 'des' when you're talking about musical instruments and 'à' when you're talking about sports. Using a nice range of verbs will also be music to the examiner's ears.

Cinema, Theatre and TV

Everyone loves a good film or TV show — and they're great to talk about in the exam. These pages cover useful vocab you can use to discuss films, plays and TV. Can someone pass me the popcorn?

Regarder un film — *Watching a film*

Vocabulary

le cinéma	*cinema*	le film d'action	*action film*
regarder	*to watch*	l'histoire d'amour (f)	*romance*
voir	*to see*	l'acteur / l'actrice	*actor / actress*
le film	*film*	le personnage	*character*
le billet	*ticket*	**H** les effets spéciaux (m)	*special effects*

Question

Est-ce que tu aimes aller au cinéma ?

Do you like to go to the cinema?

Simple Answer

Non, je préfère regarder des films chez moi.

No, I prefer to watch films at home.

Extended Answer

Oui, je suis membre d'un club de cinéma. J'y vais une fois par semaine, parce que les billets sont moins chers. J'adore discuter des nouveaux films avec les autres membres.

Yes, I am a member of a cinema club. I go once a week because the tickets are less expensive. I love discussing new films with the other members.

J'adore voir des films d'action au cinéma. Les effets spéciaux sont étonnants sur grand écran.

Mon frère aime les mêmes films que moi, donc nous les regardons ensemble.

Je dois acheter deux billets de cinéma pour le nouveau film ce week-end.

I love seeing action films at the cinema. The special effects are amazing on the big screen.

My brother likes the same films as me, so we watch them together.

I need to buy two cinema tickets for the new film this weekend.

horror films — des films d'horreur

romantic films — des histoires d'amour

comedies — des films comiques

Aller au théâtre — *Going to the theatre*

Vocabulary

la pièce	*play, piece*	montrer	*to show*
le théâtre	*theatre, drama*	rire	*to laugh*
passionnant(e)	*exciting, thrilling*	**H** le titre	*title*
		la scène	*stage, scene*
la star	*star, celebrity*		

Ce soir, je vais au théâtre pour voir une nouvelle pièce.

Je n'ai pas aimé la scène d'ouverture car la musique était trop forte.

Cependant, la pièce était intéressante et moderne, et les acteurs étaient drôles.

Tonight, I'm going to the theatre to see a new play.

I didn't like the opening scene because the music was too loud.

However, the play was interesting and modern, and the actors were funny.

a musical — une comédie musicale

the plot — l'intrigue

Qu'est-ce qu'il y a à la télé ? — *What's on TV?*

Vocabulary

la télé(vision)	television / TV
l'émission (f)	*TV programme*
le programme	*schedule*
l'écran (m)	*screen*
la télé-réalité	*reality TV*
la célébrité	*celebrity*
Higher la série	*series*
diffuser	*to broadcast*
la pub(licité)	*advert*

'On' is usually translated as 'sur' in French, but remember, it's 'à la télé'.

Oscar and Rex could really see themselves in the main characters.

Grammar — 'qui'

'Qui' means 'who' or 'which'. It refers to the <u>subject</u> of the sentence.
La personne qui regarde la télévision.
The person <u>who</u> watches television.
Le personnage qui est mort à la fin.
The character <u>who</u> died at the end.

Mon passe-temps préféré, c'est regarder la télévision — c'est amusant.

My favourite hobby is watching television — it's fun.

relaxing — relaxant
entertaining — divertissant

J'adore les émissions qui me font rire.

I love programmes that make me laugh.

La télé-réalité est intéressante car on peut suivre la vie quotidienne des célébrités.

Reality TV is interesting because you can follow celebrities' daily lives.

the news — les informations
soap operas — les feuilletons
crime series — les séries policières

Elle aime les documentaires.

She likes documentaries.

Practice Questions

Q1 *Pierre is talking about television. Read the text, then answer the question below.*

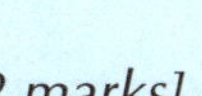

Je regarde la télévision presque tous les jours après le collège. Mon père pense que je ne fais jamais mes devoirs parce que je passe trop de temps devant la télé. Il croit que le sport est meilleur pour ma santé, et que je suis paresseux. Moi, je pense que j'ai besoin de regarder la télé pour me relaxer après une longue journée de cours.

Choose the two correct statements from the list below.

A. Pierre watches TV almost every day after school.

B. Pierre watches TV to relax after doing his homework.

C. Pierre likes watching sport on TV.

D. Pierre watches TV to relax after a long day at school.

[2 marks]

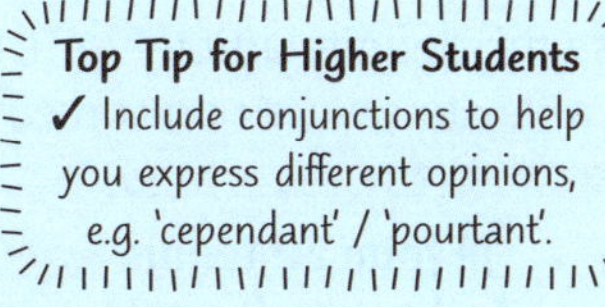

Q2 *You are writing a blog post about the films and TV shows you like to watch. Write about 90 words in French. Describe:*

- *what kinds of films and TV shows you like watching and why*
- *what types of films you enjoyed as a child*
- *what kind of film you will watch the next time you go to the cinema.*

Top Tip for Higher Students
✓ Include conjunctions to help you express different opinions, e.g. 'cependant' / 'pourtant'.

[15 marks]

This play about the French Revolution is a *pièce de résistance...*

No standing ovation for that joke? If you run out of things to say about TV shows you like, you could compare your tastes to your siblings' or parents' tastes. Next up is sports — race you to the next page...

Quick Quiz

Sport

Whether you're sporty or not, you need to learn to talk about what sports you do and give your opinion on them. The next two pages should guide you through nicely. On your marks, get set, go!

Faire du sport — *To do sport*

Vocabulary

faire	*to do (a sport)*	la promenade	*walk*	nager	*to swim*
le sport	*sport*	courir	*to run*	pratiquer	*to do, play, practise*
la santé	*health*	danser	*to dance*		
l'exercice (m)	*physical exercise*	participer (à)	*to take part (in), participate (in)*	le terrain	*ground, terrain*
actif / active	*active, energetic*	la participation	*participation*	le terrain de sport	*sports field*
sportif / sportive	*athletic, competitive, sporty, sporting*	monter	*to climb, go up*		
le vélo	*bike, bicycle*	le centre sportif	*sports centre*		
la natation	*swimming*	la piscine	*swimming pool*		
marcher	*to walk*	la course	*race*		
		le Tour de France	*Tour de France*		

Higher: nager, pratiquer, le terrain, le terrain de sport

Moi, je suis assez actif / active. Je fais du vélo cinq fois par semaine. À l'avenir, c'est mon rêve de participer à des courses comme le Tour de France.

I'm quite active. I go cycling five times a week. In the future, it's my dream to participate in races like the Tour de France.

sailing — de la voile
skiing — du ski
horse riding — de l'équitation

Je ne suis pas très sportif / sportive mais cet été j'ai beaucoup marché dans la campagne.

I am not very sporty but during the summer I walked a lot in the countryside.

Je suis sportif / sportive — *I am sporty*

Q&A Audio

Question

Est-ce que tu fais du sport souvent ?

Do you do sport often?

Simple Answer

Oui, je danse le lundi, et je cours le mercredi. Je fais aussi partie d'un club de natation.

Yes, I dance on Mondays and I run on Wednesdays. I'm also a member of a swimming club.

Grammar — adverbs of time

Use the definite article 'le' + the name of a day to say you do something on the same day each week.

Je joue au tennis le jeudi.
I play tennis on Thursdays.

Extended Answer

Oui, j'aime être actif / active. En hiver, je fais du ski — c'est ma passion. Le paysage est beau, mais le ski peut être un sport dangereux. L'année dernière, je suis tombé(e) et je me suis blessé(e).

Yes, I like to be active. In the winter, I go skiing — it's my passion. The scenery is beautiful, but skiing can be a dangerous sport. Last year, I fell and was injured.

Je travaille dans un centre sportif. Pour moi, il est important que tout le monde participe.

I work at a sports centre. For me, it's important that everyone participates.

Cette semaine, la nouvelle piscine ouvrira dans ma ville. Je vais prendre des cours de natation.

This week, the new swimming pool will open in our town. I am going to take swimming lessons.

Les sports (m) d'équipe — *Team sports*

Vocabulary

le foot(ball)	*football, soccer*	perdre	*to lose*
le match	*match*	dangereux / dangereuse	*dangerous*
la partie	*part, game, match*	la concurrence	*competition (rivalry)*
le concours	*competition*	la vitesse	*speed*
le jeu	*game*	blesser	*to hurt, injure*
l'équipe (f)	*team*	se blesser	*to hurt oneself, injure oneself*
le stade	*stadium, stage*		
gagner	*to win*		

(Higher: la concurrence, la vitesse, blesser, se blesser)

Normalement, je joue au rugby avec mes copains après l'école.

Je préfère la natation mais mes copains aiment jouer au hockey et ils sont membres d'une équipe locale.

J'adore assister aux événements sportifs au stade national à Paris.

Le week-end dernier, je me suis blessé(e) pendant une course.

Normally, I play rugby with my friends after school.

I prefer swimming but my friends like to play hockey and they are members of a local team.

I love to attend sports events at the national stadium in Paris.

Last weekend, I got injured during a race.

badminton — au badminton
basketball — au basket
netball — au netball
golf — au golf

tournaments — aux tournois

a football match — un match de foot
a game of tennis — une partie de tennis

Practice Questions

Q1 *Translate the following sentences into French.* **WRITING**

  a) In my opinion, exercise is essential for your health. *[2 marks]*

  b) I am active and I try to do sport every day. *[2 marks]*

  c) This summer, I am going to participate in a swimming competition. *[2 marks]*

  d) My sister goes to the sports centre to dance with her friends. *[2 marks]*

Q2 *Read what Lola has to say about trying a new sport and answer the questions below.*

 **READING**

Higher

> Moi, je cours pour rester en bonne santé. C'est un sport qu'on peut faire seul ou dans une équipe. On peut le faire au centre sportif, au terrain de sport, même au parc et ça ne coûte rien. Chaque semaine je sors avec une amie qui est très sportive. Elle participe à des concours et gagne souvent. Elle m'a aidée beaucoup, parce qu'au début c'était vraiment difficile. Alors, je suis en train d'améliorer ma vitesse, et maintenant, quand je fais du sport, j'ai plus confiance en moi.

  a) What sport does Lola do? *[1 mark]*

  b) According to the text, which three places can you do this sport? *[3 marks]*

  c) Give two things Lola has improved on since training with her friend. *[2 marks]*

No diving, no running, and certainly no *piscine* in the pool...

This topic gives you a good opportunity to use the imperfect tense (see p.136) — you can mention sports that you used to do. Don't forget that 'faire', 'jouer' and 'participer' will still need 'de' or 'à' in the imperfect.

Going Out and Other Hobbies

We've all got different activities we prefer — from computer games to cooking. These pages cover plenty of vocab that will be useful when you're talking about all the fun stuff you get up to.

Mes passe-temps (m) — *My hobbies*

Vocabulary

sortir	*to go out, exit, take out, release*	visiter	*to visit*	la photo	*photo*
libre	*free*	se diriger	*to make one's way*	le jeu vidéo	*video game*
le temps libre	*free time*	se relaxer	*to relax*	l'ordinateur (m)	*computer*
l'activité (f)	*activity*	voir	*to see*	le festival	*festival*
l'intérêt (m)	*interest*	lire	*to read*	le parc	*park*
s'intéresser (à)	*to be interested in*	le roman	*novel*	l'ami(e)	*friend*
		le livre	*book*	la passion	*passion*
aller	*to go*	la lecture	*reading*	le chapitre	*chapter*
				dessiner	*to draw*

Higher — la passion, le chapitre, dessiner

Question

Quel est ton passe-temps préféré ?

What is your favourite hobby?

Simple Answer

Mon passe-temps préféré, c'est la lecture. Je pense que les romans historiques sont les meilleurs.

My favourite hobby is reading. I think that historical novels are the best.

Extended Answer

J'ai une passion pour les jeux vidéo. Je joue sur mon ordinateur presque tous les jours. Au lycée, il y a un club de jeux — heureusement, il y a aussi beaucoup d'autres gens qui s'intéressent aux jeux vidéo.

I have a passion for video games. I play on my computer almost every day. At college, there is a games club — fortunately, there are lots of other people who are interested in video games too.

Je préfère aller au cinéma **que** jouer sur l'ordinateur.

I prefer going to the cinema to playing on the computer.

Pendant mon temps libre, j'adore être dehors. Quand il y a du soleil, je vais au parc avec mes amis.

In my free time, I love being outside. When it's sunny, I go to the park with my friends.

Grammar — giving opinions

Use 'j'aime' (I like), 'je préfère' (I prefer) and 'je déteste' (I hate) to give a range of opinions.

Je préfère la lecture au sport.
I prefer reading to sport.

Je déteste les jeux vidéo.
I hate video games.

Au centre commercial — *At the shopping centre*

Vocabulary

le shopping	*shopping*	acheter	*to buy*
commercial(e)	*commercial, shopping (adj.)*	coûter	*to cost*
		le prix	*price*
la course	*shopping*	le consommateur / la consommatrice	*consumer, customer*
les courses (f)	*food shopping*		
la mode	*fashion*	l'achat (m)	*purchase*

J'adore aller au centre commercial. Je fais souvent du shopping avec mes amis et on achète de nouveaux vêtements. Cependant, c'est une activité qui coûte cher.

I love to go to the shopping centre. I often go shopping with my friends and we buy new clothes. However, it's an expensive hobby.

window-shopping — du lèche-vitrines

Manger au restaurant — *Eating at the restaurant*

Vocabulary

le repas	*meal*	la table	*table*
la nourriture	*food*	emporter	*to take with, take away*
manger	*to eat*	réserver	*to reserve, book, keep*
la cuisine	*cooking, kitchen*	payer	*to pay (for)*
le dîner	*dinner*	l'addition (f)	*bill*
l'entrée (f)	*starter*	le plat	*dish*
la carte	*menu*	commander	*to order*
le serveur / la serveuse	*waiter / waitress*	l'ouverture (f)	*opening*

Higher: l'addition, le plat, commander, l'ouverture

Paul and Zara knew the importance of maintaining eye contact.

Hier soir, j'ai réservé une table au restaurant que tu aimes. La nourriture est super et les serveurs sont très sympathiques.

Last night, I reserved a table at the restaurant that you like. The food is great and the waiters are very nice.

Je voudrais payer le repas parce que c'est ton anniversaire.

I would like to pay for the meal because it's your birthday.

the drinks — les boissons

the desserts — les desserts

Est-ce qu'on peut voir la carte, s'il vous plaît ? Je pense qu'on va acheter des plats à emporter.

Can we see the menu, please? I think we will buy food to take away.

Comme entrée, je prends le poisson et un peu de pain, s'il vous plaît.

As a starter, I'll take the fish and a bit of bread, please.

For the main course — Comme plat principal

Practice Questions

Q1 Look at the two photos below. Talk in French about what is in the photos. You should talk for about a minute and say something about both photos.

SPEAKING

Top Tips for Higher Students
✓ Use time expressions such as 'être en train de' or 'venir de'.
✓ Link phrases together with conjunctions.

[5 marks]

Q2 Listen to Anaïs, Izzie, Enzo and Paul talking about activities they do in their free time. Then answer the questions below.

Higher

LISTENING

a) Why does Anaïs like drawing clothes? *[1 mark]*

b) How does Izzie relax? *[1 mark]*

c) What does Enzo prefer to do? *[1 mark]*

d) Why does Paul dislike shopping? Give two reasons. *[2 marks]*

Why do ducks make good waiters? They always bring the bill...

It can be easy to get stuck using the same phrases all the time, so try practising different ways of expressing your opinions. Using verbs like 'préférer' and 's'intéresser' will make you sound much more sophisticated.

Free-time Activities — Vocabulary

Learning all of this vocab about your hobbies will only make your free time more fun — I promise.

Music

la musique	*music*
jouer (de)	*to play (an instrument)*
l'instrument (m)	*instrument*
apprendre (à)	*to learn (to)*
chanter	*to sing*
le chanteur / la chanteuse	*singer*

la chanson	*song*
les paroles (f)	*lyrics*
écouter	*to listen (to)*
la radio	*radio*
le concert	*concert*
le membre	*member*
le groupe	*group*
populaire	*popular*

Internet (m)	*internet*
télécharger	*to download*
essayer (de)	*to try, attempt*

Higher

le rythme	*rhythm, rate*
le genre	*type, kind, sort*

Cinema, Theatre and TV

le cinéma	*cinema*
regarder	*to watch, look at*
voir	*to see*
le film	*film*
le billet	*ticket*
le film d'action	*action film*
l'histoire d'amour (f)	*romance*
l'action (f)	*action*
l'acteur / l'actrice	*actor / actress*
le personnage	*character*

la pièce	*play*
le théâtre	*theatre, drama*
passionnant(e)	*exciting, thrilling*
célèbre	*famous*
la star	*star, celebrity*
la célébrité	*celebrity*
montrer	*to show*
rire	*to laugh*
la télé(vision)	*television, TV*
l'émission (f)	*TV programme*
le programme	*schedule*

l'écran (m)	*screen*
la réalité	*reality*
la télé-réalité	*reality TV*

Higher

l'effet (m)	*effect*
les effets spéciaux (m)	*special effects*
la scène	*stage, scene*
le titre	*title*
la série	*series*
diffuser	*to broadcast*
la pub(licité)	*advert*

Sport

faire	*to do (a sport)*
le sport	*sport*
l'exercice (m)	*physical exercise*
la santé	*health*
actif / active	*active, energetic*
sportif / sportive	*athletic, competitive, sporty, sporting*
lancer	*to throw, launch*
le vélo	*bike, bicycle*
la natation	*swimming*
marcher	*to walk*
la promenade	*walk*
courir	*to run*
danser	*to dance*

monter	*to climb, go up*
participer (à)	*to take part (in), participate (in)*
la participation	*participation*
le centre	*centre*
le centre sportif	*sports centre*
la piscine	*swimming pool*
la course	*race*
le Tour de France	*the Tour de France*

Higher

nager	*to swim*
pratiquer	*to do, play, practise*
le terrain	*ground, terrain*
le terrain de sport	*sports field*
régulièrement	*regularly*

Sport — Team Sports

le foot(ball)	*football, soccer*
le match	*match*
la partie	*game, match, part*
l'événement (m)	*event*
le concours	*competition*
le jeu	*game*
l'équipe (f)	*team*
le stade	*stadium, stage*

gagner	*to win, earn, gain*
perdre	*to lose*
dangereux / dangereuse	*dangerous*

Higher

la concurrence	*competition (rivalry)*
la vitesse	*speed*
blesser	*to hurt, injure*
se blesser	*to hurt oneself, injure oneself*

Going Out

sortir	*to go out, exit, take out, release*
libre	*free*
le temps	*time, weather*
le temps libre	*free time*
le shopping	*shopping*
commercial(e)	*commercial, shopping (adj.)*
le centre commercial	*shopping centre*
la course	*shopping*
les courses (f)	*food shopping*
la mode	*fashion*
acheter	*to buy*
aller	*to go*
visiter	*to visit*
coûter	*to cost*
payer	*to pay (for)*
le prix	*price*
se diriger	*to make one's way*
voir	*to see*
le parc	*park*
le soleil	*sun*
la fête	*party, festival*

le festival	*festival*
manger	*to eat*
la nourriture	*food*
le restaurant	*restaurant*
la cuisine	*cooking*
le repas	*meal*
le dîner	*dinner*
l'entrée (f)	*starter*
la carte	*menu*
le serveur / la serveuse	*waiter, waitress, server*
le garçon	*waiter (old-fashioned)*
la table	*table*
emporter	*to take with, take away*
réserver	*to reserve, book, keep*
ouvert(e)	*open*

Higher

le consommateur / la consommatrice	*consumer, customer*
l'achat (m)	*purchase*
l'addition (f)	*bill*
le plat	*dish*
commander	*to order*
l'ouverture (f)	*opening*

Other Hobbies

le passe-temps	*hobby*
l'intérêt (m)	*interest*
intéresser	*to interest*
s'intéresser (à)	*to be interested in*
le jeu vidéo	*video game*
l'activité (f)	*activity*
lire	*to read*
le livre	*book*
la lecture	*reading*
le roman	*novel*

se relaxer	*to relax*
la photo	*photo*
l'ordinateur (m)	*computer*
l'ami(e)	*friend*
le copain	*friend, boyfriend*
la copine	*friend, girlfriend*

Higher

la passion	*passion*
le chapitre	*chapter*
dessiner	*to draw*

Section Six — Free-time Activities

Revision Summary Test for Section Six

Before you can enjoy some free time, check your knowledge with these questions.

- These questions are **hard**, but they'll really help you see **how well you know your stuff**.
- Tackle the **revision summary test** below, or scan the QR code to do it **online**.
  You can **track your progress** online and see **which areas need more work**.
- There are **sample answers** for the test here: www.cgpbooks.co.uk/BonjourExtras

Music ☑

1) 'Est-ce que tu joues d'un instrument de musique ?' Translate this question, then answer it in French. ☑

2) A French musician has given an interview: 'Je suis membre d'un groupe. J'écris les
   paroles et je chante. Nous participons à beaucoup de concerts.' What's he saying? ☑

3) Imagine you recently went to a music festival. Write two sentences about it in French. ☑

4) Translate into French: 'I used to listen to the radio but now I download songs on my phone.' ☑

Cinema, Theatre and TV ☐

5) What do these words mean in English?
   a) l'acteur   b) l'écran   c) le film d'action   d) l'émission   e) le billet   f) rire ☑

6) 'Est-ce que tu aimes aller au cinéma ? Pourquoi ? / Pourquoi pas ?' Respond in French. ☑

7) 'La télé-réalité est ennuyeuse et elle encourage les jeunes à avoir une fausse image de la
   vie normale.' Translate this statement into English and then explain whether you agree in French. ☑

8) In French, describe the last film or TV show you watched. Did you enjoy it? Why? / Why not? ☑

9) Sylvie is an actress. Translate what she says about her job: 'J'adore travailler pour le théâtre —
   c'est ma passion. Je préfère les pièces aux films parce que les personnages sont plus intéressants.' ☑

H 10) Translate these phrases into French:
   a) to watch a series   b) to broadcast   c) title   d) special effects   e) advert ☑

Sport ☑

11) Write three sentences about your favourite sport. Why do you like it and when do you play it? ☑

12) Hugo tells you: 'Je fais souvent du vélo et j'ai un concours la semaine prochaine.
    Si je gagne toutes mes courses, je vais devenir membre de l'équipe nationale française.'
    Translate his sentences into English. ☑

13) 'Do you enjoy team sports? Why? / Why not?' Answer in French. ☑

14) Write this sentence in French: 'I am quite active because exercise is good for my health.' ☑

15) Translate these words into French: a) sports centre   b) football match   c) stadium ☑

H 16) 'Je pratique la natation régulièrement mais récemment je me suis blessée,
    donc je ne peux pas nager pendant cinq semaines.' What's Nadia saying? ☑

Going Out and Other Hobbies ☐

17) Write two sentences about going shopping with a friend. Describe what you bought and why. ☑

18) 'Pendant mon temps libre, je lis un livre ou, s'il y a du soleil, je vais au parc avec un ami.'
    Translate Lola's sentence into English, then describe what you do in your own free time in French. ☑

19) In French, how would you say 'I would like to reserve a table but the restaurant isn't open yet.' ☑

20) Translate these phrases into English: a) he relaxes   b) I always pay   c) they go out often ☑

21) You're at a restaurant in France. Say that you'd like to see the menu and order food to take away. ☑

22) Translate these words into English:
    a) la consommatrice   b) le chapitre   c) l'ouverture   d) l'addition   e) l'achat   f) le plat ☑

Celebrations

Quick Quiz

There are many occasions to celebrate, and you'll need to know how to talk about them. This page has some handy vocabulary, so let's get the party started...

Remember there's also lots of online content here: www.cgpbooks.co.uk/Bonjour

Venez à la fête ! — *Come to the party!*

Vocabulary

célébrer	*to celebrate*	inviter	*to invite*
la fête	*party, festival*	la surprise	*surprise*
l'événement (m)	*event*	surprendre	*to surprise*
l'anniversaire (m)	*birthday*	**Higher** apprécier	*to appreciate, like*
le cadeau	*present, gift*	offrir (à)	*to give (someone), offer (someone)*
le gâteau	*cake*		
félicitations	*congratulations*	féliciter	*to congratulate*

The guests at the house-warming party really raised the roof.

J'ai apprécié la musique à l'événement.

I enjoyed the music at the event.

L'année dernière, j'ai reçu un beau cadeau pour mon anniversaire.

Last year, I received a beautiful gift for my birthday.

Ma tante a invité ses amis à sa fête d'anniversaire, mais je ne peux pas y aller.

My aunt invited her friends to her birthday party, but I can't go to it.

Je sais déjà qu'ils vont faire une fête surprise pour me féliciter.

I already know they're going to throw a surprise party to congratulate me.

a tasty cake — un gâteau délicieux

new headphones — de nouveaux écouteurs

wish me a happy birthday — me souhaiter un joyeux anniversaire

Grammar — talking about the (immediate) future

You can use the <u>immediate future</u> to talk about something that is <u>going to</u> happen. Use the <u>present tense</u> form of the verb '<u>aller</u>' + an <u>infinitive</u>.

Nous <u>allons donner</u> des fleurs à Maman.   *We <u>are going to give</u> some flowers to Mum.*

You can use either 'bon anniversaire' or 'joyeux anniversaire' to say 'happy birthday'.

Practice Question

Q1 *Youssou is describing his birthday celebrations. Choose the correct option to finish each sentence.*

a) To celebrate his birthday, he...
A. had an enormous party.   **B.** ate his favourite meal.   **C.** had a small family event.   *[1 mark]*

b) His parents gave him...
A. a novel.   **B.** a new computer.   **C.** a cake.   *[1 mark]*

c) The following Saturday, he...
A. went to the town centre.   **B.** spent the day alone.   **C.** watched a show with friends.   *[1 mark]*

We tore up the dance floor — we're putting in carpet instead...

You'll be the life and soul of the speaking exam if you use different tenses to add some variety to your sentences. For example, you could use the perfect tense to say what you did last year for your birthday.

Customs and Festivals

Use these pages to help you talk about the many customs and festivals in the French-speaking world.

Les fêtes religieuses — *Religious festivals*

Vocabulary

la religion	*religion*	bouddhiste	*Buddhist*	la synagogue	*synagogue*
croire	*to believe*	Noël (m)	*Christmas*	le temple	*temple*
chrétien(ne)	*Christian*	l'Aïd (m)	*Eid*	la foi	*faith*
musulman(e)	*Muslim*	l'église (f)	*church*	le dieu	*god*
juif / juive	*Jewish*	la mosquée	*mosque*	prier	*to pray*

(**Higher**: la foi, le dieu, prier)

À Noël, certains chrétiens vont à l'église pour la messe de minuit.

At Christmas, some Christians go to church for midnight mass.

Au cours du Ramadan, les musulmans ne doivent ni manger ni boire pendant la journée.

During Ramadan, Muslims must neither eat nor drink during the day.

Hanoukka est une fête juive importante.

Hanukkah is an important Jewish festival.

Easter — Pâques
Diwali — Le Diwali
Hindu — hindoue

Grammar (Higher only) — 'ne...ni...ni' (neither...nor)

To say '<u>neither</u> this <u>nor</u> that', use this structure: '<u>ne</u>' before the verb + '<u>ni</u>... <u>ni</u>...'.

Je <u>ne</u> célèbre <u>ni</u> Noël <u>ni</u> Pâques.   *I celebrate <u>neither</u> Christmas <u>nor</u> Easter.*

Question

Est-ce que tu célèbres une fête religieuse ?

Do you celebrate a religious festival?

Simple Answer

Oui, je célèbre une fête musulmane qui s'appelle l'Aïd.

Yes, I celebrate a Muslim festival called Eid.

Extended Answer

Oui, ma famille et moi célébrons l'Aïd, une fête musulmane importante. Chaque année, nous visitons la mosquée tôt le matin pour prier, puis nous mangeons des plats traditionnels et nous passons du temps ensemble.

Yes, my family and I celebrate Eid, an important Muslim festival. Each year, we visit the mosque early in the morning to pray, then we eat traditional dishes and spend time together.

La Fête Nationale — *Bastille Day*

Many events are held on <u>Bastille Day</u> to commemorate the <u>French Revolution</u>. It's the French <u>national day</u>.

Vocabulary

férié(e)	*public holiday (adj.)*	rappeler (à)	*to remind (someone)*	
la tradition	*tradition*	se rappeler	*to remember*	
traditionnel(le)	*traditional*	francophone	*French-speaking*	
historique	*historic*	unir	*to unite, join*	

(**Higher**: rappeler (à), se rappeler, francophone, unir)

Claire pulled out all the stops to make it onto the cover, but page 64 will have to do.

En France, le quatorze juillet est le jour de la Fête Nationale.

In France, 14th July is Bastille Day (a national holiday).

C'est un jour férié qui commémore les événements historiques de la Révolution française.

It's a public holiday that commemorates the historic events of the French Revolution.

Les festivals culturels — *Cultural festivals*

Vocabulary

la culture	*culture*	regarder	*to watch, look at*
culturel(le)	*cultural*	le bruit	*noise*
spécial(e)	*special*	porter	*to wear, carry*
le feu d'artifice	*firework display*	participer (à)	*to take part (in)*
le défilé	*parade, procession*	la participation	*participation*
la musique	*music*	joyeux / joyeuse	*merry, joyful, happy*
danser	*to dance*	assister à	*to attend*
le spectacle	*sight, show*		

Both 'la fête' and 'le festival' can mean 'festival'.

'Is that the parade?'
'No idea — I can't see a thing!'

J'adore les festivals culturels — il y a souvent des spectacles et des défilés dans les rues.

I love cultural festivals — there are often shows and parades in the streets.

La musique est toujours super, ce qui encourage les gens à danser.

The music is always great, which encourages people to dance.

Les festivals culturels de ma ville sont pleins de vie et tout le monde apprécie les feux d'artifice.

The cultural festivals in my town are lively and everyone likes the firework displays.

Practice Questions

Q1 Look at the two photos below. Talk in French about what is in the photos. You should talk for about a minute and say something about both photos. 

[5 marks]

Q2 Read the passage below and answer the questions.

On a demandé aux Français : « Qu'est-ce que vous allez faire le quatorze juillet ? »
- La majorité (82%) va sortir avec des amis.
- 12% vont regarder un feu d'artifice.
- Seulement 8% vont participer à un défilé.
- 34% mangeront un repas avec leur famille.
- 74% des gens assisteront à un spectacle.
- Et 18% resteront à la maison.

a) What percentage of people will be doing the following activities?

　　i) eating a meal　　**ii)** attending a show　　**iii)** participating in a procession　　[3 marks]

b) According to the text, what will 18% of people be doing?　　[1 mark]

I passed my fireworks exam with flying colours...

In your exam, it's important you can give some good examples of the things you do to celebrate different customs and festivals. If one of the activities you do isn't covered on these pages, look it up in a dictionary.

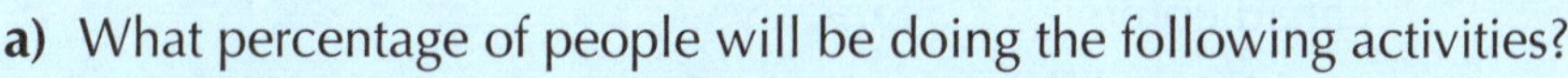

Customs, Festivals and Celebrations — Vocabulary

If you want to celebrate in style — and tell everyone about it — you'll need to nail this vocab on festivals and customs.

Celebrations

célébrer	*to celebrate*
la fête	*party, festival*
l'événement (m)	*event*
l'anniversaire (m)	*birthday*
le cadeau	*present, gift*
le gâteau	*cake*
la fleur	*flower*
félicitations	*congratulations*
inviter	*to invite*
la surprise	*surprise*
surprendre	*to surprise*
familial(e)	*family (adj.)*
donner	*to give*
recevoir	*to receive*
ouvrir	*to open*
acheter	*to buy*
envoyer	*to send*
venir	*to come*

partager	*to share*
passer	*to spend time, pass*
se passer	*to happen*
crier	*to shout, scream, cry out*

Higher

apprécier	*to appreciate, like*
profiter de	*to make the most of*
offrir (à)	*to give (someone), offer (someone)*
féliciter	*to congratulate*
le bonheur	*happiness*
la joie	*joy*

Reflexive verbs like 'se passer' take 'être' in the perfect tense. E.g. 'La fête s'est passée hier.' (*The party happened yesterday.*) See p.140 for more.

'Offrir' means the same thing as 'donner', but it's used specifically for giving gifts.

Mathilde had an unusual method of ensuring she got the entire cake to herself.

Customs and Festivals — Religion and Identity

religieux / religieuse	*religious*
la religion	*religion*
croire	*to believe*
chrétien(ne)	*Christian*
musulman(e)	*Muslim*
juif / juive	*Jewish*
bouddhiste	*Buddhist*
Noël (m)	*Christmas*
Pâques (m)	*Easter*
l'Aïd (m)	*Eid*

l'église (f)	*church*
la mosquée	*mosque*
la synagogue	*synagogue*
le temple	*temple*
le pays	*country*
la région	*region, area*
français(e)	*French*
britannique	*British*
européen(ne)	*European*
canadien(ne)	*Canadian*
américain(e)	*American*

Higher

la foi	*faith*
le dieu	*god*
catholique	*Catholic*
prier	*to pray*
africain(e)	*African*
marocain(e)	*Moroccan*
québécois(e)	*from Quebec*
belge	*Belgian*
occidental(e)	*western*

Most of the time, when you're talking about what happens during a particular festival, you say 'le jour de', e.g. 'le jour de l'Aïd' or 'le jour de la Fête nationale'. However, for some days, like Christmas or Easter, you can simply say 'à Noël' or 'à Pâques'.

Many adjectives used to describe religions or nationalities can also be used as nouns — for example, 'un(e) catholique' (*a Catholic*) or 'un(e) Canadien(ne)' (*a Canadian*).

Customs and Festivals — Traditions

férié(e)	*public holiday (adj.)*
la tradition	*tradition*
traditionnel(le)	*traditional*
historique	*historic*
la culture	*culture*
culturel(le)	*cultural*
spécial(e)	*special*
le festival	*festival*
les vacances (f)	*holiday(s)*
la date	*date*
l'an (m)	*year*
l'année (f)	*year*
la société	*society*

la Fête Nationale	*Bastille Day (French national holiday)*
la Saint-Valentin	*Valentine's Day*
local(e)	*local*
national(e)	*national*
international(e)	*international*
rappeler (à)	*to remind (someone)*
se rappeler	*to remember*
francophone	*French-speaking*
unir	*to unite, join*
la diversité	*diversity*
l'humanité (f)	*humanity*
le roi	*king*

Higher: rappeler (à), se rappeler, francophone, unir, la diversité, l'humanité (f), le roi

'An' and 'année' both mean 'year', but you sometimes use them differently, e.g. you say 'le Nouvel An' (*New Year*) but 'l'année dernière' (*last year*).

Customs and Festivals — Entertainment

le feu	*fire*
le feu d'artifice	*firework display*
la lumière	*light*
le défilé	*parade, procession*
la musique	*music*
danser	*to dance*
le concert	*concert*
la chanson	*song*
chanter	*to sing*
le spectacle	*sight, show*
regarder	*to watch, look at*
voir	*to see*
le bruit	*noise*
porter	*to wear, carry*
participer (à)	*to take part (in)*
la participation	*participation*
le repas	*meal*
la cuisine	*cooking*
le vin	*wine*

Don't forget that you usually add 'x' instead of 's' to nouns ending in '-eu' to make them plural, e.g. 'les feux d'artifice' (*firework displays*). See p.121 for more on plurals.

fou / folle	*crazy*
l'expérience (f)	*experience*
l'intérêt (m)	*interest*
préparer	*to prepare, get ready*
organiser	*to organise*
s'organiser	*to get organised*
découvrir	*to discover*
prendre	*to take*
brûler	*to burn, be on fire*
vif / vive	*lively*
joyeux / joyeuse	*merry, joyful, happy*
assister à	*to attend*
le plat	*dish*

Higher: brûler, vif / vive, joyeux / joyeuse, assister à, le plat

Revision Summary Test for Section Seven

The party's not over yet — here's a smattering of summary questions to keep you on your toes.

- Yep, these questions are **hard** — they'll really help you see **how well you know your stuff**.
- Tackle the **revision summary test** below, or scan the QR code to do it **online**.
  Use the CGP RevisionHub to **track your progress** and see **which areas need more work**.
- You can find **sample answers** here: www.cgpbooks.co.uk/BonjourExtras

Celebrations ☐

1) 'Qu'est-ce que tu fais normalement pour célébrer ton anniversaire ?' Answer in French. ☑

2) How would you say the phrases below in French?
   a) birthday cake   b) congratulations   c) beautiful flowers   d) happy birthday ☑

3) 'J'ai envoyé un SMS à mes cousins pour les inviter à une fête de famille
   mais ils ne peuvent pas venir.' Translate Coralie's sentence into English. ☑

4) Describe your ideal party. Answer in French and try to give as much detail as you can. ☑

5) 'Ma famille essaie de me surprendre pour mon anniversaire chaque année, mais je n'aime
   pas les surprises.' What does Lucien's family do every year? Answer in English. ☑

6) 'When I receive a gift, I don't like to open it immediately.' Translate Carla's sentence into French. ☑

Higher 7) 'Quand c'est l'anniversaire d'un ami, j'adore organiser la plus grande fête possible et lui
   offrir des cadeaux.' What does Pierre like to do for his friends' birthdays? Answer in English. ☑

8) What do these words mean in English?   a) profiter de   b) apprécier   c) le bonheur ☑

Customs and Festivals ☑

9) How many words related to religion and religious festivals can you name in French?
   There are at least 14 you need to know (plus 4 for Higher tier). ☑

10) 'Vous célébrez quelles fêtes traditionnelles dans ta famille ? Comment vous les célébrez ?'
    Try to write at least three sentences in French, adding as much detail as you can. ☑

11) 'Ma sœur et moi préférons passer Pâques avec nos cousins américains car les traditions sont plus
    amusantes là-bas.' Why does Lilian prefer to spend Easter in the U.S.? Answer in English. ☑

12) 'Qu'est-ce que tu penses des traditions de ton pays ou ta région ?' Answer in French. ☑

13) How do you say the following verbs in French? a) to discover   b) to carry   c) to sing   d) to see ☑

14) 'Pour la Saint-Valentin, mon copain a préparé mon repas préféré. Il a aussi acheté du vin.
    Nous avons passé une super soirée.' What did Amina do for Valentine's Day? Answer in English. ☑

15) 'Le 14 juillet est la fête nationale en France. Chaque année, je regarde le feu d'artifice
    et je participe au défilé.' What's Jean-Luc saying about Bastille Day? Answer in English. ☑

16) How do you say the words below in French?
    a) light   b) cooking   c) interest   d) crazy   e) holiday(s)   f) society ☑

17) What do these two French people say about a party they recently attended? Answer in English.
    a) 'Je trouvais la musique trop forte, alors je suis restée dans le jardin, près du feu.'
    b) 'J'ai pris trop de temps à m'organiser, mais après mon arrivée, j'ai beaucoup chanté et dansé.' ☑

18) 'Est-ce que tu aimes aller voir des spectacles et des concerts ?' Answer in French. ☑

19) 'Les jours de fête, j'aime porter des vêtements traditionnels et prendre des selfies.'
    What does Estelle like to do when there's a special celebration? Answer in English. ☑

Higher 20) How would you say the words below in French?
    a) African   b) Catholic   c) from Quebec   d) Moroccan   e) Belgian   f) western ☑

21) 'Le français unit les gens — le nombre de pays où on le parle démontre
    la diversité du monde francophone.' Translate this sentence into English. ☑

Quick Quiz

Favourite Celebrities

Time to put what you've learned about jobs and people to use — this section is all about celebrities. Remember what they say about never meeting your hero...

Don't forget you can access your online content here: www.cgpbooks.co.uk/Bonjour

Ma célébrité préférée — *My favourite celebrity*

Vocabulary

célèbre	*famous*	le concert	*concert*		le héros / l'héroïne (f)	*hero*
la célébrité	*celebrity*	le spectacle	*show*		la tournée	*tour*
la star	*star, celebrity*	le groupe	*group*		inspirer	*to inspire*
suivre	*to follow*	la mode	*fashion*	**Higher**	s'inspirer (de)	*to be inspired (by)*
écouter	*to listen to*	le style	*style*		respecter	*to respect*
regarder	*to watch*	**H** le rôle	*role*			

Le groupe est devenu célèbre à cause de son style et de ses belles voix.

The group became famous because of their style and their beautiful voices.

their unique lyrics — ses paroles uniques

Le style de l'influenceuse était à la mode.

The influencer's style was in fashion.

their nice personalities — ses personnalités agréables

Ma chanteuse préférée est en tournée en Europe, donc je vais la voir en concert.

My favourite singer is on tour in Europe, so I am going to see her in concert.

on stage — sur scène

Q&A Audio

Question

Qui est ta célébrité préférée ? Pourquoi ?

Who is your favourite celebrity? Why?

Simple Answer

J'aime le joueur de foot Gabriel Bernaut parce qu'il est passionnant à regarder.

I like the football player Gabriel Bernaut because he is exciting to watch.

Extended Answer

Mon héroïne, c'est l'actrice Marianne Cotillon. Je l'adore dans tous ses rôles, au cinéma comme à la télé, notamment dans 'Maurice et Moi', une série très amusante.

My hero is the actress Marianne Cotillon. I love her in all her roles, in films and on the TV, notably in 'Maurice and I', a really funny series.

Practice Questions

Q1 *Listen to this extract from a podcast in which two people discuss their favourite celebrities. There are **two** correct statements in each list below. Choose the correct statements in each list.*

Listening Track 12

a) A. Margot's favourite celebrity is a singer.

   B. She dresses like her favourite celebrity.

   C. Margot wants to be a dancer.

b) A. André is a politician.

   B. André shares his hero's views.

   C. André has met his hero. *[4 marks]*

Q2 *Write a blog post about your favourite celebrity. You should write about 50-90 words in French. Describe:*

Top Tip for Higher Students
✓ Use Higher-tier adjectives to describe your celebrity.

- who they are and what they do
- what you like about them.

[10 marks]

There were too many fans at the launch party — I got a chill...

Discussing your favourite celebrities is a great way to show off all those adjectives you've learned. Jot down a few celebrities and some adjectives you can use to describe them to help you prepare for the exam.

Celebrity Life

Lights, camera, action — the life of the rich and famous may have its perks, but it isn't all glamorous. These pages will help you talk about the positive and negative aspects of fame.

La vie d'une star — *The life of a star*

Vocabulary

la carrière	*career*	la télé(vision)	*TV, television*	le / la porte-parole	*spokesperson*
les médias (m)	*media*	la réalité	*reality*	la presse	*the press*
Internet (m)	*internet*	l'émission (f)	*TV programme*	la marque	*brand, mark*
la vidéo	*video*	le cinéma	*cinema*	l'image (f)	*picture, image*
la photo	*photo*	le journal	*newspaper*	la richesse	*wealth*
le selfie	*selfie*	l'argent (m)	*money*	puissant(e)	*powerful*

(Higher: le / la porte-parole, la presse, la marque, l'image, la richesse, puissant(e))

Les célébrités sont souvent invitées à participer à des émissions de télé-réalité.

Celebrities are often invited to take part in reality TV shows.

J'ai pris une photo avec un auteur célèbre que j'ai vu dans la rue, et puis j'ai partagé l'image en ligne.

I took a photo with a famous author who I saw in the street, and then I shared the image online.

Il suit beaucoup d'influenceurs sur les réseaux sociaux.

He follows lots of influencers on social media.

Les avantages (m) d'être célèbre — *The advantages of being famous*

Vocabulary

positif / positive	*positive*	l'occasion (f)	*opportunity*
spécial(e)	*special*	la sécurité	*safety*
populaire	*popular*	bénéficier (de)	*to benefit (from)*
extraordinaire	*extraordinary*	reconnaître	*to recognise*
le succès	*success*	l'ouverture (f)	*opening*
le prix	*prize*	unique	*unique*

(Higher: bénéficier (de), reconnaître, l'ouverture, unique)

The group's success was about to reach new heights...

Si son film a beaucoup de succès, on peut gagner un prix.

If your film has a lot of success, you can win an award.

earn money — gagner de l'argent

gain fans — avoir plus de fans

Les stars bénéficient de certains avantages comme être invitées à des fêtes et recevoir des cadeaux.

Celebrities benefit from certain advantages like being invited to parties and receiving gifts.

special treatment — un traitement de faveur

Question

Est-ce que tu voudrais être célèbre ? Pourquoi / pourquoi pas ?

Would you like to be famous? Why / why not?

Simple Answer

Oui, je veux être artiste célèbre car je voudrais vendre mes tableaux.

Yes, I want to be a famous artist because I would like to sell my pictures.

Extended Answer

Non, je n'aimerais pas être célèbre. Je pense qu'il vaut mieux être heureux et passer du temps en famille qu'être riche mais devoir voyager tout le temps.

No, I would not like to be famous. I think that it's better to be happy and spend time with family than to be rich but to have to travel all the time.

Les inconvénients (m) — *The disadvantages*

Vocabulary

négatif / négative	*negative*	la victime	*victim*	la critique	*criticism, critic*
l'inquiétude (f)	*worry, anxiety*	le scandale	*scandal, uproar*	critiquer	*to criticise*
public / publique	*public (adj.)*	secret / secrète	*secret (adj.)*	déclarer	*to report*
l'annonce (f)	*announcement*	la honte	*shame*	annoncer	*to announce*

(The middle and right groups are marked **Higher**.)

Malheureusement, les célébrités peuvent être victimes de harcèlement.

Unfortunately, celebrities can be victims of harassment.

of a scandal — d'un scandale

Il est impossible de garder un peu de secret dans sa vie — les journaux rendent public chaque détail.

It is impossible to keep your life secret — the newspapers make every detail public.

La presse critique souvent les stars sans connaître la réalité de leur quotidien.

The press often criticises celebrities without knowing the reality of their daily life.

Grammar — Preposition + infinitive

When followed by an infinitive, the preposition '<u>pour</u>' means '<u>to</u>' do something and '<u>sans</u>' means '<u>without</u>' doing something. See p.116 for more on prepositions.

J'ai pris ma voiture <u>pour éviter</u> les fans. **I took my car <u>to avoid</u> the fans.**

Il est devenu célèbre <u>sans essayer</u> de l'être. **He became famous <u>without trying</u>.**

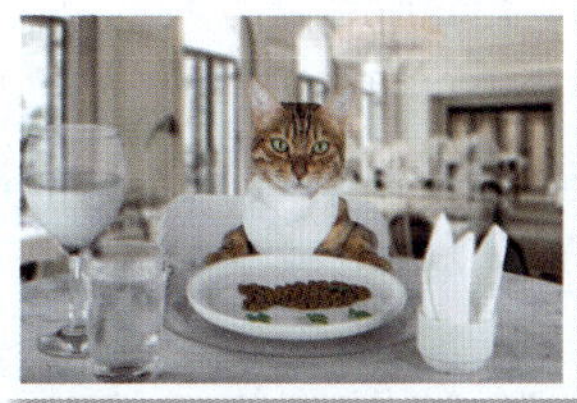

Since becoming famous, Céline had got used to a certain standard of living.

Practice Questions

Q1 *Answer these questions out loud in French.*

- *Quels sont les avantages d'être célèbre ?*
- *À ton avis, à quoi ressemble la vie d'une célébrité ?*
- *Quelle célébrité veux-tu rencontrer ? Pourquoi ?* [6 marks]

(SPEAKING)

Top Tips for Higher Students
✓ Give more than one detail for each question.
✓ Give the reason behind your answer.

Q2 *Read this extract from a newspaper interview with Amar Requin, a famous actor. Then answer the questions below in English.*

(READING)

Je m'occupe de mon nouveau film en ce moment. J'ai l'occasion de travailler avec des personnes formidables et dans des lieux extraordinaires. L'histoire se passe en Tunisie, mais on fait le film au Maroc, un pays riche en culture. Je peux faire ce que j'aime dans un bel endroit chaque jour. Cela dit, ma famille me manque beaucoup — c'est la pire partie de mon travail. Mes enfants m'appellent le soir et ils me font toujours sourire. Après avoir fini ce projet, j'espère partir en vacances avec eux. J'ai besoin de me relaxer loin de l'attention des médias.

a) Name two things Amar is enjoying about making his new film. [2 marks]

b) Where is Amar's new movie being filmed? [1 mark]

c) What does Amar say is the worst part of his job? [1 mark]

d) What is he going to do when he has finished making the film? Why? [2 marks]

(The Q2 block is marked **Higher**.)

Opticians are really famous — they're always in the public eye...

You can use real-life examples to add detail when you talk about celebrities. Give your opinion on why celebrity life does or doesn't appeal to you, and you'll be on your way to some award-winning answers.

Celebrity Culture — Vocabulary

Stop the presses — here's a whole heap of exciting vocab all about celebrities for you to discover...

Favourite Celebrities

célèbre	famous
la célébrité	celebrity
la star	star, celebrity
le personnage	character, individual, person
la personnalité	personality
l'identité (f)	identity
la génération	generation
suivre	to follow
l'auteur(e)	author
l'influenceur / l'influenceuse	influencer
l'acteur / l'actrice	actor
le chanteur / la chanteuse	singer
chanter	to sing

la chanson	song
la musique	music
les paroles (f)	lyrics
écouter	to listen to
voir	to see
regarder	to watch
le concert	concert
le spectacle	show, sight
le tour	tour, turn
le groupe	group
le sport	sport
l'équipe (f)	team
jouer (à un sport)	to play (a sport)
la politique	politics
la mode	fashion, way
le style	style
porter	to wear, carry

le rôle	role
le héros / l'héroïne	hero
la voix	voice
la série	series
la scène	stage, scene
la tournée	tour, round

Higher

présenter (à)	to present, show, introduce someone (to someone else)
représenter	to represent
diriger	to direct, guide
se diriger	to make one's way
inspirer	to inspire
s'inspirer (de)	to be inspired (by)
respecter	to respect

Celebrity Life — Career and Lifestyle

la carrière	career
les médias (m)	media
Internet (m)	internet
la vidéo	video
la photo	photo
le selfie	selfie
la télé(vision)	TV, television
la réalité	reality
l'émission (f)	TV programme
le cinéma	cinema
le film	film
le journal	newspaper
les journaux (m)	newspapers

l'article (m)	article
l'influence (f)	influence
la société	society
culturel(le)	cultural
le mariage	marriage, wedding
riche	rich
l'argent (m)	money
local(e)	local
national(e)	national
international(e)	international
voyager	to travel

Higher

le / la porte-parole	spokesperson
le public	public, audience
la presse	the press
l'établissement (m)	establishment
la marque	brand, mark
l'image (f)	picture, image
la richesse	wealth
puissant(e)	powerful
principal(e)	main
réel(le)	real

Celebrity Life — Positives and Negatives

positif / positive	positive
spécial(e)	special
populaire	popular
extraordinaire	extraordinary
fier / fière	proud
le succès	success
le prix	prize, price
l'occasion (f)	opportunity
la sécurité	safety
négatif / négative	negative

l'inquiétude (f)	worry, anxiety
public / publique	public (adj.)
l'annonce (f)	announcement

Higher

bénéficier (de)	to benefit (from)
reconnaître	to recognise
l'ouverture (f)	opening
unique	unique
la victime	victim
le scandale	scandal, uproar
secret / secrète	secret (adj.)

la honte	shame
la critique	criticism, critic

Higher

critiquer	to criticise
déclarer	to announce, report
annoncer	to announce, make public

Revision Summary Test for Section Eight

I present to you (drum roll, please)... summary questions, to test your knowledge on this section.

- Yep, these questions are **hard** — they'll really help you see **how well you know your stuff**.
- Tackle the **revision summary test** below, or scan the QR code to do it **online**.
  Use the CGP RevisionHub to **track your progress** and see **which areas need more work**.
- You can find **sample answers** here: www.cgpbooks.co.uk/BonjourExtras

Favourite Celebrities ☐

1) How would you say the words below in French?
   a) fashion   b) to wear   c) to watch   d) song   e) famous   f) personality

2) Give the feminine version of these masculine words: a) l'acteur   b) le chanteur

3) Describe your favourite sportsperson or team in French. Say what they are good at.

4) 'Est-ce que tu préfères écouter de la musique chez toi ou voir un concert en personne ?'
   Translate the question and respond in French. Make sure you explain your answer.

5) 'What forms of media do you use to keep up with your favourite celebrities?' Answer in French.

6) How would you say the words below in English?
   a) suivre   b) les paroles   c) la politique   d) le personnage   e) chanter   f) l'identité

7) In French, talk about a famous person you consider to be a hero and explain how they inspire you.

8) A newspaper article reads: 'Ces chanteurs représentent la voix d'une génération. Quand
   ils montent sur scène, c'est toujours un spectacle extraordinaire.' Translate these sentences.

Celebrity Life ☑

9) Write down the English for the words and phrases related to celebrity life below.
   a) l'émission de télé-réalité   b) l'inquiétude   c) le prix   d) la sécurité

10) Pauline says: 'Les célébrités super riches ont un style de vie très agréable.' What is she saying?

11) A Belgian influencer said this in an interview: 'I love to travel and then share my experiences online.
    I try to visit a new country every year.' Translate his words into French.

12) Claire, a famous author, spoke to the press about her latest book.
    Which of the sentences below best describes what she did?
    a) Elle a eu l'occasion de voyager beaucoup.   c) Elle a écrit plus de dix-sept livres.
    b) Elle a connu un succès national.   d) Elle a discuté de sa carrière avec un journaliste.

13) 'Do you follow celebrities on social media? Why? / Why not?' Answer in French.

14) How would you say the words below in French?
    a) positive   b) negative   c) cultural   d) announcement   e) money

15) 'Est-ce que tu penses que la vie d'une star est facile ou difficile ?'
    Translate the question into English, then answer it in French. Make sure you explain your answer.

16) Lucien, an actor, is a private person who does not like having his personal life on display.
    Which of the following is he most likely to do?
    a) parler de sa vie sur un site Internet populaire   c) poster des selfies en ligne tous les jours
    b) avoir un mariage très public   d) éviter l'attention des journaux

17) In French, describe two advantages of being a celebrity and two disadvantages.

18) 'If you were going to be a celebrity, what would you want to be famous for?' Answer in French.

19) 'I believe that it's important to make public the actions of celebrities, especially when they are at the
    centre of a scandal. You must always report it to the press.' Translate these sentences into French.

20) How do you say the words below in French?
    a) spokesperson   b) shame   c) wealth   d) audience   e) brand   f) criticism   g) powerful

Where to Go

It's no good planning a seaside break to Switzerland. That's why it's important to know where to go...

Les pays du monde — *The countries of the world*

Head to the CGP RevisionHub
for all your online content:
www.cgpbooks.co.uk/Bonjour

Vocabulary

le pays	*country*	le Québec	*Quebec*	l'Asie (f)	*Asia*
l'Angleterre (f)	*England*	la Réunion	*Reunion Island*	l'Europe (f)	*Europe*
la Belgique	*Belgium*	les Alpes (f)	*the Alps*	la Corse	*Corsica*
le Canada	*Canada*	les Pyrénées (f)	*the Pyrenees*	Londres	*London*
la France	*France*	la Manche	*the English Channel*	la province	*province*
le Maroc	*Morocco*	la Méditerranée	*the Mediterranean*	francophone	*French-speaking*
le Sénégal	*Senegal*	le monde	*world*	occidental(e)	*western*
la Suisse	*Switzerland*	la Tunisie	*Tunisia*	mondial(e)	*worldwide, global*
la région	*region*	l'Afrique (f)	*Africa*		

Je vais au Québec, une province du Canada.	*I'm going to Quebec, a province of Canada.*	
Les Pyrénées se trouvent dans le sud de la France.	*The Pyrenees are located in the south of France.*	*are situated — se situent*
Le Maroc est un pays d'Afrique du nord.	*Morocco is a country in North Africa.*	*a French-speaking country — un pays francophone*
La Réunion est une région française.	*Reunion is a French region.*	*an overseas department — un département d'outre-mer*

Grammar — to go to...

To say you're 'going to' a country, you need the correct form of 'aller' (*to go*) and the correct preposition. Use:

• au for masc. sing. countries starting with a consonant.

• aux for plural countries.

• en for masc. sing. countries starting with a vowel and all fem. sing. countries.

If you're going to a town or city, you just need 'à'.

Benoît was the proud owner of the world's first franco-phone.

Le climat à l'étranger — *The climate abroad*

Vocabulary

le climat	*climate*	chaud(e)	*hot*	l'hiver (m)	*winter*	l'automne (m)	*autumn*
le temps	*weather*	froid(e)	*cold*	le printemps	*spring*	la météo	*weather forecast*
la pluie	*rain*	la saison	*season*	l'été (m)	*summer*		

Elle adore le climat du sud de la France — il n'y a pas besoin de regarder la météo parce qu'il fait toujours beau.	*She loves the climate in the south of France — there's no need to look at the forecast because the weather is always nice.*	*warm — chaud*
Quelle est la meilleure saison pour aller en Suisse ? Je déteste la pluie.	*What is the best season to go to Switzerland? I hate rain.*	*snow — la neige*

Où vas-tu cet été ? — *Where are you going this summer?*

Vocabulary

les vacances (f)	*holiday(s)*	national(e)	*national*
le projet	*plan*	international(e)	*international*
l'échange (m)	*exchange*	rêver (à / de)	*to dream (about)*
l'étranger / l'étrangère	*foreigner, stranger*	aller	*to go*
étranger / étrangère	*foreign*	**H** pratiquer	*to practise*
à l'étranger	*abroad*	annuel(le)	*annual, yearly*
la langue	*language*		

Cet été, nous allons en Corse, une île de la Méditerranée.

This summer, we're going to Corsica, an island in the Mediterranean.

> to Cyprus — à Chypre
>
> to Majorca — à Majorque

Je passe mes vacances annuelles à l'étranger.

I spend my annual holiday abroad.

> annual leave — congés annuels

J'essaie de pratiquer le français avant d'aller en vacances.

I am trying to practise French before going on holiday.

Q&A Audio

Question

Quels sont tes projets pour les vacances ?

What are your plans for the holidays?

Simple Answer

Je vais faire un échange à l'étranger, au Maroc.

I'm going to do an exchange programme, in Morocco.

Extended Answer

À la fin août, j'irai au Sénégal pendant trois semaines avec deux amis. Nous aimons visiter les pays francophones.

At the end of August, I will go to Senegal for three weeks with two friends. We like visiting French-speaking countries.

Practice Questions

Q1 Read this email from Françoise about her holidays and answer the questions below in English.

> Les vacances d'été sont enfin arrivées ! Mais je ne suis pas contente : ma famille n'a pas de projets pour les vacances. Moi, je voudrais aller en Suisse parce que je veux voir les Alpes. Ma sœur voudrait passer les vacances au Canada. Elle veut voir son amie au Québec. Ma mère préfère rester en France parce qu'elle veut visiter des musées. Cependant, mon père veut aller en Belgique pour faire du camping.

READING

a) How does Françoise want to spend the holidays? Why? *[2 marks]*

b) Where does her sister want to go? Give **two** details. *[2 marks]*

c) What does her mum want to do? Give **two** details. *[2 marks]*

d) What would her dad like to do? Give **two** details. *[2 marks]*

Q2 You are writing an email to your penfriend about holidays. You should write about 90 words in French. Describe:

- *your favourite holiday destination*
- *a trip you have taken recently*
- *a place you would like to visit.*

WRITING

Top Tip for Higher Students
✓ Use complex constructions like 'venir de' (to have just done).

[15 marks]

The world is your oyster*...

*Terms and conditions apply

Remember, 'en' goes with feminine countries and regions, and 'au' goes with most masculine ones. As you learn each country, try putting it in the sentence 'Je suis allé(e)...' — make sure you use the right preposition.

Accommodation and Travel

When it comes to a holiday (or an exam), it's all in the preparation. So book your tickets and pack your bags — make sure to bring the vocab on this page with you...

Le logement — *Accommodation*

Vocabulary

l'hôtel (m)	*hotel*	coûter	*to cost*	le séjour	*stay*
l'appartement (m)	*apartment, flat*	cher / chère	*expensive*	l'accueil (m)	*welcome, reception*
la place	*room, space*	la vue	*view*	la réception	*reception*
la chambre	*bedroom*	la mer	*sea*	le bagage	*luggage*
le camping	*camping*	le bord	*edge, side*	la valise	*suitcase*
sale	*dirty*	la côte	*coast*	le coût	*cost*
propre	*clean*	la plage	*beach*	la plainte	*complaint*
réserver	*to book*	l'île (f)	*island*	l'étage (m)	*floor (of a building)*
chercher	*to look for*	la campagne	*countryside*	le paysage	*landscape, scenery*
rester	*to stay*	la forêt	*forest*		
dormir	*to sleep*	la montagne	*mountain*		

(Higher: le séjour, l'accueil, la réception, le bagage, la valise, le coût, la plainte, l'étage, le paysage)

J'ai pris une chambre dans un hôtel qui n'est pas cher.
I'm staying at a hotel that isn't expensive.
→ *a luxury hotel —* un hôtel de luxe

Ils font du camping au bord de la mer.
They are camping at the seaside.
→ *in Nice —* à Nice

Je voudrais réserver une chambre pour deux personnes au deuxième étage.
I'd like to reserve a room for two people on the second floor.
→ *the mountains —* les montagnes

Ils veulent un grand appartement avec vue sur la forêt.
They want a big apartment with a view of the forest.
→ *the town centre —* le centre-ville

Le transport — *Transportation*

Vocabulary

l'avion (m)	*aeroplane*
le vol	*flight*
voler	*to fly*
la voiture	*car*
le bateau	*boat, ship*
le train	*train*
le vélo	*bike, bicycle*
l'aéroport (m)	*airport*
la gare	*railway station*
le billet	*ticket*

Q&A Audio

Question

Est-ce que tu aimes voyager en avion ?
Do you like travelling by plane?

Simple Answer

Oui, l'avion est le moyen de transport le plus sûr.
Yes, aeroplanes are the safest mode of transport.

Extended Answer

J'ai peur de prendre l'avion parce que j'imagine toujours le pire. Mais les avions sont si pratiques et si rapides !
I'm scared of flying because I always imagine the worst. But planes are so practical and fast!

Je suis allé(e) à l'aéroport en train, mais j'ai perdu mon billet.
I went to the airport by train, but I lost my ticket.
→ *to the central station —* à la gare centrale

Tu peux emprunter mon vélo.
You can borrow my bike.
→ *their motorhome —* leur camping-car

À quelle heure part le bus ? — *What time does the bus leave?*

Vocabulary

partir	*to leave*	le retour	*return*	
retourner	*to return*	rapide	*fast, quick*	
revenir	*to come back*	vite	*fast, quickly*	
arriver	*to arrive*	se rendre	*to get to, go to*	
le voyage	*journey*	la durée	*duration, length*	
le départ	*departure*	direct(e)	*direct*	
l'arrivée (f)	*arrival*	la vitesse	*speed*	
		le retard	*delay*	

*(se rendre, la durée, direct(e), la vitesse, le retard marked **Higher**)*

Grammar — 'monter', 'descendre'

Use 'monter <u>dans</u>' to say 'to get <u>on</u>'.
Use 'descendre <u>de</u>' to say 'to get <u>off</u>'.

Je monte <u>dans</u> le train.
I get <u>on</u> the train.

Il descend <u>du</u> bus.
He gets <u>off</u> the bus.

Nous descendons à la prochaine gare.
We're getting off at the next station.

À quelle heure arrive le bus ?
What time does the bus arrive? — high-speed train — TGV (train à grande vitesse)

Nous ne pouvons pas retourner sur l'île parce que nous avons raté le bateau.
We can't go back to the island because we missed the boat. — leave the island — quitter l'île

Son vol part à 18h00 et arrivera à 19h30 s'il n'est pas en retard.
Her flight leaves at 18:00 and will arrive at 19:30 if it's not late.

Practice Questions

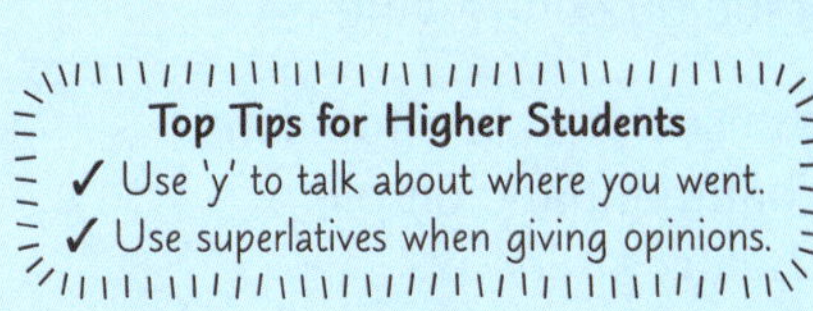

Q1 You are talking to your French friend about holiday accommodation. Respond to your friend's questions in French.

> Quelle sorte de logement préfères-tu ?
> Décris ton endroit préféré pour passer les vacances.
> Quel est ton moyen de transport préféré ?
> Qu'est-ce que tu penses du camping ?
> **H** Décris un logement où tu es passé(e) quelques jours.

SPEAKING

Top Tips for Higher Students
✓ Use 'y' to talk about where you went.
✓ Use superlatives when giving opinions.

[10 marks]

Q2 Listen to Mark talking about a recent journey, then decide which three of the statements below are true.

LISTENING

A. Mark flew from Marseille to Newcastle.
B. Mark's flight was late.
C. Mark will take the train back.
D. Plane tickets home were too expensive.
E. Mark prefers travelling by boat.
F. The boat is slower than the plane.

Listening Track 13

I'm not sure that'll get you very far, Mark…

[3 marks]

*(Q2 marked **Higher**)*

'Le camping'? It's like they're not even trying…

French examiners are like travel websites — they want you to share your views on where you've stayed and how you got there. Keep them happy by including lots of opinions and extra details about your travels.

What to Do

Stuck for things to do while you're on holiday? Got a burning desire to describe your favourite tourist attraction in French? If so, you're in luck. These pages are full of things to do while you're away.

En vacances, j'ai visité... — *On holiday, I visited...*

Use 'nouvel' and 'bel' before masculine words that start with a vowel.

Vocabulary

la capitale	*capital city*	le musée	*museum*	nouveau / nouvel / nouvelle	*new*
la ville	*town*	la piscine	*swimming pool*	beau / bel / belle	*beautiful*
le centre	*centre*	la tour	*tower*	visiter	*to visit*
le quartier	*district, quarter*	le restaurant	*restaurant*	la visite	*visit*
le bâtiment	*building*	le café	*café*	la frontière	*border*
le château	*castle*	le site	*site*	le lac	*lake*
le marché	*market*	le lieu	*place*	la rivière	*river*
le magasin	*shop*	l'entrée (f)	*entrance*	ancien(ne)	*ancient*
acheter	*to buy*	historique	*historic*		

Higher: la frontière, le lac, la rivière, ancien(ne)

Que faire à... ? — *What is there to do in...?*

Quand je vais en vacances, j'aime visiter les sites historiques et les châteaux de la région.

When I go on holiday, I like to visit the region's historic sites and castles.

On peut acheter des croissants au marché.

You can buy croissants at the market.

Les enfants aiment tous la nouvelle piscine du centre-ville.

The children all like the new swimming pool in the town centre.

Le musée d'art se situe dans un bâtiment ancien plein de beaux tableaux.

The museum of art is located in an ancient building full of beautiful paintings.

Roman ruins — ruines romaines

nature reserves — réserves naturelles

the new cafés — les nouveaux cafés

Jean-Marie still wasn't sure what it was supposed to be.

Grammar — 'beau' and 'nouveau'

Some adjectives have <u>irregular</u> feminine and plural forms, e.g. <u>beau</u> and <u>nouveau</u> — see p.121 for more.

la **belle** tour	the *beautiful* tower
les **beaux** quartiers	the *beautiful* districts
les **belles** îles	the *beautiful* islands
la **nouvelle** ville	the *new* town
les **nouveaux** musées	the *new* museums
les **nouvelles** piscines	the *new* swimming pools

Question

Qu'est-ce que tu as fait en vacances ?

What did you do on holiday?

Simple Answer

J'ai visité un château et je suis allé(e) à la plage.

I visited a castle and I went to the beach.

Extended Answer

J'ai décidé d'aller au musée pour découvrir l'histoire de la région. Ça m'a beaucoup intéressé(e). J'ai fait aussi une visite guidée du centre-ville.

I decided to go to the museum to discover the history of the region. It interested me a lot. I also went on a guided tour of the town centre.

Les activités (f) — *Activities*

Vocabulary

la cuisine	*cooking*	la photo	*photo*		la vague	*wave*
la glace	*ice cream*	découvrir	*to discover*		nager	*to swim*
la culture	*culture*	la découverte	*discovery*		central(e)	*central*
la nature	*nature*	passer	*to spend (time)*		l'addition (f)	*bill*
la promenade	*walk*	se passer	*to happen*		commander	*to order, tell*
le / la touriste	*tourist*	se relaxer	*to relax*		profiter de	*to enjoy*
prendre	*to take*	apprendre	*to learn*			

(Higher: la vague, nager, central(e), l'addition (f), commander, profiter de)

Axelle a pris de belles photos du lac — elle aime bien la nature.

Axelle took some beautiful photos of the lake — she really likes nature.

Traoré déteste nager dans la mer à cause des grandes vagues.

Traoré hates swimming in the sea because of the big waves.

of the cold water — de l'eau froide

Cette ville est connue pour sa culture riche et sa cuisine unique.

This town is known for its rich culture and unique cuisine.

Normalement, je m'achète une glace quand je vais à la plage.

Normally, I buy myself an ice cream when I go to the beach.

order — commande

Practice Questions

Q1 Read the following text about Lizzie's holiday plans, then answer the questions below in English.

READING

Cet été, je vais passer deux semaines à Cherbourg pour améliorer mon français. Je vais habiter chez une famille française. Leur appartement se situe dans un bâtiment ancien. À Cherbourg, je vais visiter un musée intéressant avec d'autres touristes et faire une promenade au centre-ville. S'il fait beau, je vais probablement aller manger une glace dans un café. Le week-end, je veux explorer la belle plage.

a) How long will Lizzie stay in Cherbourg? *[1 mark]*

b) Why will she go to Cherbourg? *[1 mark]*

c) Give two details about Lizzie's accommodation. *[2 marks]*

d) What will Lizzie do in Cherbourg? Give two details. *[2 marks]*

e) When will Lizzie go to the beach? *[1 mark]*

Q2 Write a blog post about a place you visited recently. You should write about 90 words in French. Write about:

WRITING

- what you did there
- what you liked or disliked about it
- where you will go next. *[15 marks]*

Top Tip for Higher Students
✓ Use both the perfect and the imperfect tenses.

How do beaches greet each other? They just wave…

Use the vocabulary on these pages to jot down a list of what there is to see and do in the area where you live, and then write a sentence in French about each place to let any tourists know what you think about it.

Travel and Tourism — Vocabulary

Learning vocab isn't quite as fun as going on holiday, but you'll be glad you did it when it comes to the exam...

Where to Go

le pays	country
l'Angleterre (f)	England
la Belgique	Belgium
le Canada	Canada
la France	France
le Maroc	Morocco
le Sénégal	Senegal
la Suisse	Switzerland
la région	region, area
le Québec	Quebec
la Réunion	Reunion Island
les Alpes (f)	the Alps
les Pyrénées (f)	the Pyrenees
la Manche	the English Channel
la Méditerranée	the Mediterranean
Paris	Paris
le monde	world
le climat	climate
le temps	weather, time
la pluie	rain
le soleil	sun
chaud(e)	hot, warm
froid(e)	cold
la saison	season
l'hiver (m)	winter
le printemps	spring
l'été (m)	summer
l'automne (m)	autumn

les vacances (f)	holiday(s)
le projet	plan
l'échange (m)	exchange
l'étranger / l'étrangère	foreigner, stranger
étranger / étrangère	foreign
à l'étranger	abroad
la langue	language
national(e)	national
international(e)	international
rêver (à / de)	to dream (about)
aller	to go

Higher

la Tunisie	Tunisia
l'Afrique (f)	Africa
l'Asie (f)	Asia
l'Europe (f)	Europe
la Corse	Corsica
Londres	London
la province	province
francophone	French-speaking
occidental(e)	western
mondial(e)	worldwide, global
global(e)	global
la météo	weather forecast
pratiquer	to practise
annuel(le)	annual, yearly

To say 'in summer / autumn / winter', it's 'en été', 'en automne' and 'en hiver'. There's an exception to learn, though — 'in spring' is 'au printemps'.

Accommodation

le logement	accommodation
l'hôtel (m)	hotel
l'appartement (m)	apartment, flat
la place	room, space
la chambre	bedroom
le camping	camping
sale	dirty
propre	clean
réserver	to reserve, book
chercher	to look for
organiser	to organise
s'organiser	to get organised
rester	to stay, remain
dormir	to sleep
coûter	to cost
l'euro (m)	euro
la livre	pound

cher / chère	expensive
complet (m)	full, complete
la vue	view
la mer	sea
le bord	edge, side
la côte	coast
la plage	beach
l'île (f)	island
la campagne	countryside
la forêt	forest
la montagne	mountain

Higher

le séjour	stay
l'accueil (m)	welcome, reception
la réception	reception

Higher

le bagage	luggage, baggage
la valise	suitcase
le chapeau	hat
le manteau	coat
le coût	cost
complète (f)	full, complete
la plainte	moan, complaint
l'étage (m)	floor (of a building)
le sol	floor, ground
le paysage	landscape, scenery

Travel

le transport	*transportation*
l'avion (m)	*aeroplane*
le vol	*flight*
voler	*to fly*
la voiture	*car*
le bateau	*boat, ship*
le train	*train*
le bus,	*bus*
l'autobus (m)	
le vélo	*bike, bicycle*
l'aéroport (m)	*airport*
la gare	*(railway) station*
la station	*station*
le billet	*ticket*
voyager	*to travel*
partir	*to leave*
retourner	*to return, go back*

To say 'by bike', 'by car' etc., you use 'en', e.g. 'en vélo'. The exception is 'à pied' (*on foot*).

revenir	*to come back, return*
arriver	*to arrive*
descendre (de)	*to go down, drive down, ride down, get off*
où	*where*
communiquer	*to communicate, pass on*
traverser	*to cross*
le voyage	*journey, trip*
le départ	*departure*
l'arrivée (f)	*arrival*
le retour	*return*
rapide	*fast, quick*
vite	*fast, quickly*
le sac	*bag, sack*

Higher

le métro	*underground, metro*
se rendre	*to get to, go to*
la durée	*duration, length*
le ticket	*ticket*
manquer	*to miss, fail to catch*
direct(e)	*direct*
la distance	*distance*
la vitesse	*speed*
le retard	*delay*
autour	*around*
la direction	*direction*

What to Do

la capitale	*capital city*
la ville	*town*
le centre	*centre*
le quartier	*district, quarter*
le bâtiment	*building*
le château	*castle, palace*
le marché	*market*
le magasin	*shop*
acheter	*to buy*
l'argent (m)	*money*
le musée	*museum*
la piscine	*swimming pool*
la tour	*tower*
la carte	*map, menu*
le restaurant	*restaurant*
le café	*café*
le site	*site*
l'endroit (m)	*place, spot*
le lieu	*place*
l'entrée (f)	*entrance*
entrer	*to enter, go in, come in*
fermer	*to close, shut*
historique	*historical*
nouveau / nouvel / nouvelle	*new*

beau / bel / belle	*beautiful*
industriel(le)	*industrial*
calme	*calm, quiet*
visiter	*to visit*
la visite	*visit, tour*
la cuisine	*cooking*
la glace	*ice cream, ice*
la culture	*culture*
la nature	*nature*
la promenade	*walk*
le / la touriste	*tourist*
prendre	*to take*
la photo	*photo*
apprendre	*to learn*
découvrir	*to discover*
la découverte	*discovery*
passer	*to spend (time)*
se passer	*to happen*
se relaxer	*to relax*
se perdre	*to get lost*
se situer	*to be situated, to take place*
se trouver	*to be situated*

Higher

la frontière	*border*
le lac	*lake*
la rivière	*river*
la vague	*wave*
nager	*to swim*
central(e)	*central*
ancien(ne)	*former, ancient*
l'addition (f)	*bill*
commander (à... de)	*to order, tell (someone to do something)*
profiter de	*to enjoy, make the most of*
accompagner	*to accompany*

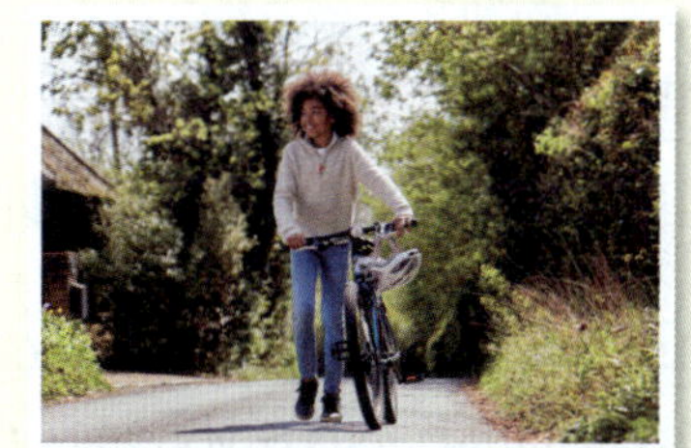

Clément liked to take his bike for walks in the sun.

Revision Summary Test for Section Nine

Before you jet off to the next section, here are some questions to test your holiday knowledge.

* These questions are **really tricky**, but they'll help you see **how well you know your stuff**.
* Tackle the **revision summary test** below, or scan the QR code to do it **online**.
  You can **keep track of your progress** online and see **which areas need more work**.
* There are **sample answers** here: www.cgpbooks.co.uk/BonjourExtras

Where to Go ☐

1) Your best friend asks you: 'Quels sont tes projets pour les vacances ?'
   Translate the question, then answer it in French, giving as much detail as you can. ☑

2) How many countries can you name in French?
   There are 7 you need to know (plus 1 for Higher tier). ☑

3) Imagine two of your friends are going on holiday to two different places.
   Say where each of them will go and what they plan to do there. ☑

4) Translate this sentence into English: 'Pendant les vacances d'été, Camille va
   faire un échange à l'étranger pour apprendre une nouvelle langue étrangère.' ☑

5) Write down the French for these places:
   a) the Pyrenees b) the Alps c) the Mediterranean d) the English Channel e) Reunion Island ☑

6) What are the names of the seasons in French? Explain which one is your favourite. ☑

Accommodation and Travel ☐

7) Write down the English for these verbs: a) voyager b) partir c) revenir d) chercher e) arriver ☑

8) You're on the phone to your French friend who is planning on visiting you. Tell them that
   the fast train costs forty euros and that they can book a place when they're at the station. ☑

9) Give the French for the verbs to do with accommodation below:
   a) to reserve b) to communicate c) to get organised d) to stay e) to sleep f) to cost ☑

10) Imagine you are going to Paris. In French, ask what there is to do in Paris and
    say that you're looking for a flat with two bedrooms that isn't too expensive. ☑

11) You're ringing a hotel. Say that you'd like to reserve a room and ask if there is:
    a) a large swimming pool   b) a beautiful view   c) an island near the hotel ☑

12) Describe a type of accommodation that you have stayed in. Give as much detail as possible. ☑

13) 'Quel moyen de transport utilises-tu normalement pour partir en vacances ?' Answer in French. ☑

Higher

14) 'I dream of travelling to Quebec, a region of Canada. However, you have to go there
    by plane so you can't take a lot of luggage.' How would you say this in French? ☑

15) Translate this announcement into English: 'Il y a un retard de trente minutes.
    La durée du vol sera deux heures et nous arriverons à onze heures du matin.' ☑

What to Do ☐

16) You're on holiday in Brittany. In French, ask a local where you can find:
    a) the museum   b) the airport   c) the tower   d) the swimming pool ☑

17) Give the English for these French verbs: a) visiter b) se passer c) se relaxer d) se perdre ☑

18) Claire is telling you about her holiday: 'Nous sommes allés à la plage tous les jours, et le
    week-end nous avons fait une promenade dans la forêt. Mon père a organisé une visite
    au château — j'ai pensé que c'était un très bel endroit.' Translate her sentences into English. ☑

19) 'Qu'est-ce que tu aimes faire en vacances ?' Answer in French. ☑

H

20) 'We like to make the most of the restaurants beside the lake and order ice creams
    at the café in the town centre.' How would you say this in French? ☑

Technology

Technology is a hot topic these days — it's difficult to imagine life without it. It's quite likely you'll get asked about its advantages and disadvantages, so go over this section carefully.

Remember there's also lots of online content here: www.cgpbooks.co.uk/Bonjour

Le monde numérique — *The digital world*

Vocabulary

la technologie	*technology*	le message	*message*	allumer	*to turn on*
l'appareil (m)	*device, apparatus*	envoyer	*to send*	recharger	*to charge*
le portable	*mobile phone, laptop*	recevoir	*to receive*	casser	*to break*
		répondre (à)	*to answer, reply (to)*	l'appel (m)	*call*
le téléphone	*telephone*			l'évolution (f)	*evolution*
l'ordinateur (m)	*computer*	enregistrer	*to record, save*	numérique	*digital*
l'appli(cation) (f)	*app(lication)*			technique	*technical*
le mail /	*e-mail*	l'outil (m)	*tool*	puissant(e)	*powerful*
l'e-mail (m)		marcher	*to work*	la puissance	*power*

Higher (bracket grouping: allumer, recharger, casser, l'appel, l'évolution, numérique, technique, puissant(e), la puissance)

Question

Est-ce que tu utilises souvent la technologie dans ta vie quotidienne ?

Do you often use technology in your everyday life?

Simple Answer

Oui, je dois utiliser mon portable tous les jours. J'envoie et je reçois beaucoup de messages.

Yes, I have to use my mobile phone everyday. I send and receive lots of messages.

Extended Answer

Oui, j'utilise beaucoup d'applis très utiles sur mes appareils, mais je pense qu'on passe trop de temps sur nos portables. Les messages ont remplacé la conversation.

Yes, I use a lot of very useful apps on my devices but I think that we spend too much time on our phones. Messages have replaced conversation.

Grammar — 'pouvoir' / 'vouloir' / 'devoir' / 'il faut' + infinitive

Some verbs can be followed directly by an infinitive (see p.133).

- **Il <u>ne peut pas vivre</u> sans son portable.**
  He <u>can't live</u> without his mobile phone.
- **Je <u>veux acheter</u> un ordinateur.**
  I <u>want to buy</u> a computer.
- **Vous <u>devez enregistrer</u> votre travail.**
  You <u>must save</u> your work.
- **<u>Il faut recharger</u> ton téléphone.**
  <u>You must charge</u> your phone.

Practice Question

Q1 Read Hugo's article about technology and decide if the statements below are true or false.

> Ma mère m'a acheté un nouveau téléphone portable pour mon anniversaire. C'est très utile parce que je peux communiquer avec mes amis tout le temps. Je peux aussi télécharger des chansons et des jeux sur Internet. Ma mère est contente car, si je ne rentre pas à la maison après l'école, elle peut m'envoyer un message. Elle aime savoir que je suis en sécurité.

a) Hugo bought a new phone. *[1 mark]*
b) Hugo downloads music from the internet. *[1 mark]*
c) Hugo's mum is glad that he has a phone. *[1 mark]*
d) Hugo doesn't bring his phone to school. *[1 mark]*

All this surfing will have me fit in no time...

...if not, I'll try phishing. Remember, 'il faut' means 'it is necessary' or 'you must'. It's common in French and is often followed by an infinitive. For example, 'Il faut faire les exercises' means 'You must do the exercises'.

The Internet

Of course, technology isn't just about phones — the internet practically runs the world, so it probably deserves a mention. It's likely to be a popular topic in the exam, so learn this vocab well.

Parler d'Internet — *Talking about the internet*

Vocabulary

l'Internet (m)	*internet*	voler (à...)	*to steal (from someone)*	la protection	*protection*
en ligne	*online*			la victime	*victim*
le site	*site*	le danger	*danger*	le risque	*risk*
le blog	*blog*	l'action (f)	*action*	l'attaque (f)	*attack*
sûr(e)	*safe, sure*	prendre	*to take*	attaquer	*to attack*
la sécurité	*security, safety*	jouer (à)	*to play (something)*	le contenu	*contents*
protéger	*to protect*	le jeu	*game*		

(Higher: la protection, la victime, le risque, l'attaque, attaquer, le contenu)

Chaque jour j'écris 100 mots pour mon blog en français.

Every day I write 100 words for my French blog.

I type — je tape

Il faut faire attention quand on donne ses informations personnelles en ligne.

You should be careful when you give out your personal information online.

your telephone number — son numéro de téléphone

L'année dernière, j'ai été victime de fraude — quelqu'un a volé mes informations bancaires.

Last year, I was the victim of fraud — someone stole my bank details.

Le streaming — *Streaming*

Vocabulary

facile	*easy*	regarder	*to watch, look at*	la série	*series*
rapide	*quick*	la télé(vision)	*television / TV*	direct(e)	*direct*
télécharger	*to download*	l'émission (f)	*TV programme*	directement	*directly*
découvrir	*to discover*	le film	*film*	diffuser	*to broadcast, diffuse*

(Higher: la série, direct(e), directement, diffuser)

Les sites de streaming proposent des podcasts, des vidéos et des séries — je les utilise souvent.

Streaming sites offer podcasts, videos and series — I often use them.

Le streaming est très utile car on peut regarder des émissions en ligne quand on veut.

Streaming is very useful because you can watch TV programmes online whenever you want.

Camille's nose was constantly streaming.

Grammar — direct object pronouns ('me', 'te', 'le', 'la', 'nous', 'vous', 'les')

A <u>direct object</u> is the person or <u>thing</u> (noun) that an action <u>is being done to</u>.

Elle regarde <u>un film</u> en ligne.   *She's watching <u>a film</u> online.*

<u>Direct object pronouns</u> (see p.112) <u>replace</u> that noun. In French, they come <u>before</u> the verb and are used to <u>avoid repetition</u>.

Elle <u>le</u> regarde en ligne.   *She's watching <u>it</u> online.*

The final letter of 'me', 'te', 'le' and 'la' is dropped and replaced with an apostrophe when they come directly before a word beginning with a vowel.

Les achats (m) en ligne — *Online shopping*

Vocabulary

le shopping	*shopping*	vendre	*to sell*	l'établissement (m)	*establishment, organisation*
l'euro (m)	*euro*	la pub(licité)	*advert*	l'achat (m)	*purchase*
la livre	*pound*	la marque	*brand, mark*	annuler	*to cancel, undo*
cher / chère	*expensive*	renvoyer	*to resend, send back*	livrer	*to deliver*
acheter	*to buy*				

(Higher: la pub(licité), la marque, renvoyer)
(Higher: l'établissement, l'achat, annuler, livrer)

Je préfère faire des achats en ligne, car je trouve souvent de bonnes marques en solde.

I prefer to shop online, because I often find good brands in the sales.

Question
Est-ce que tu fais du shopping en ligne ?
Do you shop online?

Simple Answer
Oui, j'adore acheter des vêtements en ligne. C'est rapide et facile.
Yes, I love buying clothes online. It's quick and easy.

Extended Answer
Non, j'essaie d'éviter les sites de shopping parce qu'il peut être difficile de voir la taille et la qualité des vêtements. Je dois souvent renvoyer mes achats. C'est aussi trop facile d'être influencé(e) par la publicité en ligne, et je pense que certains sites ne sont pas très sûrs.

No, I try to avoid shopping websites because it can be difficult to see the size and quality of clothes. I often have to send my purchases back. It's also too easy to be influenced by advertising online, and I think some websites are not very secure.

Practice Questions

Q1 Answer these questions out loud in French. 

    a) Qu'est-ce que tu penses du streaming ?

    b) Quels sont les dangers d'Internet ?

    c) Quel est ton avis sur le shopping en ligne ? *[6 marks]*

Top Tip for Higher Students
✓ Use interesting adverbs like 'absolument', 'évidemment' and 'régulièrement'.

Q2 In this extract from a podcast, Maxine is being interviewed about how her family uses the internet. In each list below, there is one true statement. Choose the true statement from each list. 

Listening Track 14

    a) A. Maxine's mum doesn't like using the internet.

        B. Her mum thinks shopping online is more expensive than the supermarket.

        C. Her mum prefers online shopping to going to the supermarket. *[1 mark]*

    b) A. Her dad uses the internet too much.

        B. Her dad thinks the internet is bad for your health.

       C. Her dad doesn't use the internet at work. *[1 mark]*

    c) A. Maxine is helping her brother write a blog about streaming sites.

        B. Her brother uses the internet to study.

       C. Her brother uses the internet to watch programmes. *[1 mark]*

Tightrope walkers love the internet — they're always online...

You might have lots of opinions about the internet that you're just dying to share with the examiners, but if you don't, remember that it's fine to make something up — just make sure you use lots of interesting vocab.

Social Media

Social media is great for making friends — I've got nine hundred and they always remember my birthday... Before you go scrolling, learn how to talk about the pros and cons in French.

Les réseaux sociaux — *Social networks*

Vocabulary

social(e)	*social*	la conversation	*conversation*	le compte	*account, count*	
les médias (m)	*media*	le dialogue	*dialogue*			
le réseau	*network*	la communication	*communication*	l'image (f)	*picture, image*	
utiliser	*to use*	la génération	*generation*	l'utilisation (f)	*use*	
poster	*to post*	l'influence (f)	*influence*	la communauté	*community*	
suivre	*to follow*	l'influenceur /	*influencer*	s'inscrire (à)	*to join, enrol (in)*	
partager	*to share*	l'influenceuse				
la photo	*photo*	moderne	*modern*	unir	*to unite, join*	
la vidéo	*video*	populaire	*popular*	le débat	*debate*	
le selfie	*selfie*	disponible	*available*			

The right-hand column (le compte … le débat) is marked **Higher**.

J'aime bien poster des vidéos en ligne pour les partager avec mes amis.

I really like posting videos online to share them with my friends.

Mon copain n'est pas disponible pour un appel vidéo.

My friend is not available for a video call.

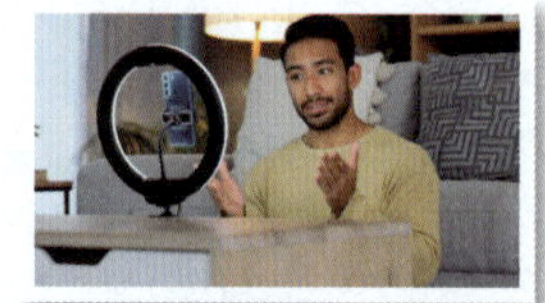

It only took Ali 40 minutes to realise he hadn't pressed record...

Une communauté en ligne — *An online community*

Question

Est-ce que tu utilises souvent les réseaux sociaux ?

Do you often use social networks?

Simple Answer

Oui, j'utilise les réseaux sociaux chaque jour. J'aime suivre mes amis.

Yes, I use social networks every day. I like to follow my friends.

Extended Answer

Oui, j'adore les réseaux sociaux. Je poste des photos sur mon compte au moins une fois par jour. Normalement, je passe une heure par jour en ligne à communiquer avec d'autres jeunes.

Yes, I love social networks. I post photos on my account at least once a day. Normally I spend an hour a day online communicating with other young people.

J'utilise les réseaux sociaux pour suivre les influenceurs qui mettent des vidéos en ligne.

I use social networks to follow influencers who put videos online.

companies — les entreprises

Les réseaux sociaux me permettent de chatter avec d'autres jeunes qui partagent les mêmes intérêts que moi. Je trouve la communauté en ligne très sympathique.

Social networks allow me to chat to other young people who share the same interests as me. I find the online community very friendly.

close-knit — très unie

Il y a beaucoup de débats autour des réseaux sociaux — c'est difficile de décider si c'est une bonne chose pour les ados ou pas.

There are lots of debates around social networks — it's hard to decide if they're a good thing for teenagers or not.

of worries — d'inquiétudes

Les inconvénients (m) — *Disadvantages*

Vocabulary

diminuer	*to lower, decrease*
inquiétant(e)	*worrying, disturbing*
l'inquiétude (f)	*worry, anxiety*
le souci	*worry, concern*
négatif / négative	*negative*

Higher
réagir	*to react*
le commentaire	*comment, remark*
harceler	*to bully, harass*
souffrir	*to suffer*

Grammar — 'de' (preposition)

Many set phrases like '<u>à cause de</u>' and '<u>se servir de</u>' use the preposition '<u>de</u>'. Don't forget that if 'de' is followed by '<u>le</u>' or '<u>les</u>', the two words are combined:

'de' + 'le' = 'du'   **'de' + 'les' = 'des'**

À cause <u>des</u> réseaux sociaux...
As a result <u>of</u> social networks...

Elles se servent <u>du</u> système...
They make use <u>of</u> the system...

Hier soir, j'ai reçu plusieurs commentaires sur un selfie que j'ai partagé avec mes amis en ligne.

Je sais que beaucoup de jeunes souffrent à cause des gens qui les harcèlent en ligne.

Ma confiance en moi a diminué à cause de tous les commentaires négatifs sur mon blog.

Il y a des personnes très méchantes qui écrivent des choses complètement fausses sur les réseaux sociaux.

Last night, I received several comments on a selfie that I shared with my friends online.

I know that lots of young people suffer because of people who bully them online.

My self-confidence has decreased because of all the negative comments on my blog.

There are really nasty people who write completely false things on social networks.

of internet users — d'internautes

insult — insultent

anonymous — anonymes

on forums — dans les forums

Practice Questions

Q1 You are writing a short speech that you will present to your class about the impact of social media on young people. You should aim to write 90 words. Write about:

- your personal view of social media and what you use it for
- the benefits of social media
- the dangers / risks of social media.   [15 marks]

WRITING

Top Tips for Higher Students
- ✓ Use superlatives when giving your opinion.
- ✓ Include more than one detail for each bullet point.

Q2 In this interview for a local newspaper, Michael talks about how he uses social media. Listen to what Michael says and answer the questions below in English.

Higher

a) How much time does Michael spend on social media each day?   [1 mark]

b) What does Michael do whilst he is doing his homework?   [1 mark]

c) What does Michael think of social media?   [1 mark]

d) How does social media help Michael stay connected to his family?   [1 mark]

LISTENING

Listening Track 15

Anti-social? Moi? But I'm always chatting online...

If you fancy showing off your communication skills, then giving both sides of an argument will do the trick. It'll allow you to use a wide range of vocab and also give you a chance to use plenty of conjunctions.

Media and Technology — Vocabulary

The digital world can challenge us at the best of times, but learning this vocab will make your life easier during the exam.

Technology

la technologie	*technology*
l'appareil (m)	*device, apparatus*
le portable	*mobile phone, laptop*
le téléphone	*telephone*
le numéro	*number*
l'ordinateur (m)	*computer*
l'écran (m)	*screen*
la lumière	*light*
l'appli(cation) (f)	*app(lication)*
le mail / l'e-mail (m)	*e-mail*
le SMS	*SMS*
le message	*message*
envoyer	*to send*
recevoir	*to receive*
répondre (à)	*to answer, reply (to)*
enregistrer	*to record, save*
communiquer	*to pass on, communicate*

cliquer	*to click*
écouter	*to listen to*
l'outil (m)	*tool*
l'expert(e)	*expert*
marcher	*to work*

Higher

allumer	*to turn on*
recharger	*to charge (an appliance)*
casser	*to break*
l'appel (m)	*call*
rappeler	*to call back*
la réception	*reception*
l'évolution (f)	*evolution*
numérique	*digital*
technique	*technical*
puissant(e)	*powerful*
la puissance	*power*
l'objet (m)	*object, subject line*

The Internet — Going Online

l'Internet (m)	*internet*
la ligne	*line*
en ligne	*online*
le site	*site*
le blog	*blog*
le mot	*word*
sûr(e)	*safe, sure*
la sécurité	*security, safety*
protéger	*to protect*
voler (à...)	*to steal (from someone)*
le vol	*theft*
le danger	*danger*
dangereux / dangereuse	*dangerous*
la santé	*health*
l'action (f)	*action*
prendre	*to take*
jouer (à)	*to play (something)*
le jeu	*game*
facile	*easy*

rapide	*fast, quick*
télécharger	*to download*
découvrir	*to discover*
voir	*to see*
regarder	*to watch, look at*
le streaming	*streaming*
la télé(vision)	*television / TV*
l'émission (f)	*TV programme*
le film	*film*

Higher

la protection	*protection*
la victime	*victim*
le risque	*risk*
l'attaque (f)	*attack*
attaquer	*to attack*
le contenu	*contents*
la série	*series*
direct(e)	*direct*
directement	*directly*
diffuser	*to broadcast, diffuse*

The Internet — Online Shopping

le shopping	*shopping*
commercial(e)	*commercial, shopping (adj.)*
l'euro (m)	*euro*
la livre	*pound*
cher / chère	*expensive*
gratuit(e)	*free (of charge)*

Lucie's late night spending sprees were starting to get a little out of hand.

acheter	*to buy*
payer	*to pay (for)*
vendre	*to sell*
la vente	*sale*

Higher

la pub(licité)	*advert*
la marque	*brand, mark*
le consommateur / la consommatrice	*consumer, customer*
renvoyer	*to resend, send back*
l'établissement (m)	*establishment, organisation*
l'achat (m)	*purchase*
annuler	*to cancel, undo*
livrer	*to deliver*

Social Media

social(e)	*social*
les médias (m)	*media*
le réseau	*network*
utiliser	*to use*
poster	*to post*
suivre	*to follow*
chatter / tchatter	*to chat (online)*
partager	*to share*
la photo	*photo*
la vidéo	*video*
le selfie	*selfie*
la conversation	*conversation*
le dialogue	*dialogue*
la communication	*communication*
la génération	*generation*
l'ado (m/f), l'adolescent(e)	*teenager, adolescent*
jeune	*young*
la jeunesse	*youth*
l'influence (f)	*influence*
l'influenceur / l'influenceuse	*influencer*
moderne	*modern*
populaire	*popular*

nouveau / nouvel / nouvelle	*new*
disponible	*available*
diminuer	*to lower, decrease*
inquiétant(e)	*worrying, disturbing*
l'inquiétude (f)	*worry, anxiety*
le souci	*worry, concern*
négatif / négative	*negative*
la fois	*time*

Higher

le compte	*account, count*
l'image (f)	*picture, image*
l'utilisation (f)	*use*
la communauté	*community*
s'inscrire (à)	*to join, enrol (in)*
unir	*to unite, join*
le débat	*debate*
réagir	*to react*
le commentaire	*comment, remark*
harceler	*to bully, harass*
souffrir	*to suffer*

Revision Summary Test for Section Ten

Once you've recharged those brain cells, test your tech knowledge with these summary questions.

- These questions are **hard**, but they'll really help you see **how well you know your stuff**.
- Tackle the **revision summary test** below, or scan the QR code to do it **online**.
  You can **track your progress** online and see **which areas need more work**.
- There are **sample answers** for the test here: www.cgpbooks.co.uk/BonjourExtras

Technology ☐

1) How do you say the following phrases in French?
   a) tool   b) to record   c) my apps   d) your devices   e) new technologies

2) Yanis says: 'Maintenant, les jeunes préfèrent les portables aux ordinateurs.'
   What does this mean in English?

3) 'I want to reply to an e-mail, but my screen isn't working.' How would you say this in French?

4) 'Est-ce que tu utilises souvent ton portable ?' Respond in French using complete sentences.

5) Sylvie says: 'Il ne faut pas avoir un portable avant l'âge de onze ans.'
   What does this mean in English? Do you agree with her statement? Answer in French.

6) Your friend explains: 'Mon numéro de téléphone a changé, donc je dois envoyer un message
   à tout le monde.' Translate this into English.

H 7) Translate the sentence below into French:
   'This morning I broke my mobile phone — I can neither turn it on nor charge it.'

The Internet ☐

8) 'Qu'est-ce que tu fais sur Internet en général ?' Respond in French.

9) You're reading a leaflet about internet safety: 'Pour rester en sécurité sur Internet,
   il ne faut pas poster tes informations sur les sites publics, car les gens peuvent
   les voler.' What advice is the leaflet giving? Answer in English.

10) In French, explain one more way that you can protect yourself online.

11) 'En ligne tu peux découvrir des blogs intéressants, regarder des films et des émissions
    sur des sites de streaming et télécharger des jeux.' Translate this into English.

12) Translate these words into French:
    a) health   b) dangerous   c) easy   d) to buy   e) to protect   f) online shopping

13) In French, write down two advantages and two disadvantages of the internet.

Higher 14) 'Lola likes streaming sites because they broadcast series directly online.'
    How would you say this in French?

15) Translate these words and phrases into English: a) la pub   b) gratuit(e)
    c) il a annulé la vente   d) elles livrent au consommateur   e) renvoyer les achats

Social Media ☐

16) 'Do you use social media? Why / Why not?' Answer in French.

17) 'Quels sont les dangers des réseaux sociaux ?' Respond in French.

18) Translate these words into French: a) youth   b) online communication   c) to lower
    d) always available   e) worry   f) modern   g) dialogue   h) to follow influencers

19) How many things can you name that you might post on social media?
    There are at least 3 you need to know (plus 2 for Higher tier).

20) 'Théo uses social networks from time to time, but he thinks the influence of some new sites
    is worrying for his generation.' How would you say this in French?

H 21) Translate these verbs into English: a) harceler   b) souffrir   c) réagir   d) s'inscrire (à)   e) unir

Where You Live

Whether you love the rural lifestyle or you're more suited to living in urban areas, you'll need to know how to talk about where you live. Reading this page should do the trick.

Don't forget you can access your online content here: www.cgpbooks.co.uk/Bonjour

Tu habites où ? — *Where do you live?*

Vocabulary

vivre	*to live*	la rue	*street*	la ferme	*farm*
habiter	*to live*	la route	*road*	situer	*to place, put, situate*
l'habitant(e)	*resident*	le chemin	*way, path*		
l'adresse (f)	*address*	le coin	*corner*	se situer	*to be situated, take place*
le/la voisin(e)	*neighbour*	le bord	*edge, side*		
le village	*village*	la côte	*coast*	où	*where*
la ville	*town*	la montagne	*mountain*	la banlieue	*suburbs, outskirts*
la capitale	*capital city*	la forêt	*forest*	la cité	*council estate*
la région	*region, area*	la campagne	*countryside*	la province	*province*

(Higher: la banlieue, la cité, la province)

Ma mère habite *près d'une vieille ferme* dans un petit village *à la campagne*.

My mother lives near an old farm in a small village in the countryside.

Moi, je *préfère vivre dans la banlieue* d'une grande ville où il y a plus de transports publics.

I prefer to live on the outskirts of a large town where there is more public transport.

Dans ma cité, tous les voisins s'entendent bien et *c'est toujours tranquille*.

On my council estate, all the neighbours get on well and it's always quiet.

by a lake — au bord d'un lac

in the mountains — à la montagne

Grammar — using prepositions for location

Some prepositions are used to describe the location of something or someone. See p.116 for more on prepositions.

La maison se situe entre deux forêts.

Il y a une montagne près de la maison.

The house is situated between two forests.

There is a mountain near the house.

George wasn't so sure about the mountain life any more...

Practice Question

Q1 Read the following text about where Élodie lives and answer the questions below in English.

J'habite dans une petite ville qui se situe sur la côte nord-ouest de la France. Ma ville est jolie, avec beaucoup de belles plages. Cependant, il n'y a pas beaucoup à faire ici, surtout en hiver. Alors, vivre dans cette ville devient parfois ennuyeux. Un jour je voudrais habiter dans le sud-ouest du pays car il fait plus chaud là-bas et j'adore la cuisine de la région.

a) Where in France is Élodie's town situated? [1 mark]

b) What is her town like? Give two details. [2 marks]

c) Why is it sometimes boring to live there? [1 mark]

d) Why does Élodie want to live in the south-west? Give two reasons. [2 marks]

I just moved to the coast — there's so much to sea...

You might love the area you live in, or maybe you wish you lived somewhere else entirely. Either way, tell the examiner and expand on your opinions by giving reasons — 'parce que...' or 'car...' will be useful.

The Home

Ahh, home sweet home... Read this page to learn some super French vocab you can use to talk about your home. You'll have the *clés* to the *porte* before you know it...

La maison — *The home*

Vocabulary

la maison	*house, home*	la clé	*key*
l'appartement (m)	*apartment, flat*	le jardin	*garden*
le / la propriétaire	*owner*	l'animal (m)	*animal, pet*
chez	*to (the place of),*	la plante	*plant*
	at (the place of), with	la feuille	*leaf*
la porte	*door*	le sol	*floor, ground*
la fenêtre	*window*	l'étage (m)	*floor (of a building)*

Higher: la plante, la feuille, le sol, l'étage

Je suis le / la propriétaire d'une grande maison. — *I am the owner of a large house.*

Dans l'appartement où j'habite, les portes et les fenêtres sont énormes. — *In the flat where I live, the doors and the windows are enormous.*

Les animaux qui traversent mon jardin mangent toujours les feuilles de mes plantes. — *The animals that cross my garden always eat the leaves of my plants.*

a detached house — une maison individuelle

a terraced house — une maison mitoyenne

Les pièces (f) de la maison — *The rooms in the house*

Vocabulary

la pièce	*room*	la cuisine	*kitchen, cooking*
le mur	*wall*	la table	*table*
le salon	*lounge, living room*	la chaise	*chair*
la chambre	*bedroom*	les toilettes	*toilet, lavatory, bathroom*
le lit	*bed*	le bain	*bath, bathing*

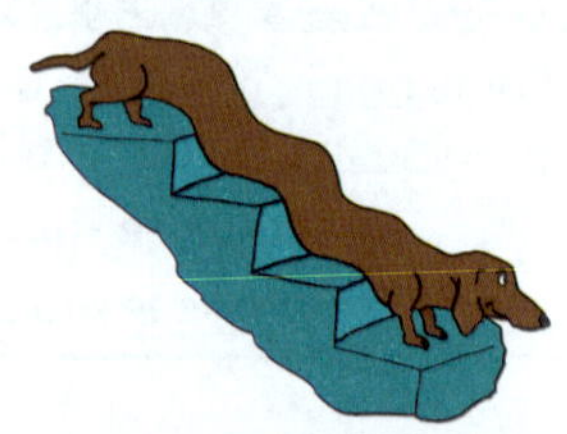

On a mis un nouveau lit dans ma chambre. — *We put a new bed in my bedroom.*

Nous avons une grande table dans la cuisine pour dîner ensemble en famille. — *We have a big table in the kitchen to eat dinner together as a family.*

Il y a deux chaises et un sofa dans le salon. — *There are two chairs and a sofa in the living room.*

a gigantic wardrobe — une armoire gigantesque

a sofa bed — un canapé-lit

Question

Décris ta maison.

Describe your home.

Simple Answer

Dans ma maison, il y a deux chambres, un salon et une cuisine.

In my home, there are two bedrooms, a living room and a kitchen.

Extended Answer

Moi, j'habite dans un appartement au troisième étage. C'est assez petit et il n'y a que deux chambres. Un jour, je voudrais habiter dans une belle maison avec un grand jardin.

I live in an apartment on the third floor. It's quite small and there are only two bedrooms. One day, I would like to live in a beautiful house with a big garden.

C'est comment chez toi ? — *What's it like at your place?*

Vocabulary

idéal(e)	*ideal*
propre	*clean, proper, own*
sale	*dirty*
énorme	*enormous*
moderne	*modern*
construire	*to build*
la construction	*construction, building*

Some adjectives have a different meaning depending on whether they go before or after a noun. See p.122 for more.

Currently under construction.
Please come back later.

Ma maison est toujours propre car je la nettoie tous les jours.

My house is always clean because I clean it every day.

messy — en désordre

Devant chez nous, il y a toujours des travaux de construction, ce qui n'est pas idéal.

Outside our place, there are always construction works, which isn't ideal.

I hate tidying up — je déteste ranger

Chez moi c'est calme puisque je n'ai qu'un voisin et il habite tout seul.

At my place it's quiet, since I only have one neighbour and he lives alone.

annoys me — m'énerve

Grammar (Higher only) — 'ne...que'

You can use the <u>negative</u> form 'ne...que' to say '<u>only</u>'. See p.141 for more on negative forms.

Il n'y a que deux appartements au premier étage.   *<u>There are only</u> two flats on the first floor.*

Practice Questions

Q1 *You receive a phone call from a French estate agent about a new home on the market. Listen to the call and choose the correct option for each question below.*

Listening Track 16

a) Where is the house situated?
   A. In the mountains
   B. In the countryside
   C. On the coast   *[1 mark]*

c) Which room is the agent's favourite?
   A. The bathroom
   B. The living room
   C. The kitchen   *[1 mark]*

b) Who is the house ideal for?
   A. A young couple
   B. A single person
   C. A family   *[1 mark]*

d) What else is great about this house?
   A. The garden is ideal for a dog.
   B. The neighbours are nice.
   C. The shops are nearby.   *[1 mark]*

Q2 *Translate the following sentences into French.*

 **Higher**

a) I clean my bedroom every weekend.
b) It's always very pleasant at my place.
c) My flat is situated on the fourth floor.
d) My uncle has several plants in his garden.
e) My house is ancient.
f) I have only lived in flats.   *[12 marks]*

Did you hear about *la maison*? It was in *pièces*, poor thing...

Sure, you could just tell the examiner you have a kitchen with a table in it. But if you want to cook up a more interesting sentence, try telling them you have a big, beautiful, red kitchen with a new table in it.

The Local Area

Your local area could be a hot topic of discussion in the exams, so it's important you know how to talk about it. Luckily for you, these pages have plenty of useful vocab to help you do just that.

Les lieux (m) d'intérêt — *Places of interest*

Vocabulary

le quartier	*quarter, district*	le centre	*centre*		le cinéma	*cinema*
la place	*square, place*	la plage	*beach*		le café	*café*
l'endroit (m)	*place, spot*	la piscine	*swimming pool*		le restaurant	*restaurant*
le lieu	*place*				social(e)	*social*
l'espace (m)	*space*	la bibliothèque	*library*		central(e)	*central*
le pont	*bridge*	la boulangerie	*bakery*		ancien(ne)	*former, ancient*
la tour	*tower*	la poste	*post office*			
le stade	*stadium*	la banque	*bank*		l'affiche (f)	*poster*
le parc	*park*	l'hôpital (m)	*hospital*		les hôpitaux (m)	*hospitals*

(Higher: central(e), ancien(ne), l'affiche (f), les hôpitaux (m))

J'allais à la boulangerie le matin.

I used to go to the bakery in the morning.

cake shop — la pâtisserie

Le week-end, mes amis et moi aimons aller au parc où il y a un café génial.

At the weekend, my friends and I like going to the park where there's a great café.

Cette ville a une tour énorme au centre et un stade de l'autre côté du pont.

This town has an enormous tower in the centre and a stadium on the other side of the bridge.

three hospitals — trois hôpitaux

Question

Tu aimes aller où dans ta ville ?

Where do you like to go in your town?

Simple Answer

J'aime faire de la natation à la piscine au centre-ville.

I like to go swimming at the pool in the town centre.

Extended Answer

J'adore aller au vieux quartier. Là-bas, il y a une belle place très ancienne avec un super restaurant qui vend des plats délicieux.

I love going to the old quarter. There's a beautiful old square with a great restaurant that sells delicious dishes.

Améliorer la ville — *Improving the town*

Vocabulary

la station	*station*	le besoin	*need*		bénéficier de	*to get, receive, benefit from*
la gare	*station, railway station*	le manque	*lack*		gérer	*to manage, handle, deal with*
		public / publique	*public*			
le véhicule	*vehicle*	local(e)	*local*		divers(e)	*varied, diverse*
l'arrêt (m)	*stop*	vert(e)	*green*		la voie	*street, route, way*
		industriel(le)	*industrial*			

(Higher: bénéficier de, gérer, divers(e), la voie)

Les habitants de cette ville bénéficient des espaces verts et de bons transports publics.

The residents of this town benefit from green spaces and good public transport.

the maintenance of roads — l'entretien des routes

Le conseil régional gère la construction de nouvelles routes.

The regional council handles the construction of new roads.

the renovation of roads — la rénovation des routes

Tu aimes faire du shopping ? — *Do you like to shop?*

Vocabulary

le marché	*market*	la vente	*sale*	commercial(e)	*commercial, shopping (adj.)*
le supermarché	*supermarket*	vendre	*to sell*	l'achat (m)	*purchase*
le magasin	*shop*	la différence	*difference*	le siège	*seat, bench*
la caisse	*checkout*	l'avantage (m)	*advantage*		
la sortie	*exit*	comparer	*to compare*		

Grammar — indirect object pronouns ('me', 'te', 'lui', 'nous', 'vous', 'leur')

Indirect objects are things that are affected by the action being done, but not directly. They often have 'to' or 'for' before them in English.

Je <u>lui</u> ai montré mon nouveau pantalon.   *I showed my new trousers <u>to him</u>.*

See p.112 for more on indirect object pronouns.

Au marché, on m'a vendu ce chapeau à prix réduit.

At the market, they sold me this hat at a discounted price.

> I bought a shirt — j'ai acheté une chemise
>
> they were selling jumpers — on vendait des pulls

Mon copain m'a donné ses achats et j'ai attendu son retour sur un siège.

My boyfriend gave me his purchases and I awaited his return on a bench.

Dans le centre commercial en ville, on vend toutes sortes de produits.

In the shopping centre in town, they sell all kinds of products.

> there are sales — il y a des soldes

Practice Questions

Q1   Look at the two photos below. Talk in French about what is in the photos. You should talk for about a minute and say something about both photos.

[5 marks]

Q2   Your French cousin is coming to visit and you are writing an email to them about your local area. You should write about 90 words in French. Describe:

- the places of interest in your local area
- something you did recently in your town
- where you will take your cousin when they visit.

Top Tips for Higher Students
✓ Use irregular verbs in the proper future, e.g. 'On ira…' (We will go…).
✓ Add interesting adjectives to nouns, e.g. 'un musée <u>formidable</u>' (*a <u>terrific</u> museum*).

[15 marks]

Talking about the local area — that sounds right up my *aller...*

Maybe you've heard it before, but I'll say it again — when you're talking about going to the different places in your local area, make sure you use 'aller + à + place'. For example, 'Je vais <u>au</u> centre commercial'.

Directions and Weather

Exams can be unfamiliar territory and it's easy to feel lost. Learn the vocab on this page to get the directions you need to reach greener pastures, bluer skies and, yep, those higher marks...

Où est... ? — *Where is...?*

Vocabulary

la droite	*the right*	entre	*between*
la gauche	*the left*	dehors	*outside*
à droite	*on the right*	partout	*everywhere*
à gauche	*on the left*	voici	*here is*
droit(e)	*right (adj.)*	tourner	*to turn, go round*
gauche	*left (adj.)*	autour	*around*
devant	*in front of*	la direction	*direction*
derrière	*behind*	indiquer	*to indicate*

Higher: tourner, autour, la direction, indiquer

The website said the beach was only 2 minutes away...

Pour arriver à la gare, tourne à droite et suis le chemin jusqu'au coin.	*To arrive at the railway station, turn right and follow the path to the corner.*
Voilà le parc du quartier, qui se trouve devant la plage.	*Here is the local park, which is located in front of the beach.*
Excusez-moi, je suis perdu(e). Vous pouvez m'indiquer comment aller au centre-ville ?	*Excuse me, I'm lost. Can you direct me to the town centre?*

to the tourist information office — à l'office de tourisme

to the art gallery — au musée d'art

C'est loin d'ici ? — *Is it far from here?*

Vocabulary

ici	*here*	le mètre	*metre*
là	*there*	le kilomètre	*kilometre*
là-bas	*over there, out there*	le nord	*north*
près	*nearby*	le sud	*south*
proche	*nearby, close*	l'ouest (m)	*west*
loin	*far*	l'est (m)	*east*
traverser	*to cross*	la position	*position*
décrire	*to describe*	relativement	*relatively*
donner	*to give*	la distance	*distance*

Higher: l'est (m), la position, relativement, la distance

Grammar — using the imperative

You can use the <u>imperative</u> form to give <u>directions</u> or <u>instructions</u>:

<u>Suivez</u> le chemin de droite.
***<u>Follow</u>** the right-hand path.*

<u>Traverse</u> la rue !
***<u>Cross</u>** the street!*

See p.142 for more on the imperative.

La distance entre ici et le pont est d'environ dix kilomètres.	*The distance between here and the bridge is around ten kilometres.*
Dites-moi, le véhicule est allé dans quelle direction ?	*Tell me, in which direction did the vehicle go?*
La frontière nord du pays se situe relativement près d'ici.	*The northern border of the country is situated relatively close to here.*

my house and my school — chez moi et mon école

where exactly — où exactement

is not too far from — n'est pas trop loin d'

Quel temps fait-il ? — *What's the weather like?*

Vocabulary

le temps	*weather*	il fait (beau)	*it is, it's (nice)*	le vent	*wind*
le climat	*climate*	froid(e)	*cold*	le brouillard	*fog, mist, haze*
le soleil	*sun*	la neige	*snow*	**H** la météo	*weather forecast*
chaud(e)	*warm, hot*	il pleut	*it rains, it's raining*	la pluie	*rain*

Le temps est génial aujourd'hui — il fait vraiment chaud et il y a du soleil.

The weather is great today — it's really hot and sunny.

breezy — il y a du vent

cloudless — il n'y a pas de nuages

Là-bas, le climat est froid et il y a toujours de la neige partout.

The climate there is cold and there's always snow everywhere.

dry — sec

damp — humide

Selon la météo, il va pleuvoir demain.

According to the weather forecast, it's going to rain tomorrow.

it's going to snow — il va neiger

it'll be icy — il y aura du gel

Q&A Audio

Question

Comment est le climat de ta région ?

What's the climate like in your area?

Simple Answer

Il fait froid et il pleut tout le temps.

It's cold and it rains all the time.

Extended Answer

Normalement, il fait assez chaud, mais récemment il y avait de la pluie et du temps froid. Je n'aime pas ça et j'espère que le soleil reviendra bientôt.

Usually it's quite hot, but recently there was some rain and cold weather. I don't like it and I hope the sun returns soon.

Practice Questions

Q1 *Read the following text about the weather in Réunion and answer the questions below in English.*

READING

La Réunion est une petite île de près d'un million d'habitants. Sur l'île, il y a beaucoup de montagnes qui sont toutes énormes et un climat tropical avec seulement deux saisons. L'été dure de novembre à avril. Pendant ces six mois, il fait chaud mais il pleut beaucoup, surtout dans le sud de l'île. De mai à octobre, c'est l'hiver et il fait généralement beau mais plus froid, surtout dans le nord et l'ouest.

a) According to the text, how many people live in Réunion? *[1 mark]*

b) What is the island's landscape like? *[1 mark]*

c) What is the weather like in the summer? Give two details. *[2 marks]*

d) What is the weather like in the winter? Give two details. *[2 marks]*

Q2 *Listen to this message your friend left on your voicemail. Complete the sentences in English.*

LISTENING

a) Cross the street and you will see... *[1 mark]*

b) Get off at the post office and... *[1 mark]*

c) Next, get off at the church, then turn right and... *[1 mark]*

d) After about 100 metres the café will be... *[1 mark]*

Higher

Listening Track 17

Left! No, the other left! Directions are hard enough in English...

In French, some verbs can be used in an impersonal way, and they take the pronoun 'il' as their subject. Most of the verbs you'll use to talk about weather are impersonal, so they'll follow this rule (e.g. 'il pleut').

Where People Live — Vocabulary

Use this vocab to make your local area (and you) stand out in the exam — or to talk about where you'd rather live...

Where You Live

exister	*to exist*
vivre	*to live*
habiter	*to live*
l'habitant(e)	*resident*
l'adresse (f)	*address*
le / la voisin(e)	*neighbour*
le village	*village*
la ville	*town*
la capitale	*capital city*
le pays	*country*
la région	*region, area*
régional(e)	*regional*
la rue	*street*
la route	*road*
le chemin	*way, path*
le coin	*corner*
le bord	*edge, side*
le bâtiment	*building*
la côte	*coast*
la montagne	*mountain*
la forêt	*forest*

la campagne	*countryside*
la ferme	*farm*
situer	*to place, put, situate*
se situer	*to be situated, take place*
où	*where*
sûr(e)	*safe*
calme	*calm, quiet*
national(e)	*national*
international(e)	*international*

Higher

la banlieue	*suburbs, outskirts*
la cité	*council estate*
le terrain	*ground, terrain*
la province	*province*
le paysage	*landscape, scenery, countryside*
le champ	*field*
la rivière	*river*
le lac	*lake*
la pierre	*stone*
tranquille	*quiet*
global(e)	*global*

The Home

la maison	*house, home*
l'appartement (m)	*apartment, flat*
le / la propriétaire	*owner*
chez	*to (the place of), at (the place of), with*
la porte	*door*
la fenêtre	*window*
la clé	*key*
le jardin	*garden*
l'animal (m)	*animal, pet*
les animaux (m)	*animals, pets*
la pièce	*room, piece*
la salle	*room*
le mur	*wall*
le salon	*lounge, living room*
la chambre	*bedroom*
le lit	*bed*
la cuisine	*kitchen, cooking*
la table	*table*
la chaise	*chair*
la boîte	*box*
la toilette	*washing*
les toilettes	*toilet, lavatory, bathroom*

le bain	*bath, bathing*
idéal(e)	*ideal*
joli(e)	*pretty, attractive*
propre	*clean, proper, own*
sale	*dirty*
énorme	*enormous*
historique	*historic*
moderne	*modern*
construire	*to build, to construct*
la construction	*construction, building*

Higher

la plante	*plant*
la feuille	*leaf*
le sol	*floor, ground*
l'étage (m)	*floor (of a building)*
l'oiseau (m)	*bird*
nettoyer	*to clean*

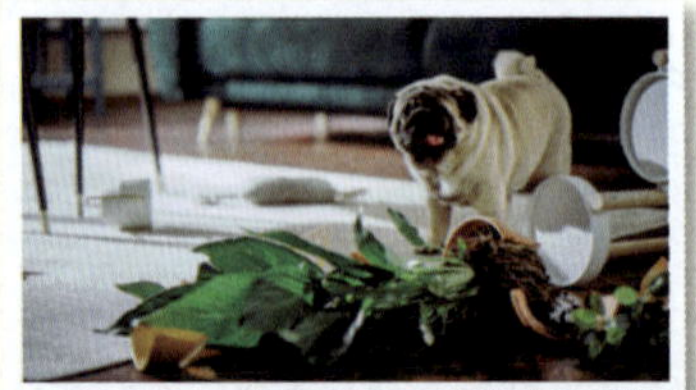

Baptiste decided to add some character to the living room.

The Local Area

le quartier	*quarter, district*
la place	*square, place*
l'endroit (m)	*place, spot*
le lieu	*place*
l'espace (m)	*space*
le pont	*bridge*
la tour	*tower*
le stade	*stadium*
l'hôtel (m)	*hotel*
le château	*castle, palace*
le musée	*museum*
le parc	*park*
le centre	*centre*
la plage	*beach*
la piscine	*swimming pool*
la bibliothèque	*library*
la boulangerie	*bakery*
la poste	*post office*
la banque	*bank*
l'hôpital (m)	*hospital*
le cinéma	*cinema*
le café	*café*
le restaurant	*restaurant*
le marché	*market*
le supermarché	*supermarket*
le magasin	*shop*
la caisse	*checkout*
la sortie	*exit*
la vente	*sale*

vendre	*to sell*
la différence	*difference*
la station	*station*
la gare	*station, railway station*
le véhicule	*vehicle*
l'arrêt (m)	*stop*
l'avantage (m)	*advantage*
le besoin	*need*
le manque	*lack*
comparer	*to compare*
social(e)	*social*
public / publique	*public*
local(e)	*local*
vert(e)	*green*
industriel(le)	*industrial*
commercial(e)	*commercial, shopping (adj.)*
l'organisation (f)	*organisation*

Higher

central(e)	*central*
ancien(ne)	*former, ancient*
l'affiche (f)	*poster*
les hôpitaux (m)	*hospitals*
bénéficier de	*to get, receive, benefit from*
gérer	*to manage, handle, deal with*
divers(e)	*varied, diverse*
la voie	*street, route, way*
efficace	*efficient, effective*
l'achat (m)	*purchase*
le siège	*seat, bench*

Directions and Weather

la droite	*the right*
la gauche	*the left*
à droite	*on the right*
à gauche	*on the left*
droit(e)	*right (adj.)*
gauche	*left (adj.)*
devant	*in front of*
derrière	*behind*
entre	*between*
dehors	*outside*
partout	*everywhere*
voici	*here is*
ici	*here*
là	*there*
là-bas	*over there, out there*
près	*nearby, close by, near*

proche	*nearby, close*
loin	*far*
traverser	*to cross*
décrire	*to describe*
donner	*to give*
le mètre	*metre*
le kilomètre	*kilometre*
le nord	*north*
le sud	*south*
l'ouest (m)	*west*
le temps	*weather*
le climat	*climate*
le soleil	*sun*
se lever	*to rise (sun)*
se coucher	*to set (sun)*
chaud(e)	*warm, hot*
il fait (beau)	*it is / it's (nice)*
froid(e)	*cold*
la neige	*snow*

il pleut	*it rains, it's raining*
le vent	*wind*
le brouillard	*fog, mist, haze*
tourner	*to turn, go round*

Higher

autour	*around*
la direction	*direction*
indiquer	*to indicate*
l'est (m)	*east*
la position	*position*
relativement	*relatively*
la distance	*distance*
la météo	*weather forecast*
la pluie	*rain*

Section Eleven — Where People Live

Revision Summary Test for Section Eleven

That's another section under your belt — time to put your knowledge to the test.

- Yep, these questions are **hard** — they'll really help you see **how well you know your stuff**.
- Tackle the **revision summary test** below, or scan the QR code to do it **online**.
  Use the CGP RevisionHub to **track your progress** and see **which areas need more work**.
- You can find **sample answers** here: www.cgpbooks.co.uk/BonjourExtras

Where You Live ☐

1) How do you say the words below in French?
   a) forest   b) farm   c) coast   d) edge   e) road   f) path   g) neighbour

2) 'Moi, j'ai deux adresses. La première est une maison dans un petit village à la campagne,
   et l'autre est un appartement situé à la montagne.' What's Xavier saying? Answer in English.

3) 'I live in the capital city of my country, and it's very international. For example, the residents
   of my street come from the four corners of the world.' Translate Marianne's sentences into French.

Higher
4) How do you say the words below in English?
   a) la banlieue   b) la cité   c) le paysage   d) le champ   e) le terrain   f) la pierre

5) 'Ma femme et moi habitions dans un vieux bâtiment qui se situait entre un grand lac
   et une rivière tranquille. J'aimais y vivre, parce que c'était très calme.'
   Where did Marc used to live and why did he like living there? Answer in English.

The Home ☑

6) 'Qu'est-ce que tu penses de ta maison ou de ton appartement ?' Answer in French.

7) How do you say the words below in French?
   a) chair   b) box   c) room   d) door   e) wall   f) key   g) bed   h) bedroom   i) owner

8) Choose one of the rooms in your home and describe it in French.

H
9) 'Je dois nettoyer le sol de mon salon souvent car j'ai beaucoup d'animaux.'
   Translate Rémie's sentence into English.

The Local Area ☑

10) How do you say the following words in French?   a) market   b) checkout   c) sale   d) to sell

11) 'Quels sont les avantages et les inconvénients d'habiter dans ta région ?' Answer in French.

12) How many buildings in the local area can you name in French? There are at least 18 in this section.

13) How do you say the words below in English?
    a) le quartier   b) le parc   c) la plage   d) l'arrêt   e) l'endroit   f) le pont   g) la sortie

H
14) 'Ici, on bénéficie de divers espaces verts. Pour les préserver, il faut encourager les entreprises
    à gérer leurs activités industrielles de façon plus efficace.' Translate these sentences into English.

Directions and Weather ☑

15) How do you say the words below in French?
    a) on the left   b) on the right   c) outside   d) over there   e) far   f) behind   g) in front of

16) How many words and expressions related to weather can you write down in French?
    There are at least 10 you need to know (plus 2 extra for Higher tier).

17) Name the compass points in French. There are 3 you need to know (plus 1 extra for Higher tier).

Higher
18) Imagine that a tourist asks you: 'Où est l'hôtel le plus proche d'ici ? Vous pouvez m'expliquer
    comment y aller ?' Translate their questions into English, then make up an answer in French.

19) 'The distance between the two towns is relatively small — it's only twenty kilometres.'
    Translate Simon's sentence into French.

Protecting the Environment

That's right — it's time to start thinking about all things green, natural and... polluted. These pages cover many of the problems poor old Mother Nature is facing, so get learning.

Head to the CGP RevisionHub for all your online content: www.cgpbooks.co.uk/Bonjour

Sauver la Terre — *Saving the Earth*

Vocabulary

protéger	*to protect*	le / la scientifique	*scientist*	transformer (en)	*to transform (into)*
le progrès	*progress*	l'expert(e)	*expert*	préserver	*to preserve, protect*
réduire	*to reduce*	l'action (f)	*action*	prévenir	*to let (someone)*
la réduction	*reduction*	l'information (f)	*information*		*know, warn*
recycler	*to recycle*	la limite	*limit*	sauver	*to rescue, save*
le recyclage	*recycling*	adapter	*to adapt*	la recherche	*research, search*
l'énergie (f)	*energy*	la coopération	*cooperation*	remplacer (par)	*to replace (with)*
diminuer	*to lower*	l'explication (f)	*explanation*	nettoyer	*to clean*

(*Higher*: la limite, adapter, la coopération, l'explication; transformer (en), préserver, prévenir, sauver, la recherche, remplacer (par), nettoyer)

Q&A Audio

Question

Qu'est-ce que tu fais pour protéger la planète ?

What do you do to protect the planet?

Simple Answer

J'essaie de recycler les déchets et j'utilise les transports publics.

I try to recycle rubbish and I use public transport.

Extended Answer

À mon avis, protéger l'environnement est très important. Je recycle quand je peux — le verre, le plastique et même mes vieux vêtements. Chaque personne doit faire un effort pour sauver la planète.

In my opinion, protecting the environment is very important. I recycle when I can — glass, plastic and even my old clothes. Everyone must make an effort to save the planet.

Grammar — 'On doit' / 'il faut'

Use 'on doit...' (from 'devoir') or 'il faut...' (from 'falloir') to say 'we must'.
The verb which follows is in the infinitive.

On doit recycler plus.
We must recycle more.

Il faut s'adapter pour protéger la planète.
We must adapt to protect the planet.

You can also use the verb 'devoir' to say that someone needs to do something.

Le gouvernement doit réagir.
The government must react.

La société ne prend pas soin de la Terre. Il y a un manque de coopération entre les pays.

Society doesn't take care of the Earth. There is a lack of cooperation between countries.

Les scientifiques et autres experts s'inquiètent de l'avenir de la planète.

Scientists and other experts are worried about the future of the planet.

Practice Question

Q1 *Listen to this extract from a podcast about the environment.*

Which two solutions to environmental problems does each person suggest? Choose the correct options from each list.

Listening Track 18

a) **A.** green energy
    B. public transport
    C. scientific research
    D. recycling   *[2 marks]*

b) **A.** preventing waste
    B. protecting wildlife
    C. using less water
    D. creating more parks   *[2 marks]*

I've given up washing in order to save the planet...

The more vocab you know the better — it will allow you to give more detailed answers. Show the examiners you really know your stuff by using the 'on doit' and 'il faut' structures too. Impressive.

Quick Quiz

Environmental Problems

You might prefer hiding away in a darkened room to roaming the hills and basking in the glories of nature, but you still need to have an opinion about environmental problems, so listen up...

Le monde naturel — *The natural world*

Vocabulary

l'environnement (m)	*environment*	le climat	*climate*	la ressource	*resource*
la terre	*earth, world, soil, land*	le ciel	*sky*	naturel(le)	*natural*
le monde	*world*	la mer	*sea*	l'espèce (f)	*species*
la planète	*planet*	l'eau (f)	*water*	mondial(e)	*worldwide, global*
la nature	*nature*	l'arbre (m)	*tree*		
la population	*population*	le bois	*wood*	le papier	*paper*
		le gaz	*gas*		

(*Higher*: l'espèce, mondial(e), le papier)

Q&A Audio

Question

Est-ce que l'environnement est important pour toi ?

Is the environment important to you?

Simple Answer

Oui, je m'intéresse beaucoup à l'environnement et j'adore découvrir la nature.

Yes, I'm very interested in the environment and I love discovering nature.

Extended Answer

Oui, je m'inquiète beaucoup pour l'environnement car, chaque jour, on peut déjà remarquer des changements dans la nature. Aujourd'hui, il y a de graves menaces pour la Terre. C'est à nous de la protéger.

Yes, I worry about the environment a lot because every day we can see the changes in nature. Today, there are serious threats to the earth. It's up to us to protect it.

Les causes (f) de la pollution — *Causes of pollution*

Vocabulary

menacer (de)	*to threaten (to)*	la poubelle	*rubbish bin*	l'usine (f)	*factory*
la menace	*threat*	le bruit	*noise*	la conséquence	*consequence*
détruire	*to destroy*	la lumière	*light*	le changement	*change*
tuer	*to kill*	conduire	*to drive*	causer	*to cause*
polluer	*to pollute*	le transport	*transport*	contribuer	*to contribute*
jeter	*to throw*	la voiture	*car*	la puissance	*power*
le plastique	*plastic*	la cause	*cause*	puissant(e)	*powerful*
les déchets (m)	*rubbish*	fabriquer	*to produce*	la circulation	*traffic*

(*Higher*: la conséquence, le changement, causer, contribuer, la puissance, puissant(e), la circulation)

Dans les grandes villes, le niveau de pollution causée par les voitures peut être dangereux.

In big cities, the level of pollution caused by cars can be dangerous.

On peut réduire la quantité de déchets plastiques dans la mer si les gens jettent leurs déchets dans la poubelle.

We can reduce the quantity of plastic waste in the sea if people throw their rubbish in the bin.

La population mondiale augmente d'année en année, donc on fabrique plus de produits et on utilise plus d'énergie.

The global population is increasing from year to year, so we produce more products and use more energy.

large companies — les grandes entreprises

packaging — les emballages

waste — gaspille

La planète en crise — *The planet in crisis*

Vocabulary

le réchauffement	*warming*	grave	*serious, grave*	brûler	*to burn, be on fire*
la catastrophe	*catastrophe, disaster*	le danger	*danger*	disparaître	*to disappear*
la crise	*crisis*	la nécessité	*necessity, need*	risquer	*to risk*
pire (adv.)	*worse, less well*	nucléaire	*nuclear*	le taux	*rate*
augmenter	*to increase*	la destruction	*destruction*	la qualité	*quality*
				la tragédie	*tragedy*

(Higher: la nécessité, nucléaire, la destruction, brûler, disparaître, risquer, le taux, la qualité, la tragédie)

Beaucoup d'espèces sont menacées par le réchauffement de la planète. Si les humains ne prennent pas soin de la nature, certaines espèces vont disparaître.

Many species are threatened by global warming. If humans don't take care of nature, some species will disappear.

by extinction — d'extinction

L'énergie nucléaire cause de nombreux débats.

Nuclear energy causes many debates.

Renewable — renouvelable

Les grandes entreprises sont responsables de la pollution de l'eau des rivières.

Large companies are responsible for water pollution in rivers.

for deforestation — du déboisement

for the environmental crisis — de la crise écologique

Léo was getting a bit too good at hide and seek — he hadn't seen anyone for hours…

Grammar — adjective position

In French, adjectives usually come after the noun. However, this isn't always the case, e.g.

Il y a une grande usine. **There is a big factory.**

Adjectives such as beau (*beautiful*), joli (*pretty*), jeune (*young*), gentil (*kind*), grand (*big*) and petit (*small*) usually come before the noun. See p.122 for more.

Le beau paysage est en danger. **Les petites actions ont un grand effet.**
The beautiful landscape is in danger. **Small actions have a big effect.**

Practice Questions

Q1 *Answer these questions out loud in French.*

- *Quelles sont les causes de la pollution ?*
- *Est-ce que le réchauffement de la planète t'inquiète ? Pourquoi ?*

SPEAKING

[4 marks]

Q2 *Read this passage written by Hugo and answer the questions below.*

READING

La pollution cause de graves problèmes pour l'environnement. Chaque jour, la situation semble être pire — je veux protéger la planète pour mes futurs enfants. Dans mon pays, on peut voir les effets de la crise sur le climat. Cet été, il y a eu des feux de forêts à cause du réchauffement de la planète. C'était une tragédie pour les animaux, et le nombre de touristes qui visitent le pays a diminué aussi. Je m'inquiète pour l'été prochain.

(Higher)

a) Why is protecting the planet important to Hugo? *[1 mark]*

b) What does he say happened during summer? *[1 mark]*

c) Give two consequences of the event that happened in summer. *[2 marks]*

d) How does he feel about next summer? *[1 mark]*

You should always mention global warming on a first date…

…it's a real ice-breaker. Remember that not all adjectives come after the noun — some come before. Make a list and learn the few that come before the noun so they don't catch you out in your exams.

Social Issues

Social problems, war, politics — this section just keeps getting better. It's enough to make you want to pull the duvet over your head and stay there. Here's something to pass the time...

Les problèmes sociaux — *Social problems*

Vocabulary

la violence	*violence*	l'avantage (m)	*advantage*		la souffrance	*suffering*
pauvre	*poor*	l'inconvénient (m)	*disadvantage*		raciste	*racist*
l'abri (m)	*shelter*	le souci	*worry, concern*		l'ennemi(e)	*enemy*
la pauvreté	*poverty*	l'inquiétude (f)	*worry, anxiety*		l'attentat (m)	*attack*
la faim	*hunger*	cacher	*to hide*	**Higher**	le choc	*shock, clash*
actuel(le)	*current*	la guerre	*war*		la lutte	*fight, struggle*
moral(e)	*moral*	l'arme (f)	*weapon, arms*		l'attitude (f)	*attitude*
le chômage	*unemployment*	le crime	*crime*		battre	*to beat, hit*

(Higher: la guerre, l'arme (f), le crime)

L'inégalité sociale entre les riches et les pauvres peut mener au conflit.

Social inequality between the rich and the poor can lead to conflict.

to political instability — à l'instabilité politique

Les guerres causent de la souffrance.

Wars cause suffering.

destruction — la destruction

Dans la société actuelle, le chômage est un problème.

In today's society, unemployment is a problem.

the crime rate — le taux de criminalité

C'était un choc de découvrir la violence des attentats terroristes.

It was a shock to discover the violence of the terrorist attacks.

La politique — *Politics*

Vocabulary

voter	*to vote*	élire	*to elect*		l'économie (f)	*economy*
le vote	*vote*	(avoir) élu	*(to have) elected*		la république	*republic*
le gouvernement	*government*				la démocratie	*democracy*
la manifestation	*demonstration, event*	la victoire	*victory*		la loi	*law*
		manifester	*to protest, demonstrate*		le commerce	*trade, commerce*
la révolution	*revolution*					
l'élection (f)	*election*	officiel(le)	*official*		libéral(e)	*liberal*
l'électeur / l'électrice	*elector, voter*	le / la porte-parole	*spokesperson*		l'impôt (m)	*tax*
		économique	*economic*			

Dans une démocratie, les électeurs doivent voter pour élire les meilleurs candidats.

In a democracy, voters must vote to elect the best candidates.

Des milliers de gens ont manifesté contre l'augmentation des impôts par le gouvernement.

Thousands of people protested against the increase in taxes by the government.

Une porte-parole a prévenu le public que la situation économique était inquiétante.

A spokesperson warned the public that the economic situation was worrying.

frightening — effrayante

Aider la société — *Helping society*

Vocabulary

la liberté	*liberty, freedom*	juste	*right, true, correct, fair*	la communauté	*community*
le / la bénévole	*volunteer*	l'individu (m)	*individual*	la volonté	*will*
développer	*to develop*	l'humain (m)	*human*	l'accord (m)	*agreement*
l'égalité (f)	*equality*	la paix	*peace*	défendre	*to defend, forbid, stand up for*
intégrer	*to integrate*	l'association (f)	*association*		
s'intégrer	*to fit in*	le / la citoyen(ne)	*citizen*	la libération	*liberation*

(Higher: l'individu, l'humain, la paix, l'association, le / la citoyen(ne))
(Higher: la communauté, la volonté, l'accord, défendre, la libération)

Q&A Audio

Question

Est-ce que tu aimes aider les autres ?

Do you like helping others?

Simple Answer

Oui, c'est important d'aider les autres. On peut aider les gens à s'intégrer dans la société.

Yes, it's important to help others. We can help people integrate into society.

Extended Answer

Oui, quand j'ai du temps libre, je suis bénévole pour une association qui aide les personnes qui vivent dans la rue. Je voudrais faire plus pour aider, mais c'est difficile — on a besoin de plus de soutien. Si les personnes sont au chômage, elles n'ont pas les moyens de payer un logement, et il est difficile de trouver un emploi quand on est sans abri.

Yes, when I have free time, I'm a volunteer for an association that helps people who live on the streets. I would like to do more to help, but it's difficult— we need more support. If people are unemployed, they don't have the means of paying for accommodation, and it's difficult to find a job when you are homeless.

Grammar — 'avoir besoin de…'

'Avoir besoin de' means 'to need' something.

Nous avons besoin d'emplois.
We need jobs.

You can also use 'avoir besoin de' with a verb, to say you need to do something.

Le gouvernement a besoin de prendre des mesures pour aider les citoyens.
The government needs to take action to help citizens.

Practice Questions

Q1 *Translate the following sentences into French.* **WRITING**
  a) Hunger is a common problem in society. [2 marks]
  b) The results of the vote are interesting. [2 marks]
  c) Last weekend, there was a demonstration. [2 marks]
  d) I am a volunteer, and I try to help others. [2 marks]

Q2 *Listen to Lucy talk about problems in society. Complete the following sentences in English.* **LISTENING** — **Listening Track 19** *(Higher)*
  a) The government recently changed the ....
  b) The new agreement about crime will improve ....
  c) According to a survey, people have negative attitudes towards ....
  d) Though the war is over, the effects of the violence will last .... [4 marks]

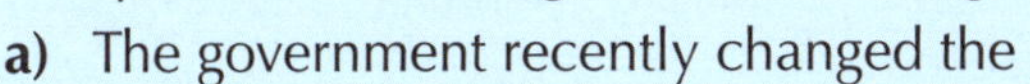

All this time I thought *chômage* was a type of French cheese...

There are a lot of new (and sometimes tricky) pieces of vocab in this section. You could write out any words you find challenging and, if you want to practise your pronunciation, you could read the sentences aloud.

Environmental and Social Issues — Vocabulary

Phewwww, I need a cup of camomile tea after all of that doom and gloom — oh wait, there's more...

Protecting the Environment

protéger	to protect
le progrès	progress
réduire	to reduce
la réduction	reduction
recycler	to recycle
le recyclage	recycling
l'énergie (f)	energy
diminuer	to lower, decrease
la science	science
le / la scientifique	scientist
l'expert(e)	expert
le chercheur / la chercheuse	researcher
rechercher	to look for, collect
l'action (f)	action
l'information (f)	information
l'effort (m)	effort

améliorer	to improve
important(e)	important
se souvenir de	to remember
sérieux / sérieuse	conscientious, responsible

Higher

conscient(e)	conscious, aware
la limite	limit
adapter	to adapt, adjust
s'adapter (à)	to get used (to)
la coopération	cooperation
l'explication (f)	explanation
transformer (en)	to transform (into)
préserver	to preserve, protect
prévenir	to let (someone) know, warn
sauver	to rescue, save

Higher

se sauver	to escape, get away
la recherche	research, search
remplacer (par)	to replace (with)
la protection	protection
nettoyer	to clean
l'utilisation (f)	use

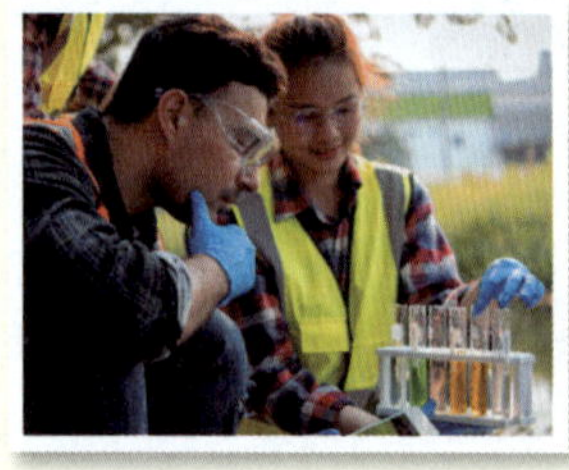

When Max said 'oui' to analysing Clare's samples, this wasn't quite what he had in mind...

Environmental Problems

l'environnement (m)	environment
la terre	earth, world, soil, land
le monde	world
la planète	planet
la nature	nature
la population	population
le climat	climate
le ciel	sky
la mer	sea
l'eau (f)	water
l'arbre (m)	tree
le bois	wood
le gaz	gas
la ressource	resource
naturel(le)	natural
menacer (de)	to threaten (to)
la menace	threat
détruire	to destroy
tuer	to kill
polluer	to pollute
le réchauffement	warming
la catastrophe	catastrophe, disaster
la crise	crisis
jeter	to throw

le plastique	plastic
les déchets (m)	rubbish
la poubelle	rubbish bin
le bruit	noise
la lumière	light
conduire	to drive
le transport	transportation
la voiture	car
la cause	cause
fabriquer	to produce, make
l'usine (f)	factory
remplir	to fill (up / in)
pire (adv.)	worse, less well
augmenter	to increase, raise
s'augmenter	to grow, expand
grave	serious, grave
le danger	danger
dangereux / dangereuse	dangerous
vide	empty
la pollution	pollution

la conséquence	consequence
l'étoile (f)	star
le papier	paper
l'espèce (f)	species
mondial(e)	worldwide, global

Higher

le changement	change
causer	to cause
contribuer	to contribute
la puissance	power
puissant(e)	powerful
la circulation	traffic
la nécessité	necessity, need
nucléaire	nuclear
la destruction	destruction
brûler	to burn, be on fire
disparaître	to disappear
risquer	to risk
le taux	rate
la qualité	quality
la quantité	quantity
la tragédie	tragedy
le pire (adv.)	the worst, the least well

Social Issues — Social Problems

le problème	*problem*
l'avantage (m)	*advantage*
l'inconvénient (m)	*snag, drawback, disadvantage, inconvenience*
le souci	*worry, concern*
la solution	*solution*
la violence	*violence*
pauvre	*poor*
l'abri (m)	*shelter*
la pauvreté	*poverty*
la faim	*hunger*
courant(e)	*current, common*
actuel(le)	*current*
moral(e)	*moral*
le chômage	*unemployment*
sale	*dirty*
inquiet / inquiète	*worried, anxious*

l'inquiétude (f)	*worry, anxiety*
inquiétant(e)	*worrying, disturbing*
cacher	*to hide*

Higher

la guerre	*war*
l'arme (f)	*weapon, arms*
le crime	*crime*
souffrir	*to suffer*
la souffrance	*suffering*
raciste	*racist*
l'ennemi(e)	*enemy*
attaquer	*to attack*
l'attaque (f)	*attack*
l'attentat (m)	*attack, assassination attempt*
le choc	*shock, clash*
commun(e)	*common*
la lutte	*struggle, fight, conflict*

Higher

lutter	*to fight, struggle*
l'attitude (f)	*attitude*
la honte	*shame*
battre	*to beat, hit*
se battre	*to fight*
la frontière	*border*
la bataille	*battle*
l'industrie (f)	*industry*
l'enquête (f)	*survey, investigation*
le débat	*debate*
l'étude (f)	*study*
la richesse	*wealth*
occidental(e)	*western*
l'humanité (f)	*humanity*

Social Issues — Politics

la politique	*politics*
voter	*to vote*
le vote	*vote*
le gouvernement	*government*
le / la président(e)	*president*
la manifestation	*demonstration, event*
la révolution	*revolution*

Higher

l'élection (f)	*election*
l'électeur / l'électrice	*elector, voter*
élire	*to elect*

Higher

(avoir) élu	*(to have) elected*
la victoire	*victory*
manifester	*to protest, demonstrate*
le parlement	*parliament*
l'état (m)	*state*
le leader	*leader*
officiel(le)	*official*
le / la porte-parole	*spokesperson, spokeswoman, spokesman*

Higher

économique	*economic*
l'économie (f)	*economy*
la république	*republic*
la démocratie	*democracy*
démocratique	*democratic*
la loi	*law*
le commerce	*trade, commerce*
libéral(e)	*liberal*
l'impôt (m)	*tax*

Social Issues — Helping Society

aider	*to help*
l'aide (f)	*help*
la société	*society*
la liberté	*liberty, freedom*
l'égalité (f)	*equality*
égal(e)	*equal*
le / la bénévole	*volunteer*
développer	*to develop*
intégrer	*to incorporate, integrate, include*
s'intégrer	*to fit in*
juste	*right, true, correct, fair*
organiser	*to organise*
s'organiser	*to get organised*

Higher

l'individu (m)	*individual*
l'humain (m)	*human*
le citoyen / la citoyenne	*citizen*
la communauté	*community*
la paix	*peace*
l'association (f)	*association*
le développement	*development*
la volonté	*will*
l'accord (m)	*agreement*
défendre	*to defend, forbid, stand up for*
contrôler	*to check, inspect, control*
la libération	*liberation*

Revision Summary Test for Section Twelve

Don't let all this vocab go to landfill — re-use and recycle it with these summary questions...

- These questions are **really tricky**, but they'll help you see **how well you know your stuff**.
- Tackle the **revision summary test** below, or scan the QR code to do it **online**.
  You can **keep track of your progress** online and see **which areas need more work**.
- There are **sample answers** here: www.cgpbooks.co.uk/BonjourExtras

Protecting the Environment ☑

1) What do these words mean in English?
   a) se souvenir   b) sérieux   c) le / la scientifique   d) diminuer   e) améliorer

2) 'If I use less energy, I am helping to protect the environment.' Translate this sentence into French.

3) In French, describe two ways you can protect the environment. Give as much detail as you can.

4) 'Il faut utiliser l'information des chercheurs et des autres experts pour faire
   des progrès et changer nos habitudes.' Translate this sentence into English.

5) 'Do you think we do enough globally to save the planet? Why / Why not?' Answer in French.

6) Translate the words below into French:
   a) to warn   b) to get used to   c) to escape   d) to replace   e) to clean

Environmental Problems ☐

7) 'Do environmental problems worry you?' Respond in French and explain your answer.

8) Translate the words below into French:
   a) world   b) tree   c) wood   d) light   e) noise   f) rubbish bin

9) 'Global warming is a threat to nature and animals.' Translate this sentence into French.

10) An environmental leaflet warns: 'La pollution commence à détruire notre planète.
    Le réchauffement de la planète est une catastrophe — il faut faire quelque chose.' What is it saying?

11) 'Dans ta région, quels sont les problèmes qui ont un effet négatif sur la nature ?' Respond in French.

12) Zoé says: 'On utilise trop de ressources tous les jours. On doit recycler les déchets plus souvent.
    C'est inquiétant parce qu'on ne pense pas à l'avenir.' Translate her words into English.

13) 'Changes to the climate have many serious consequences. It's a tragedy to see species disappear,
    forests burn and the destruction of the natural world.' Translate this passage into French.

14) 'Qu'est-ce que tu penses de l'énergie nucléaire ?' Translate the question, then respond in French.

Social Issues ☑

15) How would you say the words below in French?
    a) hunger   b) poverty   c) unemployment   d) demonstration   e) volunteer   f) right / correct

16) Louis says: 'En général, la violence n'est pas un problème dans ma région.'
    What does this sentence mean in English?

17) 'Qu'est-ce qu'on peut faire pour aider les pauvres et les personnes qui vivent dans la rue ?'
    Translate the question, then respond in French.

18) In French, explain one of the main worries you have about today's society.

19) Translate these verbs into French, then try conjugating them in the first person singular:
    a) to develop   b) to integrate   c) to organise   d) to help   e) to hide

20) Your penfriend asks you in an email: 'Quelle est la situation politique et
    économique dans ton pays ?' Translate his question, then respond in French.

21) Translate the words below into French:
    a) war   b) border   c) survey   d) spokesperson   e) to protest   f) agreement

Nouns

Nouns are words for people and objects. In French, all nouns are divided up by gender.

Every noun in French is masculine or feminine

1) Whether a noun is <u>masculine</u> or <u>feminine</u> affects loads of things. The words for '<u>the</u>' and '<u>a</u>' are <u>different</u> and, if that wasn't enough, <u>adjectives</u> change to match the gender too.

For more on how adjectives change to fit the gender, see p.121.

2) '<u>Le</u>' in front of a noun means it's <u>masculine</u>. '<u>La</u>' in front means it's <u>feminine</u>.

> le livre (m) bleu   *the blue book*

> la table (f) bleue   *the blue table*

3) When you <u>learn</u> a <u>noun</u>, learn the <u>article</u> too — don't think 'chien = dog', think '<u>le</u> chien = <u>the</u> dog'.

4) If you have to <u>guess</u> whether a noun is <u>masculine</u> or <u>feminine</u>, use these <u>rules of thumb</u>:

> <u>Masculine</u> nouns often end in...
> -age, -al, -er, -eau, -ing, -in, -ment,
> -ou, -ail, -ier, -et, -isme, -oir, -eil

> <u>Feminine</u> nouns often end in...
> -aine, -ée, -ense, -ie, -ise, -tion, -ance, -elle, -esse,
> -ière, -sion, -tude, -anse, -ence, -ette, -ine, -té, -ure

Some words have masculine and feminine versions

1) Words for people often have <u>masculine</u> and <u>feminine</u> versions to show whether the person is male or female. To form a feminine noun, <u>add 'e'</u> to the masculine noun and <u>change the article</u>.

> le président   *the president (m)*
> la présidente   *the president (f)*

2) Some nouns follow a <u>different pattern</u>. Here are a few common examples:

Masc. ending	Change	Example
-e	article only	le journaliste ⟶ la journaliste (*journalist*)
-eur	'eur' ⟶ 'rice' or 'euse'	l'acteur ⟶ l'actrice (*actor*) le chanteur ⟶ la chanteuse (*singer*)
-en	add '-ne'	le Canadien ⟶ la Canadienne (*Canadian*)

Nouns can also be made plural

1) <u>Nouns</u> in French are usually made plural by adding an '<u>s</u>' — the same as in English.

> le chien   *the dog*   ⟶   les chiens   *the dogs*

When you make a noun plural, you need to use 'les' rather than 'le' or 'la'.

2) Masculine nouns ending in '-<u>au</u>' and '-<u>eu</u>' need an '<u>x</u>' rather than an '<u>s</u>' in the plural form.

> le jeu   *the game*   ⟶   les jeux   *the games*

3) Nouns already ending in '<u>s</u>' or '<u>x</u>' do not change in the plural.

> le choix   *the choice*   ⟶   les choix   *the choices*

Grammar Questions

Add 'le' or 'la' to these words and then put the whole thing into its plural form.

1. cadeau (*present*)
2. piscine (*pool*)
3. maison (*house*)
4. pays (*country*)
5. voiture (*car*)
6. prix (*prize*)
7. langue (*language*)
8. gâteau (*cake*)

You've not learnt the gender of each word? We'll have noun of that...

The gender of each noun is included in the handy vocab lists throughout the book. No need to thank me...

Articles

'The' and 'a' are pretty useful words, so make sure you're a pro at using them in French.

'Un', 'une', 'le', 'la', 'l'', 'les' — *'A' and 'the'*

'Le', 'la' and 'les' are definite articles.
'Un' and 'une' are indefinite articles.

1) The word for '<u>a</u>' depends on the <u>gender</u> of the <u>noun</u> (see p.109).

'<u>Un</u>' is used with masculine words...

un café (m)   *a coffee*

...and '<u>une</u>' is used with feminine ones.

une boisson (f)   *a drink*

2) The word for '<u>the</u>' is <u>different</u> depending on the <u>gender</u> and <u>number</u> of the <u>noun</u>:

Masculine singular	Feminine singular	Before vowels / 'h' (sometimes)	Masc. or fem. plural
le	la	l'	les

3) For words starting with a <u>vowel</u>, 'le' or 'la' is shortened to '<u>l'</u>'. This makes them <u>easier</u> to say.

l'avion (m)   *the aeroplane*

l'émission (f)   *the programme*

4) Most words starting with '<u>h</u>' also take '<u>l'</u>' instead of 'le' or 'la'. Sadly, there's <u>no rule</u> for when this happens — you just have to <u>learn</u> it.

l'homme (m)   *the man*

'À' and 'de' change before 'le' and 'les'

1) '<u>À</u>' *(to / at)* and '<u>de</u>' *(of / from)* are <u>prepositions</u> (see p.116).

2) <u>Be careful</u> when you use them before a <u>definite article</u> (le/la/l'/les). They <u>combine</u> with 'le' and 'les' to make <u>new words</u>.

	le	la	l'	les
à +	au	à la	à l'	aux
de +	du	de la	de l'	des

Je reste à	+	le collège.	=	Je reste au collège.	*I'm staying at school.*
Je viens de	+	le Canada.	=	Je viens du Canada.	*I come from Canada.*
Je parle à	+	les élèves.	=	Je parle aux élèves.	*I'm talking to the students.*

'Du', 'de la', 'de l'' or 'des' — *'Some' or 'any'*

1) If you want to say '<u>some</u>' or '<u>any</u>', use '<u>de</u>' combined with the correct <u>definite article</u>. These are called <u>partitive articles</u>.

Je veux du pain.   *I want some bread.*

2) In <u>negative</u> sentences (see p.141), you <u>only</u> use '<u>de</u>', regardless of the gender or whether it's singular or plural.

Je n'ai pas de pain.   *I haven't got any bread.*

3) You also just use '<u>de</u>' after most <u>quantities</u> — such as '<u>beaucoup de</u>' *(lots of)* or '<u>un peu de</u>' *(a bit of)*.

J'ai un peu de pain.   *I have a bit of bread.*

4) '<u>De</u>' becomes '<u>d'</u>' before a word beginning with a <u>vowel</u>.

un verre d'eau   *a glass of water*

Grammar Questions

Fill in the gaps with either 'de', 'du', 'de la' 'des', 'au' or 'à la'.

1. L'homme a un peu ...... pain.
2. L'étudiant vient ...... Maroc.
3. Je vais ...... piscine.
4. Il va ...... marché.
5. Elle mange ...... viande.
6. On a ...... légumes.

Personally, I prefer French articles about cheese...

A definite article used before some adjectives forms a noun, e.g. 'seul' *(alone)* becomes 'le seul' *(the only one).*

Subject and Emphatic Pronouns

I hate to *subject* you to more grammar, but I can't *emphasise* enough how useful pronouns are...

Subject pronouns replace the subject of the sentence

1) Subject pronouns are words like 'I' and 'you':

I	je
You (informal, singular)	tu
He / she / it / one / we	il / elle / on
We	nous
You (formal, plural)	vous
They	ils / elles

'Il' means 'he', or 'it' for a masculine noun. 'Elle' means 'she', or 'it' for a feminine noun.

'On' is a bit like 'one' in English. It often means 'we', e.g. 'on doit recycler' (*we must recycle*).

Use 'vous' in formal situations, e.g. when talking to your teacher, or when you're talking to more than one person. Use 'tu' when talking to one person in an informal situation.

'Ils' is for a group of masculine nouns, or a mixture of masculine and feminine. 'Elles' is for a group of feminine nouns.

2) Subject pronouns can replace the subject (the person or thing doing the action in a sentence). Using them means you don't have to keep saying the same noun over and over again.

Mon frère est médecin. Il travaille à l'hôpital.   *My brother is a doctor. He works at the hospital.*

'My brother' can be replaced with 'he' to sound less repetitive.

Emphatic pronouns emphasise who you are talking about

1) Emphatic pronouns make it really clear who you're talking about.

2) They can be used in lots of different ways:

Me	moi
You (informal sing.)	toi

Him / her / it	lui / elle
Us	nous
You (formal, plural)	vous
Them (m / f)	eux / elles

Higher

C'est qui ? Moi ! C'est moi !
Who is it? Me! It's me!

Use them if the word is on its own or comes after 'c'est'.

Écoutez-moi !   *Listen to me!*

Use them for giving orders (see p.190 for more on how to do this).

Il est plus petit que toi.   *He's smaller than you.*

They're used for comparing people or things — the emphatic pronoun goes after 'que' (than).

Ce sac est pour moi.   *This bag is for me.*

They can come after prepositions such as 'for' or 'with'.

Must. Think. Of. Better. Jokes.

3) *Higher* You can add '-même' on the end of a singular emphatic pronoun to say '-self'.

Je le fais moi-même.   *I do it myself.*   Elle l'a écrit elle-même.   *She wrote it herself.*

Grammar Questions

Unscramble the words in these sentences and then translate them into **English**.

1. un achète il billet

2. pour cadeau est le toi

3. moi plus que est elle bavarde

4. avez joué moi vous avec

5. [H] elle eux mange avec [H]

6. la lui-même il envoyé lettre a

At last, my evil pronoun plan is working — moi ha ha ha ha...

You'll soon get to know subject pronouns as they're frequently used in spoken and written French. If you're struggling to find the subject in a sentence, it'll be the person or thing performing the action of the verb.

Object Pronouns

Now that you've mastered subject and emphatic pronouns, object pronouns are up next. They're a bit different from subject pronouns — they replace the person or thing affected by an action.

There are different pronouns for the direct object...

The direct object is the person or thing that the action is being done to — direct object pronouns replace the noun used as the direct object:

Me	You (inf. sing.)	Him / her / it	You (formal, pl.)		Us	Them
me	te	le / la	vous	**H**	nous	les

Remember, if <u>me</u>, <u>te</u>, <u>le</u> or <u>la</u> are followed by a word beginning with a vowel, they become <u>m'</u>, <u>t'</u>, or <u>l'</u>.

Il voit son amie.   *He sees his friend.* ⟶ Il la voit.   *He sees her.*

...and for the indirect object

Indirect objects are things that are affected by the action being done, but not directly. They often have 'to' or 'for' before them in English:

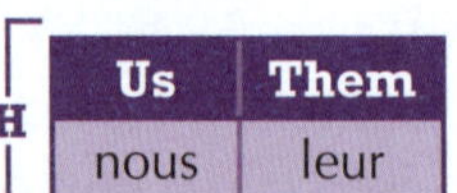

Il donne le cadeau à son amie.
He gives the present to his friend.

Me	You (inf. sing.)	Him / her / it	You (formal, pl.)		Us	Them
me	te	lui	vous	**H**	nous	leur

Il lui donne le cadeau.
He gives the present to her.

Object pronouns usually go before the verb

1) In French, you put the object pronoun before the verb.

Je la mange.   *I eat it.*

2) The perfect tense is a compound tense — a tense which uses 'avoir' or 'être' before the main verb. With compound tenses, the pronouns go before both verbs.

Elle l'a acheté.   *She bought it.*

3) Certain verbs (e.g. 'vouloir', 'pouvoir', 'devoir') are often used with the infinitive of another verb. The object pronouns go between them.

Je peux le faire.   *I can do it.*

4) In negative sentences, 'ne' goes before the object pronoun and 'pas' goes after the verb. See p.141 for more about negatives.

Il ne l'aime pas.   *He doesn't like him.*

Grammar Questions

Rewrite each sentence below, replacing the word or phrase in **bold** with the correct pronoun.

E.g. Lola donne le livre **à son cousin**. ⟶ *Lola lui donne le livre.*

1. Maria aime **le chien**.
2. J'ai lu **le livre**.
3. Je ne vois pas **toi et ton ami**.
4. Elle a envoyé le mail **à son père**.
5. Ils parlent **à moi et Pierre**.
6. Il ne visite pas **les musées**.

I used to be pro-nouns, but now I object to them...

Keep an eye out for the difference between direct object pronouns and indirect object pronouns in the third person singular form. Use 'le' / 'la' for direct object pronouns and 'lui' for indirect object pronouns.

Quick Quiz

Relative and Interrogative Pronouns

Woohoo, this section really is a pronoun party. These ones help to link bits of a sentence together.

Relative pronouns add detail

1) <u>Relative pronouns</u> introduce <u>extra information</u> about something you've mentioned in your sentence.

2) '<u>Qui</u>' is used if you're referring to the <u>subject</u> of a clause — the person or thing <u>doing</u> the action.

> la femme qui a acheté le livre   *the woman who bought the book*

3) '<u>Que</u>' is used to refer to the <u>object</u> of the clause —
the person or thing that something's <u>being done to</u>.

> le livre que la femme a acheté   *the book that the woman bought*

4) You can also use '<u>où</u>' as a relative pronoun to mean both '<u>where</u>' and '<u>when</u>'.

> La ville où il habite est jolie.
> *The town where he lives is pretty.*

> le jour où je suis parti(e)
> *the day when I left*

A clause is a group of words that has a subject and a verb. For more on verbs, see p.131.

Vincent was devastated to be saying goodbye to his suitcase.

(Higher)

You can use 'qui' and 'que' to ask questions

1) In questions, '<u>qui</u>' and '<u>que</u>' are <u>interrogative pronouns</u>.
'<u>Qui</u>' means '<u>who</u>', and '<u>que</u>' means '<u>what</u>'.

> Qui parle ?   *Who is speaking?*

> Que savez-vous ?   *What do you know?*

See p.8-9 for more on questions.

2) After <u>prepositions</u> (words such as '<u>with</u>' or '<u>for</u>' — see p.116),
'qui' stays the same but 'que' changes to 'quoi'.

> Tu parles avec qui ?   *Who are you talking to?*

> De quoi parles-tu ?   *What are you talking about?*

There are a few ways to say 'this', 'that' and 'it'

1) '<u>Ce</u>' can be used with '<u>est</u>' or '<u>sont</u>'
to mean '<u>it is</u>' or '<u>they are</u>'.

> C'est super. *It's super.*

> Ce sont bons. *They are good.*

2) '<u>Ça</u>' can be used in a sentence to mean '<u>this</u>' or '<u>that</u>'.

> Je n'aime pas faire ça. *I don't like doing that.*

3) '<u>Ceci</u>' and '<u>cela</u>' also mean '<u>this</u>' and '<u>that</u>'. They don't have to agree in gender or number
with the nouns they are replacing. They usually refer to things that aren't very specific.

> Ceci est intéressant.   *This is interesting.*

> Cela n'est pas vrai !   *That isn't true!*

'Cela' is a more formal way to say 'ça' (that).

(Higher)

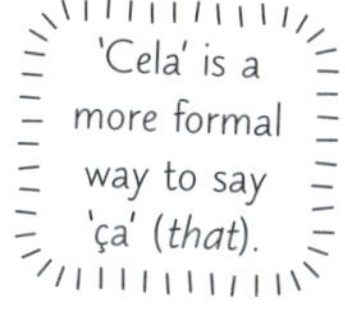

My friend didn't know the difference between 'qui' and 'que'...

...I told him it's all relative. 'Qui' is often followed by a verb, whilst 'que' is followed by a noun or pronoun.

Indefinite and Adverbial Pronouns

There are even more pronouns for unspecified things — read on for more...

Use indefinite pronouns for unspecified things

Indefinite pronouns refer to general, unspecific things, such as 'everyone' and 'something'.

quelqu'un	*someone*	plusieurs	*several*
tout le monde	*everyone*	tout	*all, everything*
quelque chose	*something*	**H** chacun(e)	*each one*

Tout le monde aime le chocolat.
Everyone likes chocolate.

Y — There, it, them

'Y' and 'en' are adverbial pronouns.

Higher

1) 'Y' can mean 'there'. It replaces the noun for a location which has already been mentioned.

Elle va à la banque.   *She's going to the bank.* → Elle y va.   *She's going there.*

2) It can also mean 'it' or 'them' when it replaces 'à' + a noun after a verb.

Je pense à cette idée.   *I'm thinking about this idea.* → J'y pense.   *I'm thinking about it.*

En — Of it, of them, some, any

Higher

1) 'En' has a few meanings — depending on the context, it can mean 'of it', 'of them', 'some' or 'any'.

As-tu peur des oiseaux ? Oui, j'en ai peur.   *Are you scared of birds? Yes, I'm scared of them.*

As-tu des légumes ? Non, je n'en ai pas.   *Have you got any vegetables? No, I don't have any.*

2) It means 'it' or 'them' when it replaces 'de' + a noun after a verb.

Tu as besoin d'aide.   *You need help.* → Tu en as besoin.   *You need it.*

3) 'En' can be used alongside 'y' in the phrase 'il y a' to say 'there are some'.

Il y a... *There is / There are...* → Est-qu'il y a des fleurs ? Oui, il y en a.
Are there any flowers? Yes, there are some.

Lara fell over three hours ago, but the smell was just so nice…

Grammar Questions

Translate these sentences into **French**, making sure you're using the correct pronouns.

1. Several finished their homework.
2. Everyone knows that it is true.
3. Someone bought the book.

Higher
4. I'm reflecting on it.
5. Do you know the castle? I've been there.
6. There are lots of them.

Why did the tall man take five cans of beans on his flight?

Because he wanted more legume. Ahem. Some indefinite pronouns, such as 'tout le monde' (*everyone*), are singular, even though they refer to multiple people or things. Conjugate the following verb with this in mind.

Section Thirteen — Nouns, Articles & Linking Words

Conjunctions

Conjunctions link words together. They help make your French sound more natural and more sophisticated too — because nothing says sophistication like accurate French conjunctions...

Use conjunctions to make longer sentences

1) Here are some <u>common</u> conjunctions:

mais	*but*	ou	*or*	donc	*therefore, so*	⌐ ne...ni	*neither...nor*
et	*and*	puis	*then, so*	ensuite	*next*	∟ en plus	*in addition, also*

2) Some conjunctions <u>link</u> two <u>clauses</u> or <u>sentences</u> together. They make the sentences sound more <u>natural</u>.

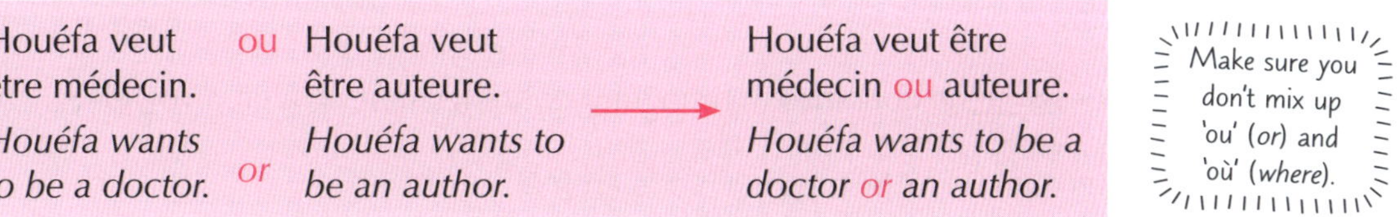

J'aime protéger la planète.	donc	Je recycle mes déchets.
I like to protect the planet.	*so*	*I recycle my rubbish.*

→ J'aime protéger la planète, donc je recycle mes déchets.

I like to protect the planet, so I recycle my rubbish.

This picture was made from 100% recycled material.

3) '<u>Ou</u>' (*or*) is used to give <u>more than one</u> option.

Houéfa veut être médecin.	ou	Houéfa veut être auteure.
Houéfa wants to be a doctor.	*or*	*Houéfa wants to be an author.*

→ Houéfa veut être médecin ou auteure.

Houéfa wants to be a doctor or an author.

Make sure you don't mix up 'ou' (*or*) and 'où' (*where*).

Some conjunctions add extra information to a sentence

1) Some conjunctions can also add <u>extra detail</u> to a <u>sentence</u>.

2) Often these conjunctions introduce a <u>reason</u> for something happening, a <u>contradiction</u> or a <u>condition</u>.

parce que	*because*	par contre	*on the other hand*	si	*if, whether*
car	*because, for*	par exemple	*for example*	même si	*even if*
cependant	*however*	comme	*like, as*	**H** puisque	*as, because*

Je déteste fumer parce que c'est mauvais pour la santé.
I hate smoking because it's bad for your health.

Même si l'exercice est difficile, il faut le faire.   *Even if exercise is difficult, you must do it.*

Some conjunctions can go at the beginning of sentences too.

Grammar Questions

Fill in the gaps with either 'comme', 'si', 'et' or 'mais'. You can only use each conjunction once.

1. Je voudrais un thé ..... une glace.
3. Je veux sortir, ... je dois finir mes devoirs.
2. ..... tu voles mon pain, je vais être triste.
4. ..... je suis fatigué, je vais me coucher tôt.

Even after all these clauses, Santa's still my firm favourite...

You probably already know lots of the conjunctions on this page — it's good practice to add them into your work as much as you can. Keep doing that, and you'll be sounding fluent in no time. Got it? Great.

Prepositions

Prepositions may not be much to look at, but size is no guarantee of power. These fellas are some of the most useful words in French — and, luckily, they're also some of the easiest to pronounce.

À — 'to', 'in' or 'at'

1) <u>Prepositions</u> are short words like 'to' and 'from'. They let you add <u>extra information</u> to sentences.

2) <u>À</u> can mean '<u>to</u>', '<u>in</u>' or '<u>at</u>'. It changes to '<u>au</u>' and '<u>aux</u>' when it's followed by '<u>le</u>' and '<u>les</u>' (see p.110).

Je suis à la maison. *I'm at home.*	Il va aux toilettes. *He's going to the toilet.*	J'habite au Canada. *I live in Canada.*

You can't use 'à' for feminine countries, or singular countries beginning with a vowel. Look at the section on 'en' below to find out more.

3) Some <u>verbs</u> are <u>followed</u> by '<u>à</u>' when they go before a <u>noun</u> or <u>another verb</u>. Here are some examples:

s'intéresser à	*to be interested in*	réussir à	*to succeed in*
jouer à	*to play (a game)*	penser à	*to think about*

'En' — 'in' or 'to'

1) '<u>En</u>' is used instead of '<u>à</u>' for <u>feminine</u> countries and singular countries starting with a <u>vowel</u>.

Hugo habite en Angleterre. *Hugo lives in England.*	Je vais en France en mai. *I'm going to France in May.*

2) You should use '<u>en</u>' to say <u>how long</u> an action takes:

Elle a lu l'article en cinq minutes.   *She read the article in five minutes.*

Higher

3) You <u>don't</u> need 'le', 'la' or 'les' after 'en'.

Il partira en hiver.   *He will leave in the winter.*

4) 'En' is also used before <u>present participles</u> to mean 'while' or 'by' (see p.143).

Elle est tombée en courant.   *She fell while running.*

Tom left in hope of catching some winter sun. He arrived looking like an idiot.

De — 'of' or 'from'

1) '<u>De</u>' often means '<u>of</u>'.

French doesn't use apostrophes to show belonging — it uses 'de' instead.

un groupe d'étudiants *a group of students*		les vêtements de ma sœur *my sister's clothes*

2) 'De' can also mean '<u>from</u>'. It changes to '<u>du</u>', '<u>de la</u>' or '<u>des</u>' when used with a <u>definite article</u> (see p.110).

Chérif revient de la plage.   *Chérif is coming back from the beach.*

3) Some <u>verbs</u> are <u>followed by 'de'</u> when they go <u>before a noun</u>. Learn these important examples:

changer de	*to change*	jouer de	*to play (an instrument)*
avoir besoin de	*to need*	partir de	*to leave*

Chez Natalie — *At Natalie's*

These prepositions are <u>really important</u> for your exams — try to learn them all.

avec	*with*	à cause de	*because of*	par	*by, per*	parmi	*among*
sans	*without*	chez	*at (the place of)*	malgré	*despite*	**H** vers	*towards*

Lots of prepositions relate to time

1) Prepositions of <u>time</u> tell you <u>when</u> something happened <u>in relation to</u> something else.

pour	*for*	avant (de)	*before*	jusque	*up to, until*
pendant	*during*	après	*after*	**H** depuis	*for, since*

'Jusque' is normally followed by 'à' or 'en', e.g. 'jusqu'à la fin' (*until the end*).

2) Use '<u>pendant</u>' for actions that have <u>already happened</u>, or <u>will happen</u> in the future, but <u>aren't happening</u> now.

> J'ai travaillé dans un hôtel pendant deux ans. *I worked in a hotel for two years.*

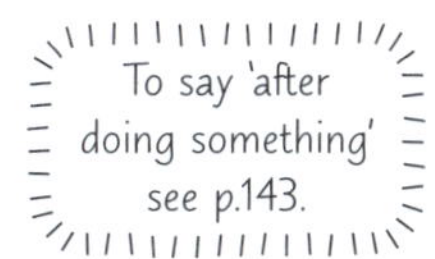

3) '<u>Pour</u>' (*for*) is used very similarly to in English, but with time, it's <u>only used</u> in the <u>future tense</u>.

> Myriam va aller en Suisse pour une semaine. *Myriam is going to go to Switzerland for a week.*

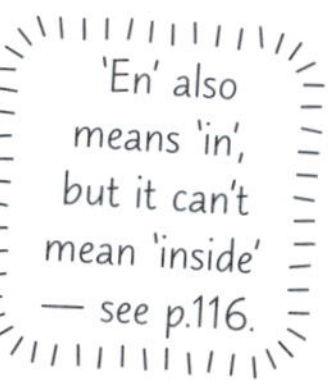

Higher

4) Use '<u>depuis</u>' for actions that <u>began in the past</u>, but are <u>still continuing</u> today (see p.133).

> J'habite à la campagne depuis trois mois. *I've lived in the countryside for three months.*

5) You can use '<u>avant de</u>' with an <u>infinitive</u> to say '<u>before</u> doing something'.

> Avant de partir, j'ai mangé avec ma famille. *Before leaving, I ate with my family.*

To say 'after doing something' see p.143.

Use prepositions to describe position

1) Some prepositions describe the <u>location</u> of <u>something</u> or <u>someone</u>.

sur	*on*	à côté de	*next to*	dans	*in*
sous	*under*	derrière	*behind*	devant	*in front of*

'Dans' is also used to say how much time will pass before an event. E.g. 'dans cinq minutes' (*in five minutes*).

'En' also means 'in', but it can't mean 'inside' — see p.116.

2) '<u>Dans</u>' (*in*) is normally used to describe when something is <u>actually inside</u> something else.

> Mon livre est dans mon sac. *My book is in my bag.*

Grammar Questions

Choose the correct preposition to complete each sentence below.

1. Je suis (à / chez) Nadia avec Tom.
2. La route passe (sous / dans) le pont.
3. Je joue (au / du) foot.
4. Il était en vacances (pendant / pour) deux semaines.
5. Il y a un train (à / dans) deux minutes.
H 6. Je travaille à la boulangerie (depuis / par) six mois. **H**

Depuis or not depuis — that is the question...

Make sure you learn the prepositions on this page — they'll help you to express time, location or direction.

Nouns, Articles & Linking Words — Grammar List

All the essential info from this grammar section is listed on these pages — they're handy to turn to for a quick recap.

Determiners

A determiner is a word that comes before a noun in a sentence. They provide extra information about the quantity of the noun, and what it is referring to.

le	*the (m)*
la	*the (f)*
les	*the (pl.)*
un	*a, an (m)*
une	*a, an (f)*
du	*some (m)*
de la	*some (f)*
des	*some (pl.)*
ce / cet	*this, that (m)*
cette	*this, that (f)*
ces	*these, those*

Subject Pronouns

Subject pronouns replace the person or thing doing the action.

je	*I*
tu	*you (sing. informal)*
il	*he, it (m)*
elle	*she, it (f)*
on	*everyone, you, one, we (informal)*
nous	*we*
vous	*you (formal, pl.)*
ils	*they (m)*
elles	*they (f)*

Direct Object Pronouns

Direct object pronouns replace the person or thing the action is being done to.

me	*me*		nous	*us*
te	*you (sing. informal)*	H	vous	*you (pl.)*
vous	*you (sing. formal)*		les	*them*
le	*him, it (m)*			
la	*her, it (f)*			

Indirect Object Pronouns

Indirect object pronouns replace the person or thing that is being affected by the action, but not directly.

me	*me*		nous	*us*
te	*you (sing. informal)*	H	vous	*you (pl.)*
vous	*you (sing. formal)*		leur	*them*
lui	*him, her, it*			

Nouns

In French, all nouns are either masculine or feminine.
Common endings for masculine nouns are:

-age, -al, -er, -eau, -ing, -in, -ment, -ou, -ail, -ier, -et, -isme, -oir, -eil

Common endings for feminine nouns are:

-aine, -ée, -ense, -ie, -ise, -tion, -ance, -elle, -esse, -ière, -sion, -tude, -anse, -ence, -ette, -ine, -té, -ure

Most masculine nouns describing people can be made feminine:

le président	→	la président**e**	*president*
le journaliste	→	la journaliste	*journalist*
le chant**eur**	→	la chant**euse**	*singer*
l'act**eur**	→	l'act**rice**	*actor*
l'Européen	→	l'Européen**ne**	*European*

There are also different ways of making singular nouns plural:

le chien	→	les chien**s**	*dog(s)*
le château	→	les château**x**	*castle(s)*
le concours	→	les concours	*competition(s)*

You can add definite articles (le/la/les) before some adjectives to form nouns. E.g. 'français' (*French*) becomes 'les Français' (*French people*).

Negative Subject Pronouns

H	personne ne + verb	*nobody + verb*
	rien ne + verb	*nothing + verb*

See p.123 for more on possessive adjectives.

'À' and 'de'

Some articles change when combined with 'à' or 'de':

à + le	→	au
à + les	→	aux
de + le	→	du
de + les	→	des

Possessive Adjectives

Possessive adjectives show that something belongs to someone.

mon	*my (m)*
ma	*my (f)*
mes	*my (pl.)*
ton	*your (m)*
ta	*your (f)*
tes	*your (pl.)*
son	*his / her / its (m)*
sa	*his / her / its (f)*
ses	*his / her / its (pl.)*
notre	*our (m/f)*
nos	*our (pl.)*
votre	*your (m/f)*
vos	*your (pl.)*
leur	*their (m/f)*
leurs	*their (pl.)*

Emphatic Pronouns

Emphatic pronouns emphasise who you are talking about.

moi	*me*		eux	*them (m)*
toi	*you (sing. inf.)*		elles	*them (f)*
lui	*him, it (m)*		moi-même	*myself*
elle	*her, it (f)*		toi-même	*yourself (sing. inf.)*
nous	*us*		lui-même	*himself*
vous	*you (formal, pl.)*		elle-même	*herself*

(Higher: lui, elle, nous, vous) — (Higher: moi-même, toi-même, lui-même, elle-même)

Reflexive Pronouns

Reflexive pronouns refer back to a person or thing and mean 'self'.

me	*myself*
te	*yourself (sing. informal)*
se	*himself / herself itself / oneself*
nous	*ourselves, each other*
H vous	*yourselves, each other*
se	*themselves, each other*

See p.140 for more on forming reflexives.

Indefinite Pronouns

Indefinite pronouns refer to nouns that are general and unspecific.

quelqu'un	*somebody, someone*
tout le monde	*everybody, everyone*
quelque chose	*something*
plusieurs	*several*
tout	*all, everything*
certains	*some people*
H chacun(e)	*each person*

Adverbial Pronouns

'Y' and 'en' replace nouns and adverbs. 'Y' replaces the noun for a location that has already been mentioned. 'Y' is also used with verbs followed by 'à'.

E.g. Il est allé à Nice. ➝ Il y est allé.
He went to Nice. ➝ *He went there.*

'En' replaces the noun after expressions of quantity.

E.g. Nous avons trois oiseaux. ➝ Nous en avons trois.
We have three birds. ➝ *We have three of them.*

'En' is also used with verbs followed by 'de'.

Relative Pronouns

Relative pronouns introduce extra information about something already mentioned in the sentence.

'Qui' and 'que' can also be used as interrogative pronouns — see p.113.

'Qui' refers to the subject of a clause — the person or thing doing the action.

E.g. J'ai un frère qui est médecin.
I have a brother who is a doctor.

'Que' refers to the object of the clause — the person or thing that something's being done to.

E.g. L'ordinateur que j'utilise est cassé.
The computer that I use is broken.

'Où' can mean 'where' or 'when'.

E.g. Le collège où j'ai étudié a fermé.
The school where I studied has closed.

Demonstrative Pronouns

Demonstrative pronouns replace things in a sentence that are unspecific. They don't have to agree in gender or number.

ça	*that, it*	➝ J'aime ça.
ce	*it*	➝ C'est bon.
ceci	*this*	➝ Ceci est intéressant.
H cela	*that*	➝ J'adore cela.

Prepositions

à	*at, to, in, on*		pendant	*during*
en	*in, by, on, to, at*		sur	*on*
de	*of, from*		sous	*under*
avec	*with*		à côté de	*next to*
sans	*without*		derrière	*behind*
à cause de	*because of*		devant	*in front of*
chez	*at (the place of)*		dans	*in*
par	*by, per*		entre	*between*
malgré	*despite, in spite of*		voilà	*right, there, here*
			sauf	*except*
avant (de)	*before*		depuis	*since, for*
après	*after*		vers	*towards*
jusque	*to, up to, until*		dès	*from, as soon as*
pour	*for, in order to*		parmi	*among*
contre	*against*			

Conjunctions

mais	*but*
et	*and*
ou	*or*
puis	*then, so*
donc	*so, therefore*
ensuite	*next*
parce que	*because*
car	*because, for*
cependant	*however*
par contre	*on the other hand*
par exemple	*for example*
comme	*like, as*
si	*if, whether*
même si	*even if*
ne...ni	*neither...nor*
H puisque	*as, because*
en plus	*in addition, also*

Revision Summary Test for Section Thirteen

You've powered through this grammar section. Before a well-earned rest, try these questions.

- These questions are **hard**, but they'll really help you see **how well you know your stuff**.
- Tackle the **revision summary test** below, or scan the QR code to do it **online**.
  You can **track your progress** online and see **which areas need more work**.
- There are **sample answers** for the test here: www.cgpbooks.co.uk/BonjourExtras

Nouns and Articles

1) For each of these words, swap the indefinite article ('un' or 'une') for the definite
   article ('le', 'la', or 'l''): a) une maison   b) un thé   c) un hôpital   d) une heure

2) Make these nouns feminine: a) l'écrivain   b) l'étudiant   c) le serveur   d) le chrétien

3) Make these nouns plural: a) la rue   b) le pays   c) le chien   d) le jeu   e) le niveau

4) Fill in the blanks with 'à' combined with the correct definite article ('le', 'la', 'l', 'les'),
   then translate each sentence into English.   a) Je vais ..... campagne.
   b) Elle habite ..... Maroc.   c) Tu as demandé ..... profs ?   d) Je m'intéresse ..... sciences.

5) Fill in the blanks with the correct article ('de', 'du', 'de la' or 'des').   a) Je viens ..... Sénégal.
   b) Je mange beaucoup ..... fromage.   c) Il n'a pas ..... fleurs.   d) J'ai acheté ..... viande.

6) Translate these phrases into French: a) I want some food and water.   b) I won some money.

Pronouns

7) In French, list all the subject pronouns and emphatic pronouns you need to know for your tier.

8) Rewrite the sentences below, replacing each phrase in bold with the correct object pronoun.
   a) Je regarde **la pièce**.   b) Tom lit **le journal**.   c) Tu envoies la lettre **à ton oncle**.

9) Translate these indefinite pronouns into French: a) everyone   b) something   c) several

10) Translate this sentence into French: 'I watched that yesterday — it's funny.'

11) Fill in the gaps in these sentences with 'quoi', 'qui' or 'que' :
   a) ..... aime le théâtre ?   b) ..... fabriquent-ils ?   c) On a besoin de ..... pour la recette ?

12) Circle the relative pronoun in each phrase and then translate the phrase into English.
   a) le pays où j'ai passé mes vacances   b) le blog que j'ai lu hier soir

13) How do you say this in French: 'Me? I prefer to do it myself.'

14) Rewrite the sentences below, replacing each phrase in bold with the correct object pronoun.
   a) Elle déteste **les chiens**.   b) Je vais parler **à mes amis** demain.

15) Use 'y' or 'en' to fill in the gaps in these sentences. Then translate them into English.
   a) Tu ..... es déjà allée ?
   b) J'ai oublié les gâteaux. Est-ce que tu peux m'..... acheter ?
   c) On va ..... aller demain.

Conjunctions and Prepositions

16) Translate these conjunctions into English: a) ensuite   b) par contre   c) donc   d) comme

17) Fill in the gaps using an appropriate conjunction, then translate each sentence into English.
   a) Je vais rester à la maison ..... j'ai mal à la tête.
   b) J'ai oublié mon sac ..... je dois retourner au collège.

18) Fill in each gap with 'à' or 'de': a) aider .....   b) avoir besoin .....   c) réussir .....

19) Translate these sentences into French:
   a) The dog is under the table.   c) It's my brother's bag.   e) The party is at Camille's.
   b) There's a café next to the park. d) I think about you.   f) She's going to France for two days.

20) Translate the following sentences into French:
   a) Before swimming, I would like to run.   b) She's been waiting for you since 09:30.

Adjective Agreement

Adjectives are ideal for adding detail to your sentences — they'll help you bag the higher marks.

French adjectives agree with the thing they're describing

1) <u>Adjectives</u> are words used to <u>describe</u> things, for example 'beautiful', 'sad', 'funny' and 'difficult'.

2) In French, most adjectives <u>change</u> to match the <u>gender</u> and <u>number</u> of the noun they're <u>describing</u>.

3) You often add '<u>-e</u>' to the adjective if the noun being described is <u>feminine</u> (see p.109).

le livre vert	*the green book*		la table verte	*the green table*

You don't need to add an 'e' if the adjective already ends in 'e', or an 's' if the adjective already ends in 's'.

4) Add '<u>-s</u>' to the adjective if the noun being described is <u>plural</u> (see p.109). This means that with <u>feminine plurals</u>, you're adding '<u>-es</u>'.

des romans intéressants	*interesting novels*		des idées intéressantes	*interesting ideas*

Some adjectives have their own rules

Adjectives with <u>certain endings</u> follow <u>different</u> rules:

Ending	Examples	Masculine singular	Feminine singular	Masculine plural	Feminine plural
-al	génial (*brilliant*), normal (*normal*)	génial	géniale	géniaux	géniales
-x	heureux (*happy*), sérieux (*responsible*)	heureux	heureuse	heureux	heureuses
-en	quotidien (*daily*), végétarien (*vegetarian*)	quotidien	quotidienne	quotidiens	quotidiennes
-er	dernier (*last*), cher (*expensive*)	dernier	dernière	derniers	dernières
-el	industriel (*industrial*), essentiel (*essential*)	industriel	industrielle	industriels	industrielles
-f	sportif (*sporty*), positif (*positive*)	sportif	sportive	sportifs	sportives

Some adjectives are iRREGuLaR

1) These adjectives are <u>irregular</u>.

2) Some <u>change</u> before <u>masculine singular</u> nouns starting with a <u>vowel</u> or a mute '<u>h</u>' because it's <u>easier</u> to say.

3) Some adjectives <u>never change</u>, e.g. '<u>super</u>' (*great*).

Masc. sing.	Before a masc. sing. noun starting with a vowel	Fem. sing.	Masc. plural	Fem. plural
vieux (*old*)	vieil	vieille	vieux	vieilles
beau (*beautiful*)	bel	belle	beaux	belles
nouveau (*new*)	nouvel	nouvelle	nouveaux	nouvelles
fou (*mad*)	fol	folle	fous	folles
long (*long*)	long	longue	longs	longues

Grammar Questions

Translate these phrases into **French**, making sure the adjectives agree.

1. a proud mother
2. a traditional meal
3. a sad girl
4. a blue door
5. the dangerous dogs
6. the new neighbours
7. the first day
8. an international star

I swear those adjectives and nouns are up to something...

...they're always in agreement. The ending of your adjective depends on the gender and number of the noun you're describing — the adjective almost always needs to agree. Don't forget those irregulars either.

Quick Quiz

More Adjectives

Adjectives have various functions — they can be indefinite, possessive or demonstrative. Or they can just be descriptive. Whew, sounds exhausting... they need to put their feet up and enjoy a brew.

Most adjectives go after the word they're describing...

1) In French, <u>most</u> adjectives follow the <u>noun</u> (the word they're describing).

> J'ai une voiture rapide.   *I have a fast car.*

Adjectives are always masculine singular after 'c'est', e.g. 'c'est nouveau' (*it's new*).

> Je suis entré(e) dans la chambre bleue.   *I entered the blue bedroom.*

2) You can also <u>use adjectives</u> in sentences with <u>verbs</u> such as '<u>être</u>' (*to be*) and '<u>devenir</u>' (*to become*). The adjective still needs to <u>agree</u> with the noun though.

> Ils sont prêts maintenant.
> *They are ready now.*

> Elle devient grande.
> *She is becoming tall.*

Tillie's desire for a wild ride would remain unfulfilled — John refused to go over 20mph...

...but there are some odd ones which go before

1) These adjectives almost always go <u>before</u> the noun:

bon(ne)	*good*	vieux / vieil / vieille	*old*	petit(e)	*small, short*
mauvais(e)	*bad*	nouveau / nouvel / nouvelle	*new*	grand(e)	*big, tall*
jeune	*young*	beau / bel / belle	*beautiful*	joli(e)	*pretty*
haut(e)	*high*	premier / première	*first*	faux / fausse	*false*

Adjectives have to agree, regardless of whether they come before or after the noun.

> J'ai une petite maison avec un joli jardin et une belle vue.
> *I have a small house with a pretty garden and a beautiful view.*

2) Some adjectives <u>change meaning</u> depending on whether they go <u>before</u> or <u>after</u> a word. For example, 'ancien(ne)' means '<u>former</u>' before a noun, but '<u>ancient</u>' after it. '<u>Propre</u>' is another example:

> ma propre maison   *my own house*

> ma maison propre   *my clean house*

Indefinite adjectives describe words in a more general way

1) '<u>Quelque</u>' (*some*), '<u>chaque</u>' (*each*), '<u>plusieurs</u>' (*several, many*), '<u>même</u>' (*same*), '<u>autre</u>' (*other*) and '<u>tout</u>' (*all*) are all examples of <u>indefinite adjectives</u>.

2) 'Chaque' and 'plusieurs' are <u>invariable</u> — they <u>never</u> change form to agree with the <u>gender</u> or <u>quantity</u> of the word they're describing.

3) 'Quelque', 'même' and 'autre' <u>don't</u> have a set of <u>different</u> forms for masculine or feminine, but they do add an '-s' when they change from <u>singular</u> to <u>plural</u>.

> J'ai acheté quelques bonbons au magasin.   *I bought some sweets at the shop.*

4) 'Tout' has different forms for <u>masculine</u>, <u>feminine</u> and <u>plural</u>.

Masc. sing.	Fem. sing.	Masc. pl.	Fem. pl.
tout	toute	tous	toutes

Words like 'my' and 'your' show who an object belongs to

1) <u>Possessive adjectives</u> show that something <u>belongs</u> to someone. They go <u>before the noun</u>.

notre cousin   *our cousin*

	My	Your (inf. sing.)	His / her / its	Our	Your (formal, pl.)	Their
Masculine singular	mon	ton	son	notre	votre	leur
Feminine singular	ma	ta	sa	notre	votre	leur
Plural	mes	tes	ses	nos	vos	leurs

2) They <u>match</u> the <u>thing being described</u> — <u>NOT</u> the <u>person</u> it belongs to. The <u>different</u> forms are in the table on the right.

3) So, for example, it's <u>always</u> '<u>mon</u> père' (*my father*) even if a <u>girl</u> is talking.

Voici mon père et ma mère.
Here are my dad and my mum.

This means that 'son', 'sa' or 'ses' could all mean either 'his', 'her' or 'its'. You can usually tell which one it's meant to be by using the context.

4) <u>Before vowels</u>, or words starting with 'h' that take 'l'', you use the <u>masculine</u> possessive adjective — even if the noun is <u>feminine</u>. It's <u>easier to say</u>.

Mon amie s'appelle Akiko.
My friend's called Akiko.

Ce, cet, cette, ces — *This, these*

1) To say '<u>this</u>' or '<u>these</u>', you need the right form of '<u>ce</u>':

Masculine singular	Masc. words that take 'l''	Feminine singular	Masculine or feminine plural
ce	cet	cette	ces

Choose the one that matches the noun you're describing.

2) These are <u>demonstrative adjectives</u> — they're used when you use '<u>this</u>' as a <u>describing word</u>.

Ce film est excellent.   *This film is excellent.*

Cet homme est grand.   *This man is tall.*

Aucun(e) — *no, none (of them)*

Higher

1) <u>Aucun(e)</u> can refer to both <u>objects</u> and <u>people</u>. Like most adjectives, it <u>agrees</u> with the <u>gender</u> of the noun it's describing.

2) However, it is only used in the <u>singular</u> form, even when it's describing <u>plural</u> nouns.

3) When you use '<u>aucun(e)</u>', you have to put '<u>ne</u>' <u>before</u> the <u>verb</u>.

Je n'ai aucune idée.   *I have no idea.*

You use 'veut' here because the verb needs to agree with 'aucun', not 'amis'.

Aucun de mes amis ne veut partir.   *None of my friends want to leave.*

Lucien had literally no idea what he'd come out for.

Grammar Questions

Complete these sentences using the correct translations of the words in brackets.

1. ...... père n'aime pas ...... nouvelle voiture. (my, his)
2. ...... tes amis habitent dans ...... quartier. (all, our)
3. ...... hôtel est grand. (this)
4. ...... factrice a ...... lettres. (this, their)

Without adjectives, the world would be... hmmm...

You should be using adjectives all the time, so it's vital you can use them correctly and earn those marks in the exams. Remember, proper placement is key — otherwise you may change the meaning entirely...

Quick Quiz

Comparative and Superlative Adjectives

Adjectives have other functions too — they're useful for comparing things or making strong statements. For example, you might want to say this book is the best you've ever read...

Plus...que, moins...que, aussi...que — More than, less than, as...as

1) 'Plus', 'moins' and 'aussi' can be used with adjectives to compare things. Add 'que' after the adjective to say 'than'.

These are called comparative adjectives.

> Je suis plus rapide que toi.
> *I am faster than you.*

> Layla est moins forte que moi.
> *Layla is weaker than me.*

When using comparatives, the adjectives still need to agree with the noun they're describing.

2) If you want to say something is the same, use 'aussi...que' (as...as).

> Ce film est aussi passionnant que le premier.   *This film is as thrilling as the first one.*

There are some exceptions

1) There are some odd ones out when it comes to making comparisons — just like in English.

2) With these adjectives, you don't use 'plus' or 'moins':

bon(ne)	*good*	meilleur(e)	*better*
mauvais(e)	*bad*	pire	*worse*

> Les légumes sont meilleurs qu'hier.   *The vegetables are better than yesterday.*

Adding 'le', 'la' or 'les' makes it 'the most' or 'the least'

1) You can add an article to the adjective 'meilleur' to make it a superlative. It means 'the best'.

> Ses nouvelles chansons sont les meilleures.   *Her new songs are the best.*

2) 'Le plus' and 'le moins' form superlative adjectives — they're used to say something is 'the most' or 'the least', rather than directly comparing it to something else.

3) If you're using a superlative adjective, you have to make the article (*the*) agree as well.

> Cette fleur est la plus belle.   *This flower is the most beautiful.*

> Mokhtar et Françoise sont les plus jeunes.   *Mokhtar and Françoise are the youngest.*

4) You can also add an article to the adjective 'pire' to make it a superlative. It means 'the worst'.

Higher

Grammar Questions

Translate these phrases into **French**. Remember those pesky adjective agreements...

1. Théo is smaller than Pauline.
2. I am younger than you.
3. Julie is as intelligent as Léa.
4. Spring is better than winter.
5. His ideas are the worst.
6. Poole is the biggest town.

Superlatives are just the worst...

Hopefully it's *plus* clear *que* before when it comes to using comparative adjectives. Remember — 'plus', 'moins' or 'aussi' + adjective + 'que' is the way to go. Unless something is 'meilleur' or 'pire', of course...

Adverbs

Quick Quiz

Words that describe actions are called adverbs. Like adjectives, they're useful for adding more detail to your French and gaining you marks. Nifty. Just keep an eye out for those bothersome exceptions.

Adverbs describe how something's being done

Gérard had finally found the perfect dance partner.

1) In English, you don't say 'I dance <u>perfect</u>' — you add '<u>-ly</u>' on the end to say 'I dance <u>perfectly</u>'. '<u>Perfectly</u>' is an <u>adverb</u>.

2) In French, you add '<u>-ment</u>' on the <u>end</u> of an <u>adjective</u> to make an <u>adverb</u>. But <u>first</u> you have to make sure it's in the <u>feminine</u> form (see p.121).

parfait (*perfect*) ⟶ parfaite (feminine form) + -ment ⟶ parfaitement (*perfectly*)

3) Unlike adjectives, <u>adverbs</u> don't have to <u>agree</u> — they're <u>describing</u> an <u>action</u>, <u>not</u> the <u>person</u> doing it.

Il danse parfaitement.
He dances perfectly.

Elle danse parfaitement.
She dances perfectly.

Elles dansent parfaitement.
They dance perfectly.

There are a few exceptions

1) Some adverbs don't follow the rules above.

2) If an adjective ends in '<u>-ant</u>' or '<u>-ent</u>', the '<u>ant</u>' or '<u>ent</u>' is replaced with '<u>-amment</u>' or '<u>-emment</u>'.

récent (*recent*) ⟶ réc- + -emment ⟶ récemment (*recently*)
patient (*patient*) ⟶ pati- + -emment ⟶ patiemment (*patiently*)
courant (*common*) ⟶ cour- + -amment ⟶ couramment (*commonly*)

'Lent' (*slow*) follows the normal rule to become 'lentement' (*slowly*).

Some adverbs don't use '-ment'

Some <u>adverbs</u> are quite <u>different</u> from their <u>adjectives</u>.

bon(ne)   *good*   ⟶   bien   *well*
mauvais(e)   *bad*   ⟶   mal   *badly*
rapide   *fast, quick*   ⟶   vite   *fast, quickly*

Je joue bien.   *I play well.*

Il écrit mal.   *He writes badly.*

Grammar Questions

Turn these adjectives into adverbs, then translate the **adverb** into **English**.

1. triste
2. négatif
3. sérieux
4. général
5. fier
6. évident
7. actuel
8. intelligent
9. heureux

Higher 10. exact
Higher 11. suffisant
Higher 12. rare

I searched fruitlessly for bananas — Clementine had them all...

It can get confusing remembering which rules apply to adjectives and adverbs. The important thing to remember is that adverbs describe the <u>action</u> of the subject — so they don't need a feminine or plural form.

More Adverbs

As well as describing how something's done, adverbs can also specify when and where it's done.

Adverbs can describe when something's being done

1) **Adverbs of time** describe <u>when</u>, or <u>how frequently</u> something happens. They are usually placed at the beginning or end of the sentence, or after the verb they are describing.

souvent	*often*	avant	*before*	tôt	*early*
parfois	*sometimes*	déjà	*already*	tard	*late*
jamais	*never*	maintenant	*now*	bientôt	*soon*

2) You can also form <u>phrases</u> to describe the <u>day</u>, <u>month</u>, <u>season</u> or <u>year</u> something happens using the adjectives '<u>dernier</u>' (*last*) and '<u>prochain</u>' (*next*). They can go at the <u>start</u> or <u>end</u> of a <u>sentence</u>.

L'année dernière, je suis allé(e) au Québec.   *Last year, I went to Quebec.*

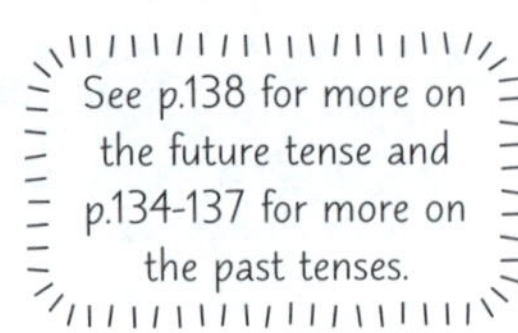

3) Words to describe <u>different days</u> can be used as adverbs.

hier *yesterday*   aujourd'hui *today*   demain *tomorrow*

Some adverbs describe location

<u>Adverbs of place</u> usually come <u>after</u> the <u>verb</u> in a phrase or sentence.

ici	*here*
là	*there*
là-bas	*over there*
partout	*everywhere*
loin	*far*
près	*nearby*

Sa voiture est là-bas.   *His car is over there.*

Il pleut partout.   *It's raining everywhere.*

Je fais mes devoirs ici.   *I do my homework here.*

If there's a direct object, e.g. 'mes devoirs', the adverb of place normally goes after it.

Phrases can be used as adverbs

You can often use <u>adverbial phrases</u> in the <u>same</u> way as <u>adverbs</u>. <u>Longer</u> adverbial phrases usually come at the <u>beginning</u> of a <u>sentence</u>.

Adverbial phrases are often really handy when you're giving your opinion on something.

en général	*in general*
par exemple	*for example*
tous les jours	*every day*

En général, j'aime les chiens.   *In general, I like dogs.*

Grammar Questions

Translate these sentences into **French**. Make sure you use the right adverbs.

1. I play football over there.
2. You ('tu') work every day.
3. I often go to town by bus.
4. There's rubbish everywhere.
5. I leave tomorrow.
6. Last year, I went to France.

Want to hear a joke about déjà vu? Oh, you've heard it before...

It's useful to remember that adverbs don't always end in '-ment', so the best way to figure out if a word is an adverb is to look at the type of word it's modifying. From there, you'll be able know where it should go.

Comparative and Superlative Adverbs

Adverbs can be used to compare how you do things, or to say you're the best or worst at something.

Comparative adverbs compare actions

1) 'Plus' is used to say someone is doing something 'more...' than someone else. Use 'que' to say 'than'.

'Que' becomes 'qu'' before a vowel.

Fatima lit plus vite qu'Axel.   *Fatima reads more quickly than Axel.*

2) You can use 'moins' to say 'less...' — use it in the same way as 'plus'.

Axel lit moins souvent que Diane.   *Axel reads less often than Diane.*

3) When something is done equally, use 'aussi...que' to say 'as...as'.

Diane lit aussi lentement que Jules.   *Diane reads as slowly as Jules.*

Emmanuel and Agathe were starting a new chapter together...

4) You can also use 'plus' or 'moins' without an adverb.

Jules lit plus que Marie.   *Jules reads more than Marie.*

'Bien' and 'mal' are the odd ones out

'Bien' (*well*) and 'mal' (*badly*) don't follow the rules. You just need to learn their comparative forms.

bien *well* ⟶ mieux *better*   mal *badly* ⟶ pire *worse*

The most, the best, the worst...

1) 'Le plus...' and 'le moins...' are superlatives — you use them to say someone does something 'the most...' or 'the least...'.

C'est Lola qui attend le plus patiemment.   *Lola waits the most patiently.*

2) You always use 'le' because adverbs don't have to agree with the person doing the action — they're describing the action itself. This is different from adjectives.

3) 'Bien' and 'mal' also have irregular superlative forms:

mieux *better* ⟶ le mieux *the best*   pire *worse* ⟶ le pire *the worst*

Higher

Grammar Questions

Fill in the gaps in these sentences by translating the words in brackets into **French**.

1. Je travaille .... toi. (as quickly as)

2. Lucie court .... Dorian. (more often than)

3. Elle mange .... vous. (less than)

Higher

4. Morgane chante .... (the best)

5. Je nage .... régulièrement. (the least)

6. Qui marche .... rapidement ? (the most)

Higher

Comparison is the thief of joy — a bit like exams...

In the reading exam, keep your eyes peeled for comparatives — they can change the meaning of a sentence.

Quick Quiz

Quantifiers and Intensifiers

Intensifiers and quantifiers seem a bit intimidating, but they're nowhere near as bad as they sound...

Intensifiers strengthen what you're saying

1) Adverbs such as '<u>trop</u>' (*too*) and '<u>assez</u>' (*quite*) can add <u>detail</u> to your sentences. They're called <u>intensifiers</u>.

2) <u>Intensifiers</u> can be used with <u>adjectives</u> — they always go <u>before</u> them. You can use them to <u>emphasise</u> the <u>adjective</u>, or to say <u>what</u> something's like.

trop	*too*	particulièrement	*particularly*
très	*very*	entièrement	*entirely*
assez	*quite*	relativement	*relatively*
vraiment	*really*	plutôt	*rather*
		extrêmement	*extremely*

Higher

Camille est trop sérieuse.
Camille is too serious.

La géographie est assez intéressante.
Geography is quite interesting.

3) The <u>adjectives</u> still have to <u>agree</u> but the <u>intensifiers don't</u>.

Cette montagne est relativement petite.   *The mountain is relatively small.*

4) You can also use intensifiers with other <u>adverbs</u>. They go <u>before</u> the adverb they modify.

Il mange vraiment lentement.   *He eats really slowly.*

J'écris très vite.   *I write very quickly.*

Quantifiers help you say how many or how much

1) <u>Quantifiers</u> let you say roughly how much of something you have, without being specific, e.g. '<u>lots</u>' or '<u>not many</u>'.

2) Many are formed using <u>adverbs</u>, followed by '<u>de</u>'.

trop de	*too much, too many*
beaucoup de	*a lot of*
un peu de	*a bit of, a little*
plusieurs	*several, many*

J'ai beaucoup de passe-temps.   *I have lots of hobbies.*

3) With <u>quantifiers</u>, '<u>de</u>' doesn't change to agree with the noun, but it changes to '<u>d'</u>' before a <u>vowel</u>.

Nous avons un peu d'argent.   *We have a bit of money.*

Il a trop d'examens.   *He has too many exams.*

Louis-Philippe decided that after he had rolled in all his money, he would invest in a new brown suit.

Grammar Questions

Translate these sentences into French.

1. She is very beautiful.
2. They have lots of friends.
3. He has a bit of water.
4. The teacher is really strict.
5. The man eats too much cheese.
6. The food is quite good.

Intensifiers will make your French incredibly good — yes, really...

It's worth remembering to scatter some of these quantifiers and intensifiers throughout your written and spoken French when you can — it'll show the examiner you're a real grammar pro. Full marks all round.

Adjectives and Adverbs — Grammar List

Here's a roundup of the words you need to describe people, things, actions... and just about anything else.

Regular Adjectives

In French, adjectives usually change to match the gender and number of the word they're describing. To make an adjective feminine, you normally add '-e' to the end.

général(e)	*general*	évident(e)	*obvious*
plein(e)	*full*	précis(e)	*precise, accurate*
haut(e)	*high*	vrai(e)	*true*
étroit(e)	*narrow, tight*	lourd(e)	*heavy*
normal(e)	*normal*	exact(e)	*exact, correct*
original(e)	*original*	suffisant(e)	*sufficient*

Other adjectives follow different rules — see p.121.

essentiel(le)	*essential*	positif / positive	*positive*
possible	*possible*	négatif / négative	*negative*
impossible	*impossible*	entier / entière	*whole, full*
pareil(le)	*the same*	ordinaire	*ordinary*
faux / fausse	*false*	régulier / régulière	*regular*
nécessaire	*necessary, required*	indispensable	*essential*
		rare	*rare*

Higher

Make most adjectives plural by adding '-s'. E.g. grande → grande<u>s</u>
However, there are some exceptions. E.g. normal → norm<u>aux</u>

See p.121 for more on how to form plural adjectives.

Irregular Adjectives

Some adjectives follow irregular patterns in French.

vieux / vieil / vieille / vieux / vieilles *old*
beau / bel / belle / beaux / belles *beautiful*

Adverbs

Adverbs are usually formed by taking the feminine version of an adjective and adding '-ment', although some are irregular.

également	*also, too, as well, equally*	simplement	*simply*
rapidement	*quickly, rapidly*	actuellement	*at present*
facilement	*easily*	effectivement	*effectively*
lentement	*slowly*	exactement	*exactly*
seulement	*only*	absolument	*absolutely*
tellement	*so much*	complètement	*completely*
bien	*well*	autrement	*differently*
mal	*badly*	certainement	*certainly*
vite	*fast, quickly*	heureusement	*fortunately, luckily*
même	*even*	parfaitement	*perfectly*
aussi	*also, too, as well*	largement	*widely*
encore	*again, yet*	évidemment	*obviously*
déjà	*already, yet*	suffisamment	*sufficiently*
alors	*so, well, then*	apparemment	*apparently*
puis	*then, so*	notamment	*notably*
surtout	*especially, above all*	ailleurs	*elsewhere*
ensuite	*next*	pourtant	*yet, nonetheless, nevertheless*
souvent	*often*		
d'abord	*first of all, firstly, to start with*		

Higher

Indefinite Adjectives

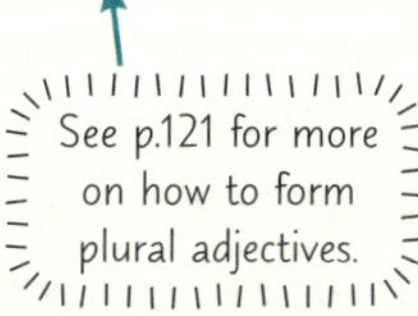

quelque	*some*
même	*same, even*
autre	*other*
chaque	*each*
certain(e)	*certain*
tout(e)	*all*
nombreux / nombreuses	*many, numerous, plentiful*

H

Remember that some adjectives come before the noun they're describing.

Quantifiers & Intensifiers

trop	*too*
trop de	*too much, too many*
très	*very*
assez	*quite*
beaucoup de	*a lot of*
un peu de	*a bit of, a little*
peu de	*few, little*
plusieurs	*several, many*
vraiment	*really*
presque	*almost*
plutôt	*rather*
extrêmement	*extremely*
particulièrement	*particularly*
entièrement	*entirely, completely*
relativement	*relatively*

Higher

Comparative & Superlative Adjectives and Adverbs

plus de	*more*
moins de	*less*
plus...que	*more...than*
moins...que	*less...than*
aussi...que	*as...as*
meilleur(e)	*better (adj.)*
mieux	*better (adv.)*
le / la / les meilleur(e)(s)	*the best (adj.)*
pire	*worse*
le / la / les plus	*the most*
le / la / les moins	*the least*
le mieux	*the best (adv.)*
le / la / les pire(s)	*the worst (adj.)*
le pire	*the worst (adv.)*

Higher

Revision Summary Test for Section Fourteen

You've hopefully got to grips with another big chunk of grammar. Have a go at some questions.

- Yep, these questions are **hard** — they'll really help you see **how well you know your stuff**.
- Tackle the **revision summary test** below, or scan the QR code to do it **online**.
  Use the CGP RevisionHub to **track your progress** and see **which areas need more work**.
- You can find **sample answers** here: www.cgpbooks.co.uk/BonjourExtras

Adjectives ☐

1) Choose the correct adjective in brackets, then translate each sentence into English.
   a) Axel a les yeux (bleu / bleus).
   c) J'aime les maisons (moderne / modernes).
   b) La (premier / première) question est difficile.
   d) Mes frères sont assez (sportifs / sportives). ☑

2) Fill in each gap by translating the adjective in brackets into French.
   a) Ces rues sont très .... (long)
   c) Hugo a une .... partenaire. (new)
   b) Je dors .... la journée. (all)
   d) Elle adore les .... fleurs. (beautiful) ☑

3) What's the French for...   a) my small dog?   b) your grey car?   c) their room?   d) our meal? ☑

H 4) Translate these phrases into French using 'aucun' or 'aucune':
   a) None of my friends are here.   b) We have no cars. ☑

Adverbs ☐

5) Circle the adverbs in these sentences, then translate each sentence into English.
   a) Aujourd'hui, je vais manger au café.   c) Il se lève souvent à six heures.
   b) Tu parles lentement.   d) Je dois aller à l'hôpital immédiatement. ☑

6) Translate these sentences into French, using the adverb form of the adjective in the brackets:
   a) He plays well. (bon)   b) She sings badly. (mauvais)   c) You run quickly. (rapide) ☑

7) Turn these adjectives into adverbs: a) facile   b) normal   c) récent   d) vrai ☑

8) Translate into French: a) The airport is quite far from the town.   c) I saw the castle over there.
                            b) Yesterday, I ran in the park.   d) I returned late last night. ☑

H 9) Turn each of these adjectives into adverbs:
   a) vif   b) efficace   c) précis   d) régulier   e) rare   f) ordinaire ☑

Comparatives and Superlatives ☐

10) Translate these sentences into French:
    a) I'm taller than you.
    c) The films are worse than the books.
    b) Eva writes as well as Toni.
    d) They go out less often than us. ☑

11) Choose the correct option to complete each sentence.
    a) Elle est aussi gentille **que / qui** son ami.   c) Cette idée est **meilleur / meilleure**.
    b) Cette maison est plus **petit / petite** que l'autre.   d) Tu joues **mieux / meilleur** que lui. ☑

12) Translate these sentences into French:
    a) His new songs are the best.
    c) She is the youngest but I am the smallest.
    b) These clothes are the least expensive.
    d) This region is the most beautiful. ☑

13) What do these sentences mean in English?
    a) Hier, le cours de maths était le pire.   b) Nous sommes les plus forts. ☑

14) Translate this sentence into French:
    'Katie studies more regularly than Léo, but Léo studies the most conscientiously.' ☑

Quantifiers and Intensifiers ☐

15) Use quantifiers or intensifiers to fill in the gaps, using the clues in brackets to help you.
    a) Elle a .... argent. (more than she needs)   c) Mon ami a .... livres. (a large amount)
    b) L'acteur a eu .... succès. (a small amount)   d) J'ai acheté .... cafés. (quite a few) ☑

Verbs in the Present Tense

You need to know the present tense inside out and back to front — it crops up all over the place.

Verbs are action words

1) A <u>verb</u> is an <u>action</u> word. 'Eat', 'sing' and 'jump' are all <u>examples</u> of English <u>verbs</u>.

2) <u>Actions</u> can take place in different <u>times</u> — or <u>tenses</u> — the past, present or future.

3) To put a verb in a <u>tense</u>, you need to know its <u>infinitive</u>, e.g. 'être' (*to be*). They're in this <u>form</u> in the <u>dictionary</u>.

The present describes something happening now

1) Use the <u>present tense</u> to describe something <u>that's occurring now</u>.

> Je mange du pain. *I am eating bread. / I eat bread.*

You can use the French present tense to say that something 'is happening' or that something 'happens'.

2) You should also use the <u>present tense</u> to describe something that <u>happens regularly</u>.

> Le lundi, je joue au football. *I play football on Mondays.*

3) <u>Verbs</u> in the present tense have <u>different endings</u>, but you always start by finding the verb's <u>stem</u>.

regarder / *to look* Begin by putting the verb in the <u>infinitive</u>.	**-er** Remove the <u>last two</u> letters of the infinitive.	**regard-** / *the stem* You're left with the <u>stem</u>.

Infinitive	Stem
parler	parl-
choisir	chois-
entendre	entend-

4) Then you add the correct <u>endings</u> to the <u>stem</u>.

5) In French, there are <u>three groups</u> of verbs — verbs ending in '<u>-er</u>', '<u>-ir</u>' and '<u>-re</u>':

The 'il'/'elle'/'on' form of the present tense for '-re' verbs doesn't have an ending.

'-er' endings

I	je	-e
you (inf. sing.)	tu	-es
he/she/it/one	il/elle/on	-e
we	nous	-ons
you (pl., formal)	vous	-ez
they (m/f)	ils/elles	-ent

'-ir' endings

I	je	-is
you (inf. sing.)	tu	-is
he/she/it/one	il/elle/on	-it
we	nous	-issons
you (pl., formal)	vous	-issez
they (m/f)	ils/elles	-issent

'-re' endings

I	je	-s
you (inf. sing.)	tu	-s
he/she/it/one	il/elle/on	—
we	nous	-ons
you (pl., formal)	vous	-ez
they (m/f)	ils/elles	-ent

E.g. 'regarder' (*to watch*)
'regard-' (the stem)
+ '-ons' ('nous' ending)
nous regardons (*we watch*)

E.g. 'choisir' (*to choose*)
'chois-' (the stem)
+ '-issent' ('elles' ending)
elles choisissent (*they choose*)

E.g. 'entendre' (*to hear*)
'entend-' (the stem)
+ nothing ('elle' ending)
elle entend (*she hears*)

Some '-ir' and '-re' verbs follow different patterns — see p.146-148.

Grammar Questions

Put the verbs below into the present tense. The subject is given in brackets.

1. parler (je)
2. trouver (tu)
3. remplir (nous)
4. répondre (je)
5. finir (elles)
6. commencer (vous)
7. perdre (on)
8. vendre (vous)

Ahhh, the present tense — it's a gift...

Regular verbs are absolutely everywhere. Do yourself a favour and learn these conjugations off by heart.

Irregular Verbs in the Present Tense

Annoyingly, irregular verbs don't follow a set pattern, so there aren't any concrete rules you can apply to them. The only way to revise them properly is to learn them off by heart. Ready, set, go...

Some of the most useful verbs are irregular

Lots of <u>important verbs</u> are <u>irregular</u> — this means that they <u>don't follow</u> the usual rules. Here are some of the <u>most common</u> ones that you <u>need to know</u> for your exams:

avoir (to have)

I have	j'ai
you (inf. sing.) have	tu as
he/she/it/one has	il/elle/on a
we have	nous avons
you (pl., formal) have	vous avez
they have	ils/elles ont

You sometimes use 'avoir' in French when you would use 'to be' in English. E.g. 'j'ai peur' (*I'm scared*), 'il a froid' (*he's cold*).

être (to be)

I am	je suis
you (inf. sing.) are	tu es
he/she/it/one is	il/elle/on est
we are	nous sommes
you (pl., formal) are	vous êtes
they are	ils/elles sont

faire (to make / do)

I make	je fais
you (inf. sing.) make	tu fais
he/she/it/one makes	il/elle/on fait
we make	nous faisons
you (pl., formal) make	vous faites
they make	ils/elles font

Remember, you don't usually pronounce the last letter of a word in French if it's a consonant. This means that some endings (e.g. 'fais' and 'fait') are spelt differently but sound exactly the same.

aller (to go)

I go	je vais
you (inf. sing.) go	tu vas
he/she/it/one goes	il/elle/on va
we go	nous allons
you (pl., formal) go	vous allez
they go	ils/elles vont

devoir (must / to have to)

I must	je dois
you (inf. sing.) must	tu dois
he/she/it/one must	il/elle/on doit
we must	nous devons
you (pl., formal) must	vous devez
they must	ils/elles doivent

'Devoir' is a verb, but 'les devoirs' is a noun meaning 'homework'.

Flo wanted to know why Phil couldn't just sit down normally...

vouloir (to want)

I want	je veux
you (inf. sing.) want	tu veux
he/she/it/one wants	il/elle/on veut
we want	nous voulons
you (pl., formal) want	vous voulez
they want	ils/elles veulent

pouvoir (to be able to / can)

I can	je peux
you (inf. sing.) can	tu peux
he/she/it/one can	il/elle/on peut
we can	nous pouvons
you (pl., formal) can	vous pouvez
they can	ils/elles peuvent

Don't mix up 'savoir' and 'connaître' — 'savoir' means to know something. To say that you know somebody, use 'connaître'.

savoir (to know)

I know	je sais
you (inf. sing.) know	tu sais
he/she/it/one knows	il/elle/on sait
we know	nous savons
you (pl., formal) know	vous savez
they know	ils/elles savent

Grammar Questions

Each verb below is spelt incorrectly. Using the verb tables above, rewrite each of the phrases correctly.

1. nous doivons
2. je veut
3. vous êtez
4. tu doix
5. elle vat
6. ils faient
7. elles pouvent
8. on saix
9. ils avont
10. nous faions

Phew — this page is so in<u>tense</u>...

It's pretty hard to speak or write French without these verbs — read this page through again, then close the book and try to write down as many of them as you can without looking. Repeat until you've got them all.

More about the Present Tense

'Really — more? What else is there to say about the present tense?' Well, I'm so glad you asked...

Verbs sometimes stay in their infinitive

1) When one verb <u>follows</u> another in a sentence or phrase, the <u>first verb</u> needs to be in the right form, but the <u>second verb</u> is <u>always</u> in the <u>infinitive</u>.

> Je veux aider les autres.   *I want to help other people.*
>
> 'Veux' is the <u>first verb</u> in the sentence — it's in the <u>first person singular</u> form of the present tense. Because '<u>aider</u>' comes <u>directly after</u> 'veux', it's in the <u>infinitive</u> form.

2) Some <u>verbs</u> can be followed <u>directly</u> by an <u>infinitive</u>, but a few verbs need a <u>preposition</u> in between.

commencer à	*to begin*	encourager à	*to encourage*	arrêter de	*to stop*
réussir à	*to succeed*	essayer de	*to try*	éviter de	*to avoid*
apprendre à	*to learn*	décider de	*to decide*		

> J'apprends à conduire la voiture de mon père.   *I'm learning to drive my dad's car.*

3) You can also use the <u>infinitive</u> as a <u>noun</u> where you'd use an '<u>-ing</u>' word in English.

> Faire du sport, c'est amusant.   *Doing sport is fun.*

'Depuis' can be used with the present tense

1) 'Depuis' means '<u>since</u>' or '<u>for</u>' (see p.117).

2) If the <u>action</u> you're talking about is <u>still going on</u> today, use the <u>present tense</u>.

> Il habite à Belfast depuis 1997.   *He's lived in Belfast since 1997.*

Even though the action began in the past, the person is still living in Belfast — so you need the present tense.

Higher

Verb phrases can tell you when something happened

1) Use '<u>être en train de</u>' to say that you're in the <u>middle</u> of doing something.

> Je suis en train de manger.   *I am in the middle of eating.*

2) '<u>Venir de</u>' followed by an infinitive means '<u>to have just done something</u>'.

> Je viens de quitter l'école.   *I've just left school.*

Higher

Marguerite could usually be found in the middle of eating.

Grammar Questions

Translate these sentences into **French**.

1. I like eating.
2. Studying is awful.
3. They ('elles') try to sing.
4. He continues to speak.
5. He has just left.
6. You've ('vous') been here since yesterday.

Honestly, I could talk infinit-iv-ely about the present tense...

There's no hard and fast way of knowing which preposition goes with which verb. They're often different to what you'd use in English, so it's best just to learn any prepositions whenever you come across a new verb.

Quick Quiz

The Perfect Tense

Now you've got the hang of the present, it's time to look at the past — that's if you can remember what life was like before revision, of course. The perfect tense can be tricky, so read carefully.

Use the perfect tense for completed actions

1) Use the perfect tense to describe an action that started and finished in the past.

2) In French, it has three parts — a subject, the present tense of 'avoir' or 'être' and a past participle.

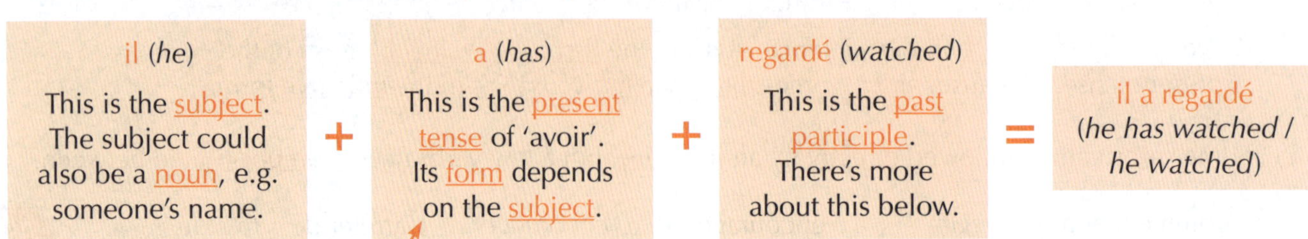

il (*he*)		a (*has*)		regardé (*watched*)		il a regardé
This is the subject. The subject could also be a noun, e.g. someone's name.	+	This is the present tense of 'avoir'. Its form depends on the subject.	+	This is the past participle. There's more about this below.	=	(*he has watched / he watched*)

3) You don't always need the 'have' part in English, but you must have it in French. For example, 'il a regardé' can be translated as 'he has watched' or 'he watched'.

Most verbs use 'avoir' in the perfect tense

1) Use the present tense of 'avoir' to make the 'have' part of the perfect tense:

avoir (to have)

I have	j'ai
you (inf. sing.) have	tu as
he/she/it/one has	il/elle/on a
we have	nous avons
you (pl., formal) have	vous avez
they have	ils/elles ont

Remember that the present tense of 'avoir' is irregular. See p.132 for other irregular verbs.

Elle a mangé.   *She has eaten. / She ate.*

Nous avons parlé.   *We've spoken. / We spoke.*

2) Get the past participle of a verb by finding the verb's stem (see p.131) and adding on the correct ending.

3) Verbs ending in '-er', '-ir' and '-re' each have a different ending:

Past participles

'-er' verbs	stem	+	é	e.g. regarder:	regard + é = regardé
'-ir' verbs	stem	+	i	e.g. choisir:	chois + i = choisi
'-re' verbs	stem	+	u	e.g. entendre:	entend + u = entendu

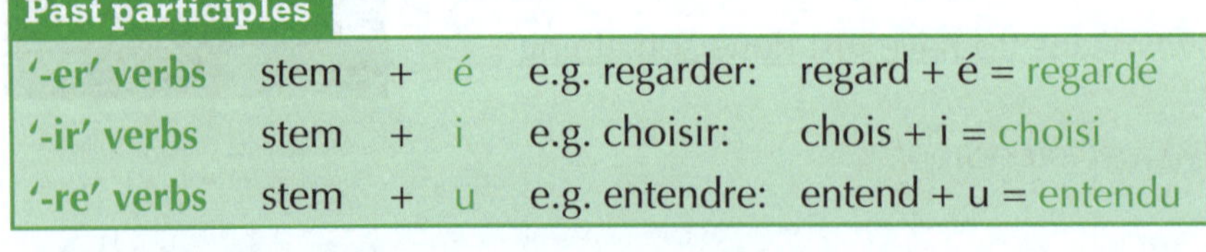

j'ai cherché   *I have searched / I searched*

vous avez dormi   *you have slept / you slept*

ils ont perdu   *they have lost / they lost*

Antoine was always losing his glasses...

4) Many '-ir' and '-re' verbs have irregular past participles — see the next page.

Irregular past participles look a bit different

1) Some verbs have <u>irregular past participles</u> — they <u>don't use</u> the same endings as regular verbs.

2) These are the most important ones:

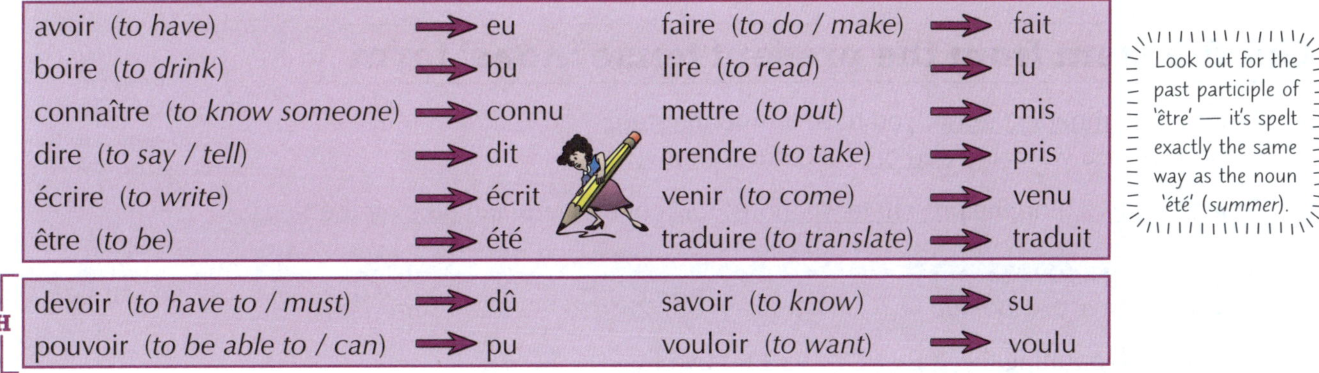

avoir *(to have)*	→ eu	faire *(to do / make)*	→ fait
boire *(to drink)*	→ bu	lire *(to read)*	→ lu
connaître *(to know someone)*	→ connu	mettre *(to put)*	→ mis
dire *(to say / tell)*	→ dit	prendre *(to take)*	→ pris
écrire *(to write)*	→ écrit	venir *(to come)*	→ venu
être *(to be)*	→ été	traduire *(to translate)*	→ traduit

Look out for the past participle of 'être' — it's spelt exactly the same way as the noun 'été' *(summer)*.

H devoir *(to have to / must)*	→ dû	savoir *(to know)*	→ su
pouvoir *(to be able to / can)*	→ pu	vouloir *(to want)*	→ voulu

Some verbs take 'être' instead of 'avoir'

To see how the present tense of 'être' is formed, see p.132.

1) A few verbs use '<u>être</u>' instead of '<u>avoir</u>' to form the <u>perfect tense</u>.

aller	*to go*	partir	*to leave*	mourir	*to die*	retourner	*to return*
venir	*to come*	sortir	*to go out*	devenir	*to become*	entrer	*to go in*
revenir	*to come back*	descendre	*to go down*	rester	*to stay*	rentrer	*to go back*
arriver	*to arrive*	monter	*to go up*	tomber	*to fall*	naître	*to be born*

2) Just like with '<u>avoir</u>' verbs, the correct <u>present tense form</u> of '<u>être</u>' is needed.

All reflexive verbs (see p.140) take 'être' in the perfect tense.

Tao est allé à l'école.   *Tao went to school.*

Il s'est levé.   *He got up.*

Verbs that take 'être' have to agree

1) <u>All verbs</u> that take 'être' in the perfect tense <u>have to agree</u> with their <u>subject</u>.

2) The <u>past participle</u> gains an '<u>s</u>' if the subject is <u>plural</u>, an '<u>e</u>' if it's <u>feminine</u> and '<u>es</u>' if it's <u>feminine and plural</u>.

When a reflexive verb is in the perfect tense, the present tense of 'être' always goes between the reflexive pronoun and the past participle.

Les filles sont parties.   *The girls have left.*

Elle s'est lavée dans la rivière.   *She washed herself in the river.*

Grammar Questions

Translate these phrases into **French**, using the **perfect tense**.
Remember to check if each verb takes 'avoir' or 'être'.

1. they ('elles') put
2. I went
3. you ('tu') said
4. we've ('nous') recycled
5. she arrived
6. he took
7. they ('ils') came back
8. I washed myself

'J'ai fini cette page.' — That's a perfect sentence, if you ask me...

Grab some paper, cover up the list of 'être' verbs above and write down as many as you can. Repeat until you can get them all without looking. For an extra challenge, write down the past participle for each one.

The Imperfect Tense

Like English, French has more than one past tense — time is complicated, after all. The imperfect tense is really useful, and dead easy to form. Once you've got the hang of it, you won't look back.

Get the stem from the present tense 'nous' form

1) To form the imperfect tense, you have to find the stem of the verb you want and add on the correct ending.

2) To get the stem, find the present tense 'nous' form of the verb and take off the '-ons'.

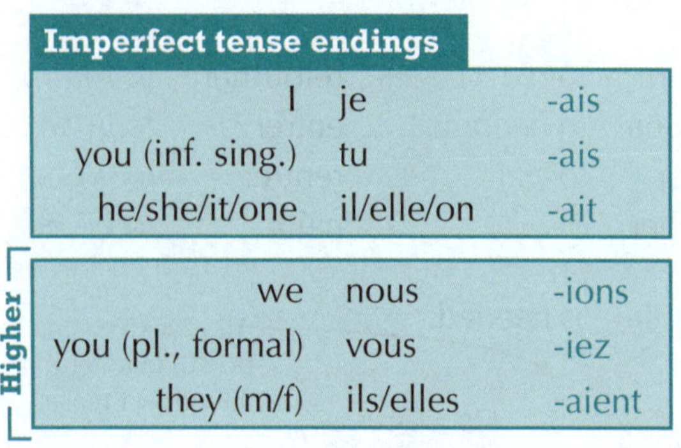

regardons
we look / we are looking

Begin by putting the verb in the 'nous' form of the present tense.

−

-ons

Remove the '-ons' from the end.

=

regard-
the stem

You're left with the stem.

> The only verb that's irregular in the imperfect tense is 'être' (see below).

> See p.131 for how to find the 'nous' form of the present tense.

3) When you've got the stem, add on the ending you need. The endings are the same for all verbs:

Imperfect tense endings		
I	je	-ais
you (inf. sing.)	tu	-ais
he/she/it/one	il/elle/on	-ait
Higher we	nous	-ions
you (pl., formal)	vous	-iez
they (m/f)	ils/elles	-aient

Tu m'attendais.   *You were waiting for me.*

Il venait le mardi.   *He used to come on Tuesdays.*

Higher
Nous faisions beaucoup de bruit.
We were making a lot of noise.

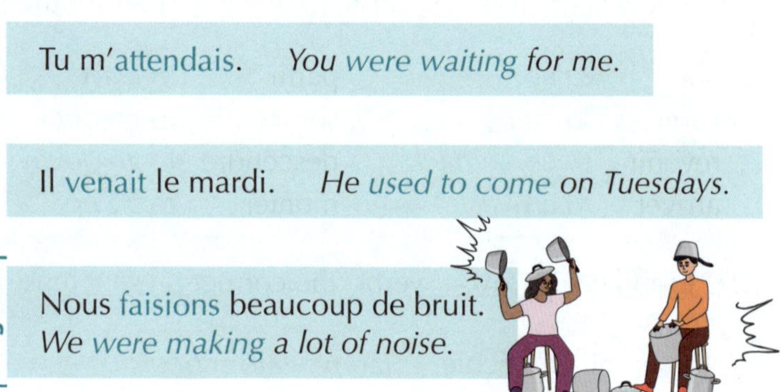

'Être', 'avoir' and 'faire' crop up a lot

1) Some verbs crop up more than others, so it's a good idea to become really familiar with them.

2) 'Être' is irregular in the imperfect tense — its stem is 'ét-'. It uses the regular endings, though:

être (to be)		
I	j'	étais
you (inf. sing.)	tu	étais
he/she/it/one	il/elle/on	était
Higher we	nous	étions
you (pl., formal)	vous	étiez
they (m/f)	ils/elles	étaient

C'était génial.   *It was great.*

'C'était' (it was) is the past tense of 'c'est' (it is). 'C'était' + an adjective is useful for descriptions.

La pièce était sale.   *The room was dirty.*

H Nous étions fatigués.   *We were tired.*

3) All the other verbs are regular — they form the imperfect tense following the normal rules.

4) Make sure you learn 'avoir' and 'faire' inside out. They're used in lots of handy phrases.

Il y avait...   *There was... / There were...*

Il faisait froid.   *It was cold.*

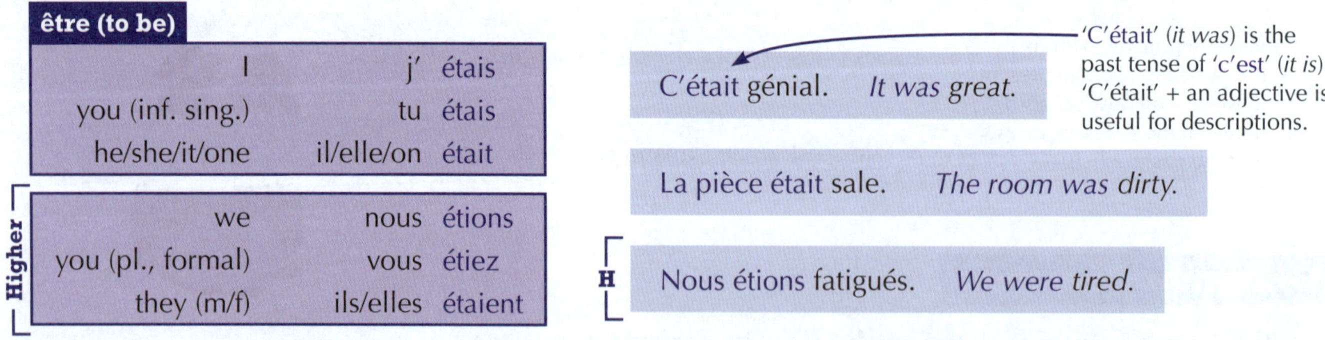

Bryn was glad he'd brought his big coat.

Use the imperfect for descriptions in the past

1) Use the <u>imperfect tense</u> to <u>describe something</u> or <u>someone</u> in the past.

Imperfect	Perfect
I was going	I went
she was running	she ran
we were waiting	we waited

C'était rouge.   *It was red.*

Il faisait chaud.   *It was hot.*

Yann était heureux de la voir.   *Yann was happy to see her.*

2) The imperfect tense can also describe an <u>action</u> that '<u>was happening</u>' in the past. It's different to the perfect tense (see p.134) because the action <u>isn't complete</u>.

J'attendais le train.   *I was waiting for the train.*

The person hadn't finished waiting for the train, so the action is incomplete.

Il parlait à l'avocat.   *He was talking to the lawyer.*

Higher

3) When one action <u>interrupts</u> another action in a past tense sentence, the <u>first action</u> is left <u>unfinished</u>. This means that it needs to be in the <u>imperfect tense</u>.

The second action is in the perfect tense.

Je lisais quand elle est arrivée.   *I was reading when she arrived.*

Il dormait quand le soleil s'est levé.   *He was sleeping when the sun rose.*

Use the imperfect for what used to happen

You also use the <u>imperfect tense</u> to talk about what you <u>used to do</u>.

You can use the imperfect for something you used to do regularly, or something you used to do in general.

J'allais au cinéma tous les jeudis.   *I used to go to the cinema every Thursday.*

Nous habitions dans la capitale du Maroc.   *We used to live in the capital of Morocco.*

Quand j'avais dix ans, je jouais de la guitare.   *When I was ten, I used to play the guitar.*

Grammar Questions

Decide whether the verbs below should be in the perfect or the imperfect tense, then translate each sentence.

1. I ran.
2. It was fun.
3. We ('on') were dreaming.
4. He was boring.
5. They ('ils') have eaten.
6. She has studied.
7. I used to play football.
8. I was buying bread.

Once upon a time, I used to have a life...

It's important you know which tense to use in different situations — generally, you use the perfect tense for completed actions and the imperfect tense for actions that took place over a longer time period. Simple.

Quick Quiz

Talking about the Future

You need to be able to talk about things that'll happen in the future, too. Don't worry — there are no crystal balls, just some good old verb conjugations. Everything you need to know is on this page.

Use 'I'm going' + infinitive

The immediate future is the easiest future tense — it uses the present tense form of 'aller' and an infinitive.

je vais (*I am going*)		danser (*to dance*)		Je vais danser.
This is the present tense of 'aller' (see p.132).	**+**	The next verb goes in the infinitive (see p.133).	**=**	(*I am going to dance.*) A sentence about the future.

Il va couper le pain.   *He's going to cut the bread.*

Ces étudiants vont voyager cet été.   *These students are going to travel this summer.*

Use 'I will' to form the proper future tense

Higher

1) Using the proper future tense in French is the same as saying 'will' in English, e.g. 'I will bake'.

2) To form the future tense of regular '-er' verbs, you need to find the verb's infinitive (see p.133) and add on the correct endings. The endings are the same for all verbs:

The endings might look familiar because they're similar to the present tense of 'avoir'.

Future tense endings

I	je	-ai		we	nous	-ons
you (inf. sing.)	tu	-as		you (pl., formal)	vous	-ez
he/she/it/one	il/elle/on	-a		they (m/f)	ils/elles	-ont

je regarderai   *I will look*   il terminera   *he will finish*

Ils mangeront des fruits.   *They will eat fruit.*

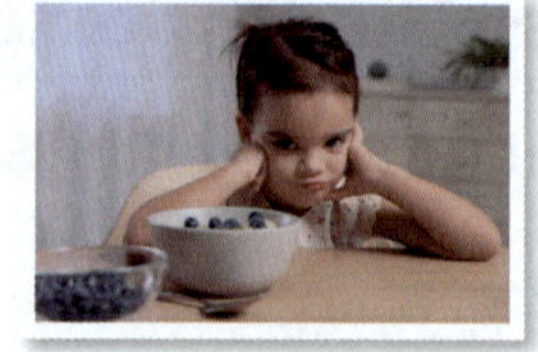

Lucie made it very clear that she definitely would not eat the fruit.

3) Some important verbs are irregular in the future tense — their stems aren't in the infinitive form:

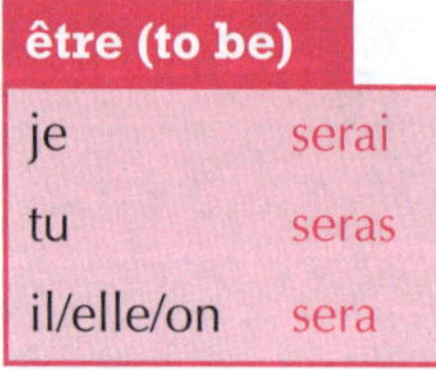

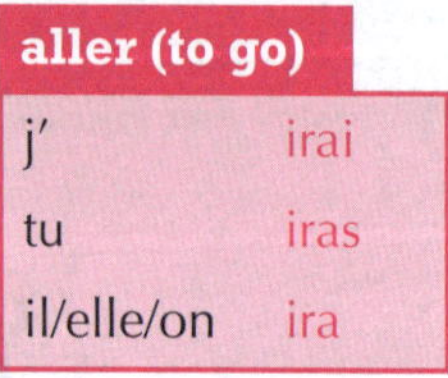

faire (to do)

je	ferai
tu	feras
il/elle/on	fera

The stems are the only irregular part of these verbs — they all use the normal endings listed above.

Grammar Questions

Put these phrases into the immediate future tense. If you're taking the Higher-tier exams, put the ones marked 'H' into the proper future too.

1. tu peux	**3.** nous finissons	**5.** elles disent	**7.** il va (H)	**9.** j'ai (H)
2. ils sont	**4.** tu regardes (H)	**6.** vous faites	**8.** elle vient	**10.** on vend

Your future will be bright — if you turn on all the lights...

Just like in English, French speakers often use the present tense to talk about something that'll happen in the near future, e.g. 'je sors ce soir' (*I'm going out this evening*) or 'ça commence demain' (*it starts tomorrow*).

The Conditional

The conditional is a bit of a mishmash of different tenses. Fortunately, you already know half of it...

'Je voudrais' — *I would like*

1) The French conditional is used when you say 'would' in English.

2) 'Vouloir' is really useful in the conditional — you can use it lots in your speaking assessment:

vouloir (to want)	
I would like	je voudrais
you (inf. sing.) would like	tu voudrais
he/she/it/one would like	il/elle/on voudrait

'Vouloir' is often followed by an infinitive. Look at p.133 for more on infinitives.

Je voudrais partir. *I'd like to leave.*

Elle voudrait du lait. *She would like some milk.*

The conditional for '-er' verbs = infinitive + imperfect endings

Higher

1) Forming the conditional is pretty straightforward for '-er' verbs — you take the verb's infinitive and add on the endings you learnt for the imperfect tense.

regarder (*to look*)	ais	je regarderais (*I would look*)
This is an infinitive ending in '-er'.	**+** This is the ending for the first person singular imperfect tense (see p.136).	**=** This is the first person singular conditional of 'regarder'.

2) Here's a reminder of the endings:

Conditional endings

I	je	-ais	we	nous	-ions
you (inf. sing.)	tu	-ais	you (pl., formal)	vous	-iez
he/she/it/one	il/elle/on	-ait	they (m/f)	ils/elles	-aient

Some important verbs have irregular stems

Higher

Some important verbs are irregular in the conditional tense — their stems aren't in the infinitive form:

avoir (to have)	
j'	aurais
tu	aurais
il/elle/on	aurait

être (to be)	
je	serais
tu	serais
il/elle/on	serait

aller (to go)	
j'	irais
tu	irais
il/elle/on	irait

faire (to do)	
je	ferais
tu	ferais
il/elle/on	ferait

The stems are the only irregular part of these verbs — they all use the normal endings listed above.

Grammar Questions

Put these verbs into the conditional. The subject has been given to you in brackets.

H
1. améliorer (vous) 3. manger (il) 5. aller (elle) 7. être (on) 9. se laver (ils)
2. disputer (il) 4. organiser (je) 6. annoncer (tu) 8. décider (elle) 10. chercher (nous)
H

Sorry, I'm afraid my love for grammar isn't unconditional...

If you're taking the Foundation paper, you need to know 'je voudrais', 'tu voudrais' and 'il/elle/on voudrait'.
If you're taking the Higher one, you also need to know regular '-er' verbs and the irregulars above. Nice.

Find the CGP RevisionHub at cgpbooks.co.uk/Bonjour

Reflexive Verbs and Pronouns

Reflexive verbs and pronouns might look and feel a little alien to English speakers, but don't be put off by them — they're actually pretty simple. You just need to know a few basic rules...

Reflexive verbs have an extra part

Reflexive pronouns	
myself	me
yourself (inf. sing.)	te
himself/herself/itself/oneself	se
ourselves	nous
yourselves (pl., formal)	vous
themselves (m/f)	se

Higher (bracket for the plural forms)

1) Reflexive verbs describe actions that you do to yourself, like washing yourself or getting yourself up.

2) These verbs look different because they've got an extra part — a pronoun that means 'self', e.g. 'se laver' (*to wash oneself*). The pronoun changes form depending on who's doing the action.

You can tell which verbs are reflexive by checking in the dictionary. If you look up 'to get up', it'll say 'se lever'.

H 3) Reflexive pronouns can also mean 'each other', e.g. 'ils se regardent' (*they look at each other*).

4) Reflexive verbs can end in '-er', '-ir' or '-re'. They form tenses in exactly the same way as other verbs:

se laver (to wash oneself)

I wash myself	je me lave	one washes oneself	on se lave
you (inf. sing.) wash yourself	tu te laves	we wash ourselves	nous nous lavons
he washes himself	il se lave	**H** you (pl., formal) wash yourselves	vous vous lavez
she washes herself	elle se lave	they wash themselves (m/f)	ils/elles se lavent

Reflexives keep their pronouns in all tenses

1) All reflexive verbs take 'être' in the perfect tense — this means they agree with their subject (see p.137).

2) The reflexive pronoun (me, te, se, etc.) always goes between the subject and the present tense of 'être'.

Je me suis levé(e) à sept heures ce matin.
I got up at seven o'clock this morning.

Elle s'est lavée.
She washed herself.

'Lavée' has an 'e' on the end here because its subject ('elle') is feminine.

3) In the immediate future tense (see p.138), the reflexive infinitive needs the pronoun that matches its subject.

Je vais me coucher. *I'm going to go to sleep.*

Il va s'organiser. *He's going to get organised.*

'Se' becomes 's'' before a word starting with a vowel.

Grammar Questions

Translate these phrases into **French**. Make sure you put the reflexive pronouns in the right places.

1. he's interested in
2. I'm going to relax
3. you ('tu') remember
4. she argued with
5. they ('elles') get up
6. we ('nous') will lie down

Reflexive verbs only think about themselves — how selfish...

For Foundation tier, you only need to know how to use singular reflexive pronouns. For Higher tier, you also need to know the plural forms. Don't worry — before you know it, using them will be, erm, a reflex...

Negative Forms

You've reached the page where you can grumble and moan. Take your stress out on two of the most important French words — 'ne' and 'pas'. (Don't worry — they're only little but they can take it.)

'ne...pas' — *not*

1) In English, you change a sentence to mean <u>the opposite</u> by adding '<u>not</u>'. In French, you add <u>two words</u> — '<u>ne</u>' and '<u>pas</u>'. They go <u>either side</u> of the <u>verb</u>.

Clémentine was not 'd'accord'.

je suis d'accord	→	je ne suis pas d'accord
I agree		*I do not agree*

'Suis' is the verb. The 'ne' goes before it, and the 'pas' goes after it.

2) For verbs in the <u>perfect tense</u> (see p.134-135), put the '<u>ne</u>' and '<u>pas</u>' <u>around</u> the bit of '<u>avoir</u>' or '<u>être</u>'.

Je n'ai pas aimé l'école.   *I did not like school.*

3) To make an <u>infinitive negative</u>, put the '<u>ne</u>' and the '<u>pas</u>' in <u>front</u> of it.

Elle préfère ne pas parler de son travail.   *She prefers not to talk about her work.*

'ne...jamais' — *never*

There are <u>other negatives</u> that work in the <u>same way</u> as 'ne...pas'. Here are some of the most common ones:

ne...jamais	*never, not ever*	ne...plus	*not any more, no longer*	ne...ni...ni	*neither...nor*
ne...rien	*nothing, not anything*			ne...que	*only, nothing but*
ne...personne	*nobody, not anyone*	ne...pas encore	*not yet*		

Je ne vais jamais à York.
I never go to York.

Il n'y a rien ici.
There's nothing here.

Elle ne voit personne.
She doesn't see anyone.

Je ne vais plus au collège.
I don't go to school any more.

Nous n'allons ni à York ni à Leeds.
We're neither going to York nor Leeds.

Tu n'as que deux heures.
You only have two hours.

Articles change to 'de' after a negative

After a <u>negative</u>, indefinite articles ('<u>un</u> / <u>une</u>') and partitives ('<u>du</u>', '<u>de la</u>', '<u>des</u>' — see p.110) become '<u>de</u>'.

Elle n'a pas de pain.   *She doesn't have any bread.*

'Ne...que' doesn't follow this rule — it keeps its articles. E.g. 'Je n'ai que du café.' (I only have coffee.)

Grammar Questions

Translate these sentences into **French**, using the negative phrases you've learnt on this page.

1. I never eat meat.
2. He doesn't like anyone.
3. I don't vape any more.
4. They ('ils') only drink tea.
5. She has neither a dog nor a bird.
6. He has not yet gone.

Learning French is positive — except for when it's negative...

Don't forget that you need two words to make French verbs negative — 'ne' before the verb, and then one of the words from above after the verb. The end result? A tasty verb sandwich. Right, time for lunch...

Giving Orders

Learning to order other people about is an important life skill, whatever language you're speaking. Putting verbs in the imperative lets you do just that — it's really useful and very easy to form.

Imperatives use the present tense

1) <u>Imperatives</u> are words that give an <u>order</u>. They often tell someone <u>to do something</u> (e.g. 'sit down').

For when to choose 'tu' or 'vous', see p.111.

2) In French, imperatives are formed using the <u>present tense</u> of the '<u>tu</u>' and '<u>vous</u>' forms of a verb. Be careful — the '<u>tu</u>' form of '<u>-er</u>' <u>verbs loses</u> its final '<u>-s</u>' in the imperative.

regarder (to watch)
regarde !   *watch! (inf. sing.)*
regardez !   *watch! (pl., formal)*

choisir (to choose)
choisis !   *choose! (inf. sing.)*
choisissez !   *choose! (pl., formal)*

attendre (to wait)
attends !   *wait! (inf. sing.)*
attendez !   *wait! (pl., formal)*

Regardez ça !
Watch this!

Choisis la rouge !
Choose the red one!

Attends le bus !
Wait for the bus!

3) The imperative forms of '<u>aller</u>' and of '<u>être</u>' are a bit <u>different</u>:

aller (to go)
va !   *go! (inf. sing.)*
allez !   *go! (pl., formal)*

Higher

être (to be)
sois !   *be! (inf. sing.)*
soyez !   *be! (pl., formal)*

Va dans le jardin !   *Go to the garden!*

Sois gentil !   *Be nice!*

Negative imperatives use 'ne...pas' normally

To make an imperative verb <u>negative</u>, put '<u>ne</u>' <u>before</u> the verb and '<u>pas</u>' or another negative <u>after</u> it (see p.141).

Ne volez pas mon tableau !   *Don't steal my painting!*

Ne sers personne !   *Don't serve anyone!*

To say 'let's', use the 'nous' form of the imperative

Claude always ordered
his cake mix in bulk.

Higher

If you want to suggest <u>doing something together</u>, you use the '<u>nous</u>' form of the imperative, which is the same as the present.

Travaillons ensemble !
Let's work together!

Construisons un château !
Let's build a castle!

Faisons du gâteau !
Let's make cake!

Grammar Questions

Translate these phrases into **French**.

1. Finish your homework! (pl.)
2. Don't organise a party! (pl.)
3. Listen! (sing.)
4. Don't drink! (pl.)
5. Don't go! (sing.)
6. Leave! (sing.)

H 7. Let's dance! **H**
8. Let's eat!

It's imperative that you learn this stuff...

Imperatives are really useful things. Next time you hear one used in English, have a think about what the French version might be — keep doing that, and you'll be an imperative expert in no time at all.

-ing Verbs

'But what if I'm doing two things at the same time and want to talk about them both?' I hear you cry. Well, dry your eyes and read on — present participles are the solution to your problem...

'Doing', 'saying' and 'thinking' are present participles

1) To form the present participle, get the imperfect stem of the verb (see p.136) and add '-ant':

Verb	Imperfect stem	Present participle
regarder	regard-	regard**ant** (*watching*)
choisir	choisiss-	choisiss**ant** (*choosing*)
partir	part-	part**ant** (*leaving*)
venir	ven-	ven**ant** (*coming*)
ouvrir	ouvr-	ouvr**ant** (*opening*)
entendre	entend-	entend**ant** (*hearing*)
prendre	pren-	pren**ant** (*taking*)
traduire	traduis-	traduis**ant** (*translating*)
connaître	connaiss-	connaiss**ant** (*knowing*)
écrire	écriv-	écriv**ant** (*writing*)

Careful — to say you're 'doing something', e.g. 'I am dreaming', you should use the present tense (see p.131-133). If you use two verbs together, e.g. 'I like writing', you use the present tense with an infinitive (see p.133).

2) 'En' + the present participle usually means 'while doing something' or 'by doing something'.

> Il lit le journal en écoutant la radio.   *He reads the paper while listening to the radio.*

3) Some verbs have irregular stems in the present participle.

Verb	Irregular stem
avoir (to have)	ay-
être (to be)	ét-
faire (to do / make)	fais-

> Elle est devenue riche en faisant des vidéos.
> *She became rich by making videos.*

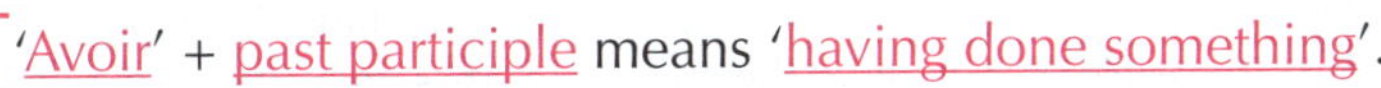

Après avoir mangé — *After having eaten*

'Avoir' + past participle means 'having done something'.

> Il regrette d'avoir envoyé le message.
> *He regrets having sent the message.*

> Après avoir payé, elles ont quitté le restaurant.
> *After having paid, they left the restaurant.*

Grammar Questions

Translate the following phrases into **French**.

1. while helping
2. by discovering
3. after having eaten
4. by staying
5. by constructing
6. after having seen
7. after having chosen
8. while enrolling

After having bought the CGP book, the student became a genius...

Present participles aren't used anywhere near as much in French as they are in English — most of the time, you'll just need the present tense. You still need to learn them though — they pop up every now and then.

Impersonal Verbs and the Passive

Passive sentences in French are structured just like passive sentences in English, so they're dead easy to recognise. But before we get there, there's some impersonal verbs to get your teeth into...

Impersonal verbs only work with 'il'

1) <u>Impersonal verbs</u> always have '<u>il</u>' as their subject. Here are some common examples:

il y a	*there is / are*	**Higher** ⌐ il est difficile de	*it's difficult to*	
il faut	*you must /*	il manque	*...is missing*	
	it is necessary to	il vaut mieux	*it's better*	
il fait beau	*it is nice (weather)*	└ il vaut la peine de	*it's worth (doing something)*	

You often use impersonal verbs to talk about the weather. For more about the weather, see p.97.

Il y a des chapeaux noirs.   *There are some black hats.*

Il y aura des gâteaux.   *There will be cakes.*

Make sure you know how to use 'il y a' in the future ('il y aura') and the imperfect ('il y avait') too.

Il vaut la peine de trouver un emploi.   *It's worth finding a job.*

2) '<u>Il faut</u>' and impersonal verb phrases ending in 'de' are always followed by an <u>infinitive</u>:

Il faut aller au lycée tous les jours.
You must go to school every day.

Il est important de recycler tes déchets.
It's important to recycle your rubbish.

See p.133 to learn more about infinitives.

Le film est regardé par... — *The film is watched by...*

1) In most sentences, there's a person or thing <u>doing</u> the verb, e.g. '<u>The fly bites</u> the man'. These are <u>active sentences</u>. In a <u>passive</u> sentence, the person or thing has <u>something done to it</u>, e.g. '<u>The man is bitten</u> by the fly'.

2) The <u>present passive</u> is formed of a <u>person</u> or <u>thing</u> followed by the <u>present tense</u> of '<u>être</u>' + a <u>past participle</u>.

Il est aidé par ses parents.   *He is helped by his parents.*

See p.134-135 for more on past participles.

Higher

3) The <u>past participle</u> has to <u>agree</u> with the <u>person</u> or <u>thing</u> that is having the <u>action done to it</u>.

La télé-réalité est regardée par beaucoup de gens.
Reality TV is watched by lots of people.

This is passive — 'reality TV' is having something done to it. 'Regardée' has an 'e' at the end as it agrees with 'la télé-réalité'.

4) The passive isn't used as often in French. French speakers often use '<u>on</u>' (*one*) with an <u>active sentence</u> instead.

'One didn't see' sounds quite formal in English, so you'd normally use the passive voice instead.

On n'a pas vu l'homme.   *One didn't see the man. / The man wasn't seen.*

Grammar Questions

Rewrite these sentences in French so they use the passive.

H
1. The owners love the dog.
2. The influencer makes a video.
3. The public elect the president.
4. The teacher adores the pupils.
5. The boy eats chicken.
6. Anna is buying trousers.
H

There's a lot to learn here, but it's nothing personal...

...No, really, I promise it isn't. It's just that impersonal verbs are so handy — especially 'il y a' and 'il faut'.

Verbs and Tenses — Grammar List

Regular Verbs

Regular verbs that end in 'er', 'ir' or 're' follow the patterns of 'parler', 'choisir' and 'entendre'.

parler (to speak)

Present
je parle
tu parles
il/elle/on parle
nous parlons
vous parlez
ils/elles parlent

Imperative
parle !
H parlons !
parlez !

Participles
(avoir) parlé
H (en) parlant

Imperfect
je parlais
tu parlais
il/elle/on parlait
nous parlions
H vous parliez
ils/elles parlaient

Future (Higher)
je parlerai
tu parleras
il/elle/on parlera
nous parlerons
vous parlerez
ils/elles parleront

Conditional (Higher)
je parlerais
tu parlerais
il/elle/on parlerait
nous parlerions
vous parleriez
ils/elles parleraient

choisir (to choose)

Present
je choisis
tu choisis
il/elle/on choisit
nous choisissons
vous choisissez
ils/elles choisissent

Participles
(avoir) choisi
H (en) choisissant

Imperfect
je choisissais
tu choisissais
il/elle/on choisissait
nous choisissions
H vous choisissiez
ils/elles choisissaient

Imperative
choisis !
H choisissons !
choisissez !

entendre (to hear)

Present
j'entends
tu entends
il/elle/on entend
nous entendons
vous entendez
ils/elles entendent

Participles
(avoir) entendu
H (en) entendant

Imperfect
j'entendais
tu entendais
il/elle/on entendait
nous entendions
H vous entendiez
ils/elles entendaient

Imperative
entends !
H entendons !
entendez !

Modal Verbs

Modal verbs crop up all over the place and are used to show possibility or necessity. They're often followed by an infinitive verb.

devoir (to have to)

Present
je dois   nous devons
tu dois   vous devez
il/elle/on doit   ils/elles doivent

Past Participle
H (avoir) dû

pouvoir (to be able to)

Present
je peux   nous pouvons
tu peux   vous pouvez
il/elle/on peut   ils/elles peuvent

Past Participle
H (avoir) pu

vouloir (to want)

Present
je veux
tu veux
il/elle/on veut
nous voulons
vous voulez
ils/elles veulent

Conditional
je voudrais
tu voudrais
il/elle/on voudrait

Past Participle
H (avoir) voulu

savoir (to know)

Present
je sais   nous savons
tu sais   vous savez
il/elle/on sait   ils/elles savent

Past Participle
H (avoir) su

Verbs and Tenses — Grammar List

Important Irregular Verbs

There are lots of verbs that don't behave themselves. Some of them, like 'être', 'faire', 'avoir' and 'aller', are pretty key.

être (to be)

Present
je suis
tu es
il/elle/on est
nous sommes
vous êtes
ils/elles sont

Imperfect
j'étais
tu étais
il/elle/on était
nous étions
H vous étiez
ils/elles étaient

Imperative
H sois !
soyez !

Future
je serai
tu seras
il/elle/on sera

Participles
(avoir) été
H (en) étant

Conditional
je serais
tu serais
il/elle/on serait

Higher

avoir (to have)

Present
j'ai
tu as
il/elle/on a
nous avons
vous avez
ils/elles ont

Imperfect
j'avais
tu avais
il/elle/on avait
nous avions
H vous aviez
ils/elles avaient

Participles
(avoir) eu
H (en) ayant

Future
j'aurai
tu auras
il/elle/on aura

Conditional
j'aurais
tu aurais
il/elle/on aurait

Higher

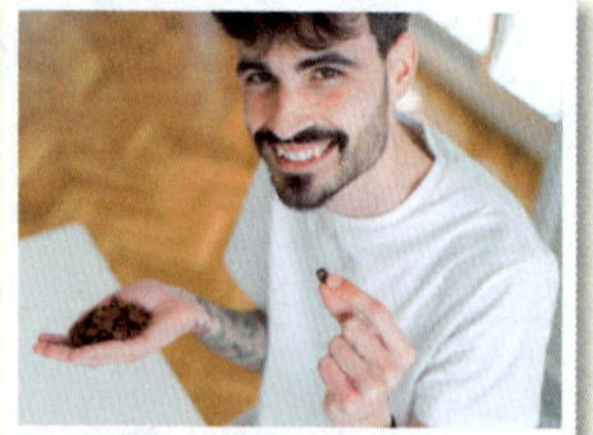

Guillaume was looking
for a raisin d'être...

faire (to do / make)

Present
je fais
tu fais
il/elle/on fait
nous faisons
vous faites
ils/elles font

Imperfect
je faisais
tu faisais
il/elle/on faisait
nous faisions
H vous faisiez
ils/elles faisaient

Imperative
fais !
H faisons !
faites !

Future
je ferai
tu feras
il/elle/on fera

Participles
(avoir) fait
H (en) faisant

Conditional
je ferais
tu ferais
il/elle/on ferait

Higher

aller (to go)

Present
je vais
tu vas
il/elle/on va
nous allons
vous allez
ils/elles vont

Imperfect
j'allais
tu allais
il/elle/on allait
nous allions
H vous alliez
ils/elles allaient

Imperative
va !
H allons !
allez !

Future
j'irai
tu iras
il/elle/on ira

Participles
(être) allé
H (en) allant

Conditional
j'irais
tu irais
il/elle/on irait

Higher

'Être', 'avoir', 'faire' and 'aller' all have irregular
stems in the future and conditional.

Anchor Verbs

Anchor verbs give you the pattern you need to be able to conjugate verbs with similar endings.

ouvrir (to open)

Verbs ending in 'vrir' normally conjugate like 'ouvrir'.

Present
j'ouvre
tu ouvres
il/elle/on ouvre
nous ouvrons
vous ouvrez
ils/elles ouvrent

Imperative
ouvre !
H ouvrons !
ouvrez !

Participles
(avoir) ouvert
H (en) ouvrant

Imperfect
j'ouvrais
tu ouvrais
il/elle/on ouvrait
nous ouvrions
H vous ouvriez
ils/elles ouvraient

traduire (to translate)

Verbs ending in 'ire' often conjugate like 'traduire'.

Present
je traduis
tu traduis
il/elle/on traduit
nous traduisons
vous traduisez
ils/elles traduisent

Imperative
traduis !
H traduisons !
traduisez !

Participles
(avoir) traduis
H (en) traduisant

Imperfect
je traduisais
tu traduisais
il/elle/on traduisait
nous traduisions
H vous traduisiez
ils/elles traduisaient

partir (to leave)

Verbs ending in 'tir' normally conjugate like 'partir'.

Present
je pars
tu pars
il/elle/on part
nous partons
vous partez
ils/elles partent

Imperative
pars !
H partons !
partez !

Participles
(être) parti
H (en) partant

Imperfect
je partais
tu partais
il/elle/on partait
nous partions
H vous partiez
ils/elles partaient

venir (to come)

Verbs ending in 'nir' normally conjugate like 'venir'.

Present
je viens
tu viens
il/elle/on vient
nous venons
vous venez
ils/elles viennent

Imperative
viens !
H venons !
venez !

Participles
(être) venu
H (en) venant

Imperfect
je venais
tu venais
il/elle/on venait
nous venions
H vous veniez
ils/elles venaient

prendre (to take)

Verbs ending in 'dre' sometimes conjugate like 'prendre'.

Present
je prends
tu prends
il/elle/on prend
nous prenons
vous prenez
ils/elles prennent

Imperative
prends !
H prenons !
prenez !

Participles
(avoir) pris
H (en) prenant

Imperfect
je prenais
tu prenais
il/elle/on prenait
nous prenions
H vous preniez
ils/elles prenaient

écrire (to write)

H Verbs ending in 'crire' conjugate like 'écrire'.

Present
j'écris
tu écris
il/elle/on écrit
nous écrivons
H vous écrivez
ils/elles écrivent

Participles
(avoir) écrit
H (en) écrivant

Imperative
écris !
écrivons !
H écrivez !

Imperfect
j'écrivais
tu écrivais
il/elle/on écrivait
nous écrivions
vous écriviez
ils/elles écrivaient

Higher

connaître (to know)

H Verbs ending in 'aître' conjugate like 'connaître'.

Present
je connais
tu connais
il/elle/on connaît
nous connaissons
H vous connaissez
ils/elles connaissent

Participles
(avoir) connu
H (en) connaissant

Imperfect
je connaissais
tu connaissais
il/elle/on connaissait
nous connaissions
vous connaissiez
ils/elles connaissaient

Higher

Imperative
connais !
connaissons !
H connaissez !

Verbs and Tenses — Grammar List

Other Irregular Verbs

The verb forms on this page are high frequency irregular verbs, so it's important you know them well.

dire (to say)

Present
je dis
tu dis
il/elle/on dit

Imperative
dis !
H disons !

Past Participle
(avoir) dit

boire (to drink)

Present
je bois
tu bois
il/elle/on boit

Imperative
bois !

Past Participle
(avoir) bu

rire (to laugh)

Present
je ris
tu ris
il/elle/on rit

Imperative
ris !

Past Participle
(avoir) ri

croire (to believe)

Present
je crois
tu crois
il/elle/on croit

Imperative
crois !

Past Participle
(avoir) cru

suivre (to follow)

Present
je suis
tu suis
il/elle/on suit

Imperative
suis !

Past Participle
(avoir) suivi

courir (to run)

Present
je cours
tu cours
il/elle/on court

Imperative
cours !

Past Participle
(avoir) couru

vivre (to live)

Present
je vis
tu vis
il/elle/on vit

Imperative
vis !

Past Participle
(avoir) vécu

Higher

recevoir (to receive)

Present
je reçois
tu reçois
il/elle/on reçoit

Imperative
reçois !

Past Participle
(avoir) reçu

voir (to see)

Present
je vois
tu vois
il/elle/on voit

Imperative
vois !

Past Participle
(avoir) vu

sourire (to smile)

Present
H je souris
tu souris
il/elle/on sourit

Imperative
souris !

Past Participle
(avoir) souri

Higher

décevoir (to disappoint)

Present
je déçois
tu déçois
il/elle/on déçoit

Imperative
déçois !

Past Participle
(avoir) déçu

Higher

s'asseoir (to sit down)

Present
je m'assieds / m'assois
tu t'assieds / t'assois
il/elle/on s'assied / s'assoit

Imperative
assieds-toi ! / assois-toi !

Past Participle
(s'être) assis

Higher

Revision Summary Test for Section Fifteen

This is it. The last revision summary. It's been an honour and a privilege... *Cries in French*
- These questions are **really tricky**, but they'll help you see **how well you know your stuff**.
- Tackle the **revision summary test** below, or scan the QR code to do it **online**.
  You can **keep track of your progress** online and see **which areas need more work**.
- There are **sample answers** here: www.cgpbooks.co.uk/BonjourExtras

The Present Tense ☑

1) Give all the present tense conjugations of these French verbs: a) jouer   b) remplir   c) attendre ☐
2) Translate these verb phrases into French: ☐
   a) I go   b) we ('nous') are   c) she wants   d) they ('elles') know   e) you ('vous') have
3) Correct these phrases: a) J'évite fumer.   b) Elle veut à sortir.   c) Nous apprenons de chanter. ☐
H 4) Translate this sentence into French: 'I have just finished my geography homework.' ☐

The Perfect and Imperfect Tenses ☑

5) Translate these sentences into French: ☐
   a) She used to dance.   b) They ('elles') danced all night.   c) I was dancing.
6) Write down the past participles of these verbs: a) parler   b) comprendre   c) partir ☐
   d) attendre   e) dire   f) avoir   g) mettre   h) prendre   i) voir   j) connaître
7) Excluding reflexive verbs, how many verbs can you think of that take 'être' in the perfect tense? ☐
   There are at least 15 you need to know.
8) Translate these verb phrases into French: a) you ('tu') ate   b) I was sleeping   c) I used to write ☐
   d) they ('ils') walked   e) you ('vous') drank   f) I have seen   g) he was doing

The Future and the Conditional ☐

9) Translate these sentences into French: a) He is going to leave.   b) They ('ils') are going to eat. ☐
10) Write down all the proper future tense conjugations of the verb 'rêver'. ☐
Higher 11) How do you say the following phrases in French? Use the proper future tense or the conditional. ☐
   a) he will be   b) you ('tu') will go   c) one would look   d) she would ask   e) I will have

Reflexives and Negation ☑

12) Give the French translations for these sentences: ☐
   a) She relaxed.   b) I am getting organised.   c) It is going to happen.   d) You ('tu') got ready.
13) Translate this passage into English: 'Il n'y avait personne sur la côte — je n'ai ☐
   jamais vu la plage comme ça en été. C'est peut-être parce qu'il n'y a rien à
   faire là-bas. J'ai décidé de ne pas acheter une glace car je n'avais pas d'argent.'
H 14) Write a sentence that includes the phrase: a) ne...plus.   b) ne...ni...ni.   c) ne...que. ☐

Imperatives, Present Participles and the Passive ☐

15) Write down the 'tu' and 'vous' imperative forms of these verbs (plus the 'let's' form for Higher tier): ☐
   a) apprendre   b) étudier   c) venir   d) aller   e) dire
16) Translate this sentence into English: 'Il faut vite rentrer chez toi parce qu'il fait mauvais.' ☐
17) Write down the present participles of these verbs: ☐
   a) conduire   b) découvrir   c) être   d) s'inscrire   e) nettoyer   f) remplir
Higher 18) Rewrite these sentences using the passive voice: ☐
   a) Joël mange un poulet.   b) Sophie achète une voiture.   c) La pollution menace les animaux.
19) Translate this sentence into French: 'It's worth going to the restaurant ☐
   because after having eaten well, you always feel better.'

Spelling and Pronunciation

French pronunciation isn't easy, so use this page to help if you're unsure how to pronounce a word. You can scan the QR code to hear the sounds and words in the tables spoken aloud.

Listening Track 20

French words aren't always pronounced as they're written

The table below shows some of the main ways of spelling common sounds in French.

Listen to the audio and practise pronouncing each sound out loud as you hear it.

Spelling	Example 1	Example 2
silent final consonant	temp**s**	froi**d**
a	**a**vril	**a**venir
i/y	i**c**i	l**y**cée
eu	h**eu**re	bl**eu**
e	m**e**	s**e**
au/eau/closed o/ô	bur**eau**	ch**ô**mage
ou	c**ou**rt	tr**ou**ver
u	f**u**tur	n**u**l
silent final e	bell**e**	sympathiqu**e**
é (-er, -ez)	pass**é**	**é**cout**er**
en/an/em/am	seulem**ent**	**em**pêcher
on/om	p**on**t	n**om**
ain/in/aim/im	chem**in**	s**im**ple
è/ê/ai	probl**è**me	f**ai**ble
oi/oy	c**oi**n	empl**oy**er
ch	pro**ch**e	re**ch**er**ch**er
ç (and soft 'c')	gar**ç**on	ly**c**ée
qu	man**qu**e	prati**qu**er
j	**j**uste	**j**uin
-tion	tradi**tion**	généra**tion**
-ien	b**ien**	entret**ien**
silent h	**h**iver	**h**ôtel
un	l**un**di	br**un**
-gn-	li**gn**e	espa**gn**ol
r	**r**evenir	app**r**end**r**e
open eu/œu	coul**eu**r	s**œu**r
open o	t**o**rt	d'acc**o**rd
-s-	égli**s**e	surpri**s**e
th	**th**é	**th**éâtre
-ill-/-ille	b**ill**et	f**ill**e
-aill-/-ail	bat**aill**e	trav**ail**

If you add an 'e' to a word ending in a silent consonant, the consonant will no longer be silent. E.g. you don't pronounce the 'd' in 'froi**d**', but you do pronounce it in 'froide'.

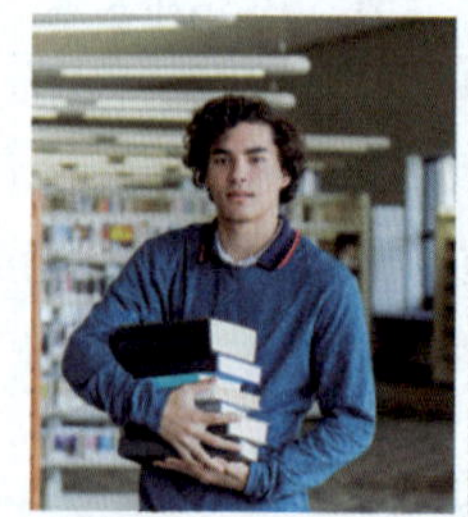
Sam decided now was the perfect time to read the French dictionary from start to finish. What a guy.

In French, you don't pronounce the 'h' at the beginning of some words.

You often pronounce the final letter of a word if the word after it begins with a vowel. This is called 'liaison'.

s-liaison	de**s** annonces	vo**s** amis
t-liaison	tou**t** en	cen**t** euros
n-liaison	to**n** oncle	so**n** avenir
x-liaison	au**x** animaux	deu**x** équipes

For example, in the phrase 'vos amis', you pronounce the 's' at the end of 'vos'.

The Listening and Speaking Exams

There are four separate exams for AQA GCSE French and each one is worth 25% of your final mark. But never mind the maths — these pages are crammed full of advice to help you tackle the exams head on.

The listening exam has two sections

1) For the listening paper, you'll listen to various recordings of people speaking in French.

2) The paper is 45 minutes long for Higher-tier students and 35 minutes long for Foundation-tier students. It's split into Section A and Section B:

> Section A is the longer section — it's worth 40 marks at Higher tier and 32 marks at Foundation tier. It contains comprehension questions in English, and you'll write your answers in English.

> Section B is a shorter dictation section — it's worth 10 marks at Higher tier and 8 marks at Foundation tier. You'll hear some short sentences and write them down in French.

3) Read the paper thoroughly before the recording begins — the questions will give you a good idea of the topics you'll be asked about. This should help you predict what to listen out for.

4) Make notes while listening to the recordings, and listen to the end, even if you think you have the answer.

5) Don't worry if you can't understand every word — just listen carefully and try to pick out the key vocab.

The speaking exam has three parts

> During your preparation time, you can make notes to use at any point during the exam.

1) Your speaking exam will be conducted and recorded by your teacher.

2) The exam is in three parts. Before you start, you'll get 15 minutes of preparation time. The time allowed for the exam is 10-12 minutes at Higher tier and 7-9 minutes at Foundation tier.

① Role-play	② Reading aloud task	③ Photo card discussion
You'll get a card with a scenario on it. It'll have five tasks — four will be notes on what you should talk about. The '?' shows you have to ask a question.	You'll get a card with several sentences in French. You'll read them aloud, then your teacher will ask you four questions related to the topic of the sentences.	You'll receive a card with two photos on it. Your teacher will ask you to talk about them and then ask you questions related to the same theme.

Try to be imaginative with your answers

You need to find ways to show off the full extent of your French knowledge. You should try to:

1) Use a range of tenses — e.g. for a question on daily routine, think of when something different happens.

> Mais demain je vais jouer au foot.   *But tomorrow I'm going to play football.*

2) Talk about other people, as well as yourself — it's fine to make people up if it helps.

> J'aime le sport, mais ma mère le déteste.   *I like sport, but my mum hates it.*

> You can use non-binary or gender-neutral pronouns in the exams — just make sure you're consistent and your adjectives agree.

3) Give loads of opinions and reasons for your opinions.

> À mon avis, il faut faire plus de recyclage.   *In my opinion, we must do more recycling.*

Silence please! I'm taking my sneaking exam...

Don't panic if you make a mistake in the speaking exam — what's important is how you deal with it.
You won't lose marks for correcting yourself, so show the examiner that you know where you went wrong.

The Reading and Writing Exams

The writing exam is a great way of showing off what you can do — try to use varied vocabulary, include a range of tenses, and pack in any clever expressions that you've learnt over the years. First up, though...

The reading exam has two sections

1) The Higher-tier reading paper is 1 hour long, and the Foundation-tier paper is 45 minutes. Both are worth 50 marks and have two sections.

2) In Section A, you'll be given a variety of French texts and then asked questions about them. The questions and answers will be in English.

   - Scan through each text first to get an idea of what it's about. Then read the questions that go with it carefully, making sure you understand what information you should be looking out for.
   - Next, go back through the text, focusing on finding the information you need. If you're having trouble with a particular question, you might want to move on and come back to it later.

3) Section B will ask you to translate several short French sentences (between 35-50 words in total) into English. The sentences will be on topics you've studied, so the vocabulary should be familiar. Here are some top tips for doing your translations:

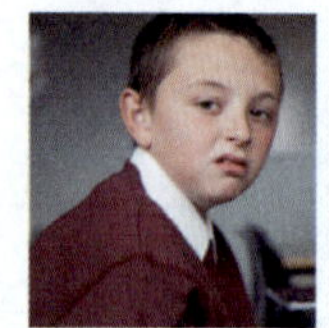

   - Translate a whole sentence at a time, rather than word by word — this will avoid any of the French word order being carried into the English.
   - Keep an eye out for different tenses — there will be a variety.
   - Read through your translations to make sure they sound natural.

James realised too late that he was sitting the Spanish paper rather than the French one.

There are various types of questions in the writing exam

1) The Higher-tier writing paper is 1 hour and 15 minutes long and the Foundation-tier paper is 1 hour and 10 minutes long. Some tasks are only for one tier, but others appear in both — these are explained below.

2) Each task is worth a different number of marks, so you should spend more time on the higher-mark tasks. For longer answers, make a quick plan before you start and remember to leave time to check your work.

Foundation

Photo Response Task (10 marks)

You'll be asked to write five short sentences in French to describe a black and white photo.

Translation Task (10 marks)

You'll translate sentences from English into French. The sentences could be on any topic you've studied. See above for some top tips for translation tasks.

Foundation

Grammar Task (5 marks)

You'll need to complete five short sentences by choosing the correct option, using your grammar knowledge.

90-word Writing Task (15 marks)

You'll be asked to write about 90 words in response to three bullet points. You'll have a choice between two questions. Make sure you write about each bullet point.

Foundation

50-word Writing Task (10 marks)

You'll be asked to produce a short piece of writing in response to five bullet points. You'll be expected to write about 50 words in total.

Higher

150-word Writing Task (25 marks)

You'll need to write about 150 words in French, based on two bullet points. There will be two questions to choose from. This task is more creative — so don't forget to include some opinions with reasons.

And lastly, don't forget your pen...

When you're nervous and stressed, it's easy to misread a question or skip question parts. For writing questions with bullet points, make sure you talk about each bullet in turn — tick them off as you go along.

Answers

The answers to the translation questions are sample answers only, just to give you an idea of one way to translate them. There may be different ways to translate these sentences that are also correct.

For dictation and translation questions, this symbol (|) shows where to divide the marks. There is 1 mark awarded for the first part of the text, and 1 mark awarded for the second.

Section One — General Stuff

Page 5: Numbers and Times

1) a) Mon frère a | dix-sept ans.
   b) C'est ma sixième | visite au musée.
   c) Elle est née en | deux mille onze.
   d) Il est quatre heures | et demie.
2) a) 16:50   b) film class   c) music
   d) theatre

Page 7: Days and Dates

2) a) 23rd March
   b) July
   c) Tuesdays and Thursdays
   d) 1995

Page 9: Questions

1) E.g. Le restaurant ferme à quelle heure ?
   E.g. Est-ce que tu veux des frites ?
   E.g. Combien coûte une glace ?
   E.g. Où sont les toilettes ?
2) Here are some questions you could have asked:
   Depuis combien de temps êtes-vous professeur ?
   Où travaillez-vous ?
   Quelle matière enseignez-vous ?
   Pourquoi aimez-vous être professeur ?
   Quelle est votre moment préférée de la journée scolaire ?

Page 11: Being Polite

1) a) (her husband's) birthday
   b) a cake
   c) in the garden
   d) There will be a fireworks display.

Page 13: Opinions

1) a) i) true   ii) false
   b) i) false   ii) false
   c) i) true   ii) false

Section Two — Identity and Relationships with Others

Page 21: My Family and Friends

2) a) her mother and her father
   b) a bird
   c) She went to the cinema.
   d) They have a tradition of watching a film together every month.

Page 23: Describing People

1) a) A and D
   b) A and C
   c) B and D

Page 25: Relationships and Partnerships

2) a) Couples who get married are happier.
   b) Weddings are too expensive.
   c) The number of same-sex marriages has increased.

Section Three — Healthy Living and Lifestyle

Page 29: Food

1) a) B   b) C   c) A   d) A

Page 31: Healthy and Unhealthy Living

2) a) A new sports centre
   b) Swimming
   c) It makes the writer feel happy.
   d) It's a good way to relax. / It's a good way to stay in shape.

Page 33: Illnesses and Treatments

1) A and C

Section Four — Education

Page 39: School Life

1) a) K   b) A   c) K
2) a) useful
   b) his brother walks too slowly
   c) tired
   d) plays football in the playground

Page 41: School Pressures and Difficulties

2) a) J'aime beaucoup | la technologie.
   b) Cette année, | je suis en seconde.
   c) Les vacances commencent | en juin.
   d) Mon ami | lève la main.

Section Five — Future Study and Work

Page 47: Education Post-16

1) a) En septembre, | je vais aller au lycée.
   b) J'ai l'occasion d'aller | à l'université de mes rêves.
   c) Mon meilleur ami / Ma meilleure amie veut | faire un apprentissage.
   d) Elle a organisé un rendez-vous | pour discuter de sa carrière.

Page 49: Career Choices and Ambitions

1) a) He wanted to work in a bakery.
   b) He wants to be a chef.
   c) He works in a restaurant kitchen.
   d) The experience will be useful. He doesn't earn a lot of money.
2) a) A and B   b) A and C

Section Six — Free-time Activities

Page 53: Music

1) a) listen to the radio
   b) i) ten years
      ii) writing lyrics for his group's songs.
   c) i) quite difficult
      ii) She can see her progress.
         OR She wants to continue with lessons.

Page 55: Cinema, Theatre and TV

1) A and D

Page 57: Sport

1) a) À mon avis, l'exercice | est essentiel pour la santé.
   b) Je suis actif / active | et j'essaie de faire du sport tous les jours.
   c) Cet été, je vais participer | à un concours de natation.
   d) Ma sœur va au centre sportif | pour danser avec ses amis.
2) a) running
   b) sports centre, sports field and park
   c) She's improving her speed. She is more confident when doing sport.

Page 59: Going Out and Other Hobbies

2) a) She loves fashion.
   b) She reads one or two chapters of a novel.
   c) He prefers staying at home and ordering a takeaway to going to a restaurant.
   d) It takes too long. At the moment it costs a lot.

Section Seven — Customs, Festivals and Celebrations

Page 63: Celebrations

1) a) C   b) B   c) C

Page 65: Customs and Festivals

2) a) i) 34%   ii) 74%   iii) 8%
   b) staying at home

Section Eight — Celebrity Culture

Page 69: Favourite Celebrities

1) a) A and B   b) B and C

Page 71: Celebrity Life

2) a) Any two from:
      the terrific people
      the extraordinary places / beautiful location
      doing what he loves
   b) Morocco
   c) missing his family
   d) He will go on holiday with his children.
      He needs to relax far from the attention of the media.

Section Nine — Travel and Tourism

Page 75: Where to Go

1) a) She wants to go to Switzerland.
      She wants to see the Alps.
   b) She wants to go to Canada.
      She wants to see her friend in Quebec.
   c) She wants to stay in France.
      She wants to visit museums.
   d) He wants to go to Belgium.
      He wants to go camping.

Page 77: Accommodation and Travel

2) B, E and F

Page 79: What to Do

1) a) Two weeks
   b) To improve her French
   c) Any two from:
      She will stay with a French family.
      She will stay in a flat.
      The flat is in an ancient building.
   d) Any two from:
      visit an interesting museum
      go for a walk around the town centre
      buy an ice cream in a café
   e) at the weekend

Section Ten — Media and Technology

Page 83: Technology

1) a) False   b) True   c) True
   d) False

Page 85: The Internet

2) a) C   b) B   c) C

Page 87: Social Media

2) a) 3 hours
   b) He chats to his friends on social media sites.
   c) It is essential.
   d) It allows him to see his cousin's photos.

Section Eleven — Where People Live

Page 91: Where You Live

1) a) on the north-west coast
   b) It is pretty.
      There are lots of beautiful beaches.
   c) There is not much to do there.
   d) It is hotter there.
      She loves the region's cuisine.

Page 93: The Home

1) a) B   b) C   c) B   d) A
2) a) Je nettoie ma chambre | tous les week-ends.
   b) C'est toujours très agréable | chez moi.
   c) Mon appartement se situe | au quatrième étage.
   d) Mon oncle a plusieurs plantes | dans son jardin.
   e) Ma maison | est ancienne.
   f) Je n'ai habité que | dans des appartements.

Page 97: Directions and Weather

1) a) almost a million
   b) It is very mountainous.
   c) It is hot.
      It rains a lot.
   d) It is generally nice.
      It is colder.
2) a) the bus stop.
   b) change buses.
   c) walk to the library.
   d) on the left.

Section Twelve — Environmental and Social Issues

Page 101: Protecting the Environment

1) a) A and D   b) B and C

Page 103: Environmental Problems

2) a) He wants to protect the planet for his future children.
   b) There were forest fires.
   c) It was a tragedy for the animals.
      The number of tourists visiting the country decreased.
   d) He is worried about it.

Page 105: Social Issues

1) a) La faim est un problème | courant dans la société.
   b) Les résultats du vote | sont intéressants.
   c) Le week-end dernier, | il y avait une manifestation.
   d) Je suis bénévole, | et j'essaie d'aider les autres.
2) a) laws on weapons
   b) community safety
   c) current politics
   d) for a long time

Section Thirteen — Nouns, Articles and Linking Words

Page 109: Nouns

1) le cadeau — les cadeaux
2) la piscine — les piscines
3) la maison — les maisons
4) le pays — les pays
5) la voiture — les voitures
6) le prix — les prix
7) la langue — les langues
8) le gâteau — les gâteaux

Page 110: Articles

1) L'homme a un peu <u>de</u> pain.
2) L'étudiant vient <u>du</u> Maroc.
3) Je vais <u>à la</u> piscine.
4) Il va <u>au</u> marché.
5) Elle mange <u>de la</u> viande.
6) On a <u>des</u> légumes.

Page 111: Subject and Emphatic Pronouns

1) Il achète un billet. *He's buying a ticket.*
2) Le cadeau est pour toi. *The present is for you.*
3) Elle est plus bavarde que moi. *She is chattier than me.*
4) Vous avez joué avec moi. *You played with me.*
5) Elle mange avec eux. *She eats with them.*
6) Il a envoyé la lettre lui-même. *He sent the letter himself.*

Page 112: Object Pronouns

1) Maria <u>l'</u>aime.
2) Je <u>l'</u>ai lu.
3) Je ne <u>vous</u> vois pas.
4) Elle <u>lui</u> a envoyé le mail.
5) Ils <u>nous</u> parlent.
6) Il ne <u>les</u> visite pas.

Page 113: Relative and Interrogative Pronouns

1) C'est une grande maison.
2) J'adore vraiment ça.
3) Tu cours avec qui ? / Avec qui cours-tu ?
4) Qu'est ce que tu veux faire ? / Que veux-tu faire ?
5) l'hôtel où j'ai dormi
6) la nourriture que j'aime manger

Page 114: Indefinite and Adverbial Pronouns

1) Plusieurs ont fini leurs devoirs.
2) Tout le monde sait que c'est vrai.
3) Quelqu'un a acheté le livre.
4) J'y réfléchis.
5) Tu connais / Vous connaissez le château ? J'y suis allé.
6) Il y en a beaucoup.

Page 115: Conjunctions

1) Je voudrais un thé <u>et</u> une glace.
2) <u>Si</u> tu voles mon pain, je vais être triste.
3) Je veux sortir, <u>mais</u> je dois finir mes devoirs.
4) <u>Comme</u> je suis fatigué, je vais me coucher tôt.

Page 117: Prepositions

1) Je suis <u>chez</u> Nadia avec Tom.
2) La route passe <u>sous</u> le pont.
3) Je joue <u>au</u> foot.
4) Il était en vacances <u>pendant</u> deux semaines.
5) Il y a un train <u>dans</u> deux minutes.
6) Je travaille à la boulangerie <u>depuis</u> six mois.

Section Fourteen — Adjectives and Adverbs

Page 121: Adjective Agreement

1) une mère fière
2) un repas traditionnel
3) une fille triste
4) une porte bleue
5) les chiens dangereux
6) les nouveaux voisins
7) le premier jour
8) une star internationale

Page 123: More Adjectives

1) <u>Mon</u> père n'aime pas <u>sa</u> nouvelle voiture.
2) <u>Tous</u> tes amis habitent dans <u>notre</u> quartier.
3) <u>Cet</u> hôtel est grand.
4) <u>Cette</u> factrice a <u>leurs</u> lettres.

Answers

Page 124: Comparative and Superlative Adjectives

1) Théo est plus petit que Pauline.
2) Je suis plus jeune que toi / vous.
3) Julie est aussi intelligente que Léa.
4) Le printemps est meilleur que l'hiver.
5) Ses idées sont les pires.
6) Poole est la plus grande ville.

Page 125: Adverbs

1) tristement — sadly
2) négativement — negatively
3) sérieusement — conscientiously / responsibly
4) généralement — generally
5) fièrement — proudly
6) évidemment — obviously
7) actuellement — currently / at present / at the moment
8) intelligemment — intelligently
9) heureusement — happily / fortunately / luckily
10) exactement — exactly
11) suffisamment — sufficiently
12) rarement — rarely

Page 126: More Adverbs

1) Je joue au foot là-bas.
2) Tu travailles tous les jours.
3) Souvent, je vais en ville en bus.
4) Il y a des déchets partout.
5) Je pars demain.
6) L'année dernière, je suis allé(e) en France.

Page 127: Comparative and Superlative Adverbs

1) Je travaille aussi vite que toi.
2) Lucie court plus souvent que Dorian.
3) Elle mange moins que vous.
4) Morgane chante le mieux.
5) Je nage le moins régulièrement.
6) Qui marche le plus rapidement ?

Page 128: Quantifiers and Intensifiers

1) Elle est très belle.
2) Elles ont beaucoup d'amis.
3) Il a un peu d'eau.
4) Le / La prof est vraiment strict(e).
5) L'homme mange trop de fromage.
6) La nourriture est assez bonne.

Section Fifteen — Verbs and Tenses

Page 131: Verbs in the Present Tense

1) je parle
2) tu trouves
3) nous remplissons
4) je réponds
5) elles finissent
6) vous commencez
7) on perd
8) vous vendez

Page 132: Irregular Verbs in the Present Tense

1) nous devons
2) je veux
3) vous êtes
4) tu dois
5) elle va
6) ils font
7) elles peuvent
8) on sait
9) ils ont
10) nous faisons

Page 133: More about the Present Tense

1) J'aime manger.
2) Étudier, c'est affreux.
3) Elles essaient de chanter.
4) Il continue à parler.
5) Il vient de partir.
6) Vous êtes ici depuis hier.

Page 135: The Perfect Tense

1) elles ont mis
2) je suis allé(e)
3) tu as dit
4) nous avons recyclé
5) elle est arrivée
6) il a pris
7) ils sont revenus
8) je me suis lavé(e)

Page 137: The Imperfect Tense

1) J'ai couru.
2) C'était amusant.
3) On rêvait.
4) Il était ennuyeux.
5) Ils ont mangé.
6) Elle a étudié.
7) Je jouais au foot.
8) J'achetais du pain.

Page 138: Talking about the Future

1) tu vas pouvoir
2) ils vont être
3) nous allons finir
4) tu vas regarder, tu regarderas
5) elles vont dire
6) vous allez faire
7) il va aller, il ira
8) elle va venir
9) je vais avoir, j'aurai
10) on va vendre

Page 139: The Conditional

1) vous amélioreriez
2) il disputerait
3) il mangerait
4) j'organiserais
5) elle irait
6) tu annoncerais
7) on serait
8) elle déciderait
9) ils se laveraient
10) nous chercherions

Page 140: Reflexive Verbs and Pronouns

1) il s'intéresse à
2) je vais me relaxer
3) tu te souviens
4) elle s'est disputée avec
5) elles se lèvent
6) nous nous coucherons

Page 141: Negative Forms

1) Je ne mange jamais de viande.
2) Il n'aime personne.
3) Je ne vapote plus.
4) Ils ne boivent que du thé.
5) Elle n'a ni chien ni oiseau.
6) Il n'est pas encore parti.

Page 142: Giving Orders

1) Finissez vos devoirs !
2) N'organisez pas de fête !
3) Écoute !
4) Ne buvez pas !
5) Ne pars pas !
6) Pars !
7) Dansons !
8) Mangeons !

Page 143: -ing Verbs

1) en aidant
2) en découvrant
3) après avoir mangé
4) en restant
5) en construisant
6) après avoir vu
7) après avoir choisi
8) en s'inscrivant

Page 144: Impersonal Verbs and the Passive

1) Le chien est aimé par les propriétaires.
2) Une vidéo est faite par l'influenceur / l'influenceuse.
3) Le président est élu / La présidente est élue par le public.
4) Les élèves sont adorés par le prof.
5) Le poulet est mangé par le garçon.
6) Un pantalon est acheté par Anna.

Index

FAR45